# The Political Economy of the Environment

This book is the culmination of several years' work by a group of academics, policy makers and other professionals looking to understand how alternative economic thinking – and indeed thinking from quite different social-scientific disciplines – could enhance the mainstream economic approach to environmental and natural-resource problems. Of the editors, Dietz comes from the mainstream economics tradition, while Michie and Oughton draw explicitly on institutional and evolutionary economics. The various authors represent a range of disciplinary backgrounds and approaches. This book draws on the strengths of each and all of these approaches to analyse environmental issues and what can be done to tackle these through corporate and public policy.

The book argues the need for an interdisciplinary approach. Two themes which emerge repeatedly throughout the book are the need for an interdisciplinary theory of technological change, and the need for a similarly interdisciplinary approach to the study of human behaviour and how it influences both production and consumption choices. The two themes are of course related. Resolving environmental questions requires an understanding of their nature, of their causes and, to the extent that they are anthropogenic, of how to change human behaviour. These fundamental issues are the focus of the four chapters that form Part I of this volume. The remainder of the volume develops them in more detail.

The literature on ecological economics is beginning to shed new light on the range of policy options available. This book argues that the traditional dichotomy between taxes and regulations is a false one, as an effective policy may combine both. Moreover, these policies may be further enhanced by the use of governance structures and agreements that may evolve or be catalysed by government to manage common pool resources, such as the atmosphere or oceans. It will therefore be of great use to both academics and policy makers alike.

**Simon Dietz** is at the London School of Economics, UK.

**Jonathan Michie** is at the University of Oxford, UK.

**Christine Oughton** is at SOAS, University of London, UK.

**Routledge Studies in Contemporary Political Economy**
Edited by Jonathan Michie
*University of Oxford, UK*

This series presents a fresh, broad perspective on the key issues in the modern world economy, drawing on economics management and business, politics and sociology, economic history and law.

Written in a lively and accessible style, it presents focused and comprehensive introductions to key topics, demonstrating the relevance of political economy to major debates in economics and to an understanding of the contemporary world.

**Global Instability**
The political economy of world economic governance
*edited by Jonathan Michie and John Grieve Smith*

**Reconstructing Political Economy**
The great divide in economic thought
*William K. Tabb*

**The Political Economy of Competitiveness**
Employment, public policy and corporate performance
*Michael Kitson and Jonathan Michie*

**Global Economy, Global Justice**
Theoretical objections and policy alternatives to neoliberalism
*George F. DeMartino*

**Social Capital Versus Social Theory**
Political economy and social science at the turn of the millennium
*Ben Fine*

**A New Guide to Post Keynesian Economics**
*Steven Pressman and Richard Holt*

**Placing the Social Economy**
*Ash Amin, Angus Cameron and Ray Hudson*

**Systems of Production**
Markets, organisations and performance
*Edited by Brendan Burchell, Simon Deakin, Jonathan Michie & Jill Rubery*

**New Economy, New Myth**
*Jean Gadrey*

**Hollywood Economics**
How extreme uncertainty shapes the film industry
*Arthur de Vany*

**Bilateral Trade Agreements in the Asia-Pacific**
Origins, evolution, and implications
*Edited by Vinod K. Aggarwal and Shujiro Urata*

**Creative Industries and Developing Countries**
Voice, choice and economic growth
*Edited by Diana Barrowclough and Zeljka Kozul-Wright*

**The Political Economy of the Environment**
An interdisciplinary approach
*Simon Dietz, Jonathan Michie and Christine Oughton*

# The Political Economy of the Environment

An interdisciplinary approach

**Edited by Simon Dietz, Jonathan Michie and Christine Oughton**

 Routledge
Taylor & Francis Group

LONDON AND NEW YORK

First published 2011
by Routledge
2 Park Square, Milton Park, Abingdon, Oxon OX14 4RN

Simultaneously published in the USA and Canada
by Routledge
711 Third Avenue, New York, NY 10017

*Routledge is an imprint of the Taylor & Francis Group, an informa business*

Typeset in Times by Wearset Ltd, Boldon, Tyne and Wear
Printed and bound in Great Britain by TJI Digital, Padstow, Cornwall

*British Library Cataloguing in Publication Data*
A catalogue record for this book is available from the British Library

*Library of Congress Cataloging in Publication Data*
A catalog record for this book has been requested

ISBN: 978-0-415-43753-0
ISBN: 978-0-203-83067-3
ISBN: 978-0-415-68200-8

# Contents

# Contributors

**Terry Barker**, Director, Cambridge Centre for Climate Change Mitigation Research (4CMR), University of Cambridge and Chairman, Cambridge Econometrics, Cambridge.

**Carlo Carraro**, Professor of Environmental Economics and Econometrics, University of Venice, Fondazione ENI Enrico Mattei (FEEM) and Euro-Mediterranean Center on Climate Change.

**Enrica de Cian**, University of Venice, Fondazione ENI Enrico Mattei (FEEM) and Euro-Mediterranean Center on Climate Change.

**Emma Dawnay**, Freelance political economist.

**Simon Dietz**, Deputy Director, Grantham Research Institute on Climate Change and the Environment, and Lecturer in Environmental Policy, Department of Geography and Environment, London School of Economics and Political Science.

**Timothy J. Foxon**, RCUK Academic Fellow, Sustainability Research Institute and Centre for Climate Change Economics and Policy, University of Leeds.

**Sir David F. Hendry**, Professor of Economics, and Director, Institute for Economic Modelling, Oxford Martin School, University of Oxford.

**Tim Jackson**, Professor of Sustainable Development and Director of the Research group on Lifestyles, Values and Environment (RESOLVE), University of Surrey.

**Jonathan Köhler**, Fraunhofer-Institut für System- und Innovationsforschung ISI Sustainability and Infrastructure Systems, Germany.

**Jonathan Michie**, Professor of Innovation and Knowledge Exchange, Director, Department for Continuing Education and President, Kellogg College, University of Oxford, UK.

**Lea Nicita**, Fondazione ENI Enrico Mattei (FEEM) and Euro-Mediterranean Center on Climate Change.

**Christine Oughton**, Professor of Management Economics, Department of Financial and Management Studies, SOAS, University of London.

**Hetan Shah**, Director of New Economics at the New Economics Foundation.

**Prashant Vaze**, Chief Economist Consumer Focus.

**Lorraine Whitmarsh**, School of Psychology, Cardiff University and Tyndall Centre for Climate Change Research.

# Acknowledgements

We are grateful to the Economic and Social Research Council for funding a series of seminars that enabled the ideas in this book to be presented, discussed and debated (ESRC Research Seminar grant, no. RES-451–26–0545). We are also grateful to the universities of Oxford, Leeds, Cambridge, Bolzano (Italy) and SOAS, University of London for hosting the seminars at which this material was discussed. Michie and Oughton are grateful to the Environment Agency for originally commissioning their paper on the role of institutional and evolutionary economics in understanding environmental decision making, and in particular to Henry Leveson-Gower for organising a seminar at which that paper was presented, and for then encouraging us to maintain and develop the network of heterodox economists committed to developing appropriate environmental policies. Dietz is grateful to the Grantham Foundation for the Protection of the Environment and to the Economic and Social Research Council for the support of his research. Oughton would like to thank the Faculty of Economics and Management, University of Bolzano for generous funding of the research seminar held in Bolzano in March 2009.

We are grateful to Sandra Gee for collating the material for the book (as well as having assisted in organising the Oxford seminar). Finally, we are grateful to the staff at Routledge for the production of the book, in particular Thomas Sutton (Associate Editor, Routledge Research: Economics) and Simon Holt (Editorial Assistant, Routledge Research: Economics).

Figures 8.1 and 8.2 reproduced with kind permission from Springer Science+Business Media: *Environmental Economics and Policy Studies*. The Costs of Greenhouse Gas Abatement: A Meta-Analysis of Post-SRES Mitigation Scenarios. Vol5(2);2002:135-166. Terry Barker, Jonathan Köhler and Marcelo Villena.

# 1 Environmental challenges of the twenty-first century and the need for interdisciplinary political economy

*Simon Dietz, Jonathan Michie and Christine Oughton*

In 2008, the Organisation for Economic Cooperation and Development (OECD) published the latest in its regular series of audits of the state of the environment, taking a global perspective and looking out to 2030 (OECD 2008). Noting that progress had been made on, for example, pollution from industrial sources (in OECD member states at least) and emissions of ozone-depleting substances, the OECD nevertheless flashed a 'red-light' warning on several environmental issues, including climate change, biodiversity loss and water scarcity. In many ways its findings are reminiscent of earlier reports, such as the World Bank's well-known assessment of the relationship between economic development and environmental degradation published nearly 20 years ago (World Bank 1992). In it, the Bank observed that while some environmental problems such as access to adequate sanitation appeared to improve monotonically with economic development, and others such as urban air quality appeared to improve only after a certain level of economic development had been attained, still others such as greenhouse gas emissions worsened monotonically with rising per capita incomes.[1] Thus, while some environmental problems seemed to be largely a symptom of poverty, there was little prospect that the world could grow out of this third category of problems, or at least not without an unprecedented societal response.

Both reports observe that what we might call twenty-first century environmental problems – namely those such as climate change and biodiversity loss that show no signs of being 'decoupled' from economic development – are of a particularly intractable nature. What marks them out is, roughly speaking, *interconnectedness* – they are complex and usually global in nature, and their impacts may only become apparent over long time frames. Climate change is a clear example. A 'carbon footprint' is embodied in almost all of the goods and services transacted in the modern economy, thanks in large part to the burning of fossil fuels for energy.[2] Once emitted, greenhouse gases mix in the atmosphere and, through a highly complex and uncertain process, eventually cause changes to climate that are distant in time and (partly) in space from the emitter. To solve the problem by mitigation (i.e. reducing greenhouse gas emissions), it would further appear from the evidence that a broad portfolio of measures is needed, as the sheer magnitude of emissions reductions that are considered necessary ultimately overwhelms the economies of scale associated with any one currently practicable measure (e.g. Enkvist *et al.* 2007). That is, there does not appear to be a 'silver bullet', and action will be required on many fronts, including to deploy renewable energy technologies, carbon capture and storage technology, to improve energy efficiency at home and in businesses, and to reduce deforestation.

As their respective prefixes would suggest, *inter*connectedness is a powerful reason why an *inter*disciplinary approach to the political economy of the environment is essential. First, however, a note is in order on what we mean by 'political economy', which is one of those elusive terms in the social sciences, meaning different things to different people. Political economy was of course the precursor to economics – i.e. political economy *was* economics – the former term being gradually replaced by the latter towards the end of the nineteenth century, due to a preference for the scientific connotations of 'economics' (Groenewegen 2008). By the mid twentieth century, a diversity of meanings had sprung up, which continues to this day. For some, like Groenewegen (2008), political economy remains a synonym for economics. For others, political economy represents the body of work, building on the Virginia and Chicago Schools, which analyses the functioning of democratic political institutions using economic tools, based around notions of rational choice (Besley 2006). For still others, political economy also means the study of how political institutions interact with the economy, but there is more of an emphasis on an interdisciplinary approach, admitting a wider range of questions and methods. This last interpretation is in the spirit of the Routledge Studies in Contemporary Political Economy series in which this volume appears, and it is the spirit in which we intend the term to be used.

Returning to the importance of interdisciplinarity, Neil Adger and colleagues make the case in a recent paper for a 'thick' analysis of environmental decision making (Adger *et al.* 2003). They observe that successful environmental decisions are likely to be underpinned by four necessary conditions: effectiveness, efficiency, equity and legitimacy. These four conditions are necessary, because, to choose an obvious example, an ostensibly efficient policy such as a carbon tax may founder due to perceived inequities in who pays (e.g. Goulder and Parry 2008). The problem is that the various social sciences place their emphasis and concentrate their insights on subsets of the four criteria. Economics, for example, focuses on efficiency, but has relatively little to say on equity and still less on legitimacy. Conversely political science focuses on legitimacy, but has less to say on efficiency. It follows that insights from many disciplines are required for successful environmental decisions.

Yet we would argue that the need for interdisciplinarity is in fact greater than this, for what Adger and colleagues do not take issue with are the problems faced by disciplinary analyses even where they are conventionally strong. In most cases, these problems are not new, but they are amplified by environmental problems characterised by strong interconnectedness. In their various ways, all of the essays collected in this volume make this point. Two themes which emerge repeatedly are the need for an interdisciplinary theory of technological change, and the need for a similarly interdisciplinary approach to the study of human behaviour and how it influences both production and consumption choices. The two themes are of course related.

The seeds for this volume were sown by a group of academics, policy makers and other professionals looking to understand how alternative economic thinking and indeed thinking from quite different social-scientific disciplines could enhance the mainstream economic approach to environmental and natural-resource problems. Of the editors, Dietz comes from the mainstream tradition, while Michie and Oughton draw explicitly on institutional and evolutionary economics. The various authors represent a range of disciplinary backgrounds and approaches. We see it as vital to draw on the strengths of each and all of these approaches, and we have worked collaboratively to try to create an interdisciplinary practice whereby researchers genuinely listen to and seek to learn from the insights of other disciplines.

In 2004, this group formed the Heterodox Economics for Environment and Development (HEED) Network, which organised seminars and set up electronic discussion boards and mailing lists. HEED also formed the basis for an interdisciplinary course on 'Environmental Economics and Policy', taught at Birkbeck College, part of the University of London. The course moved in time with its creators and is now hosted by the University of Oxford. Some of the contributions to this volume formed lectures as part of the Birkbeck course, but opportunities to include other contributions have emerged in the process of editing, and these have greatly enriched the volume overall. It is hoped that the volume will be of interest to a wide range of readers from across the social sciences and indeed the sciences. Most of its chapters are expositional, and as such the volume is likely to be of most value to students of environmental studies, both at the advanced undergraduate and postgraduate level, and to the interested non-specialist.

## 1 Foundations

Any scientific enquiry proceeds by questions and their resolution (Kuhn 1962). Resolving environmental questions requires an understanding of their nature, of their causes and, to the extent that they are anthropogenic, of how to change human behaviour. These fundamental issues are the focus of the four chapters that form Part 1 of this volume. The remainder of the volume develops them in more detail.

David Hendry's chapter, 'Climate change: lessons for our future from the distant past', starts by considering the nature of scientific evidence and its reliability, noting that for various epistemological reasons, science is often dogged by uncertainty. Despite this, advances in science and understanding have proceeded throughout history via the accumulation of theoretical and empirical evidence: not all questions have been resolved, but significant advances have been made in our understanding. In this chapter Hendry argues that analysis of our distant past (some 500 million years ago to the present day) provides valuable lessons for understanding and dealing with climate change today.

The argument for looking at the very long run (now with respect to economic, rather than geological, history) has also been underlined by the recent financial crisis. As Reinhardt and Rogoff (2008, p. 1) note:

> The economics profession has an unfortunate tendency to view recent experience in the narrow window provided by standard datasets. With a few notable exceptions, cross country empirical studies on financial crises typically begin in 1980 and are limited in several other important respects. Yet an event that is rare in a three decade span may not be all that rare when placed in a broader context.

A point that is reinforced by congressional evidence from Alan Greenspan, former Chairman of the US Federal Reserve (Greenspan 2008, pp. 2–4):

> What went wrong with global economic policies that had worked so effectively for nearly four decades? … A Nobel Prize was awarded for the discovery of the pricing model that underpins much of the advance in derivatives markets. This modern risk management paradigm held sway for decades. The whole intellectual edifice, however, collapsed in the summer of last year because the data inputted into the risk management models generally covered only the past two decades, a period of euphoria.

Hendry's chapter starts by reviewing the theoretical evidence on natural and anthropogenic causes of climate change. This lays the foundation for a detailed discussion of evidence on the extinctions of major species over the past 500 million years and the role of climate change in them. Hendry's evaluation of the (very) long-run evidence shows that: (i) all major extinctions appear to be due to climate change, though the causes differ; and (ii) long-run changes in $CO_2$ and methane concentrations are correlated with temperature and climate change.

However, as Hendry is acutely aware, correlation is not the same as causation and so this leaves open the question of the role of human activity and pollution in climate change. In Section 6 of the chapter Hendry provides an account of why we can be sure that human activity is responsible. Of course, we cannot be so sure about how much temperatures will rise in the future and what the precise effects will be. Hence, there are arguments for a precautionary approach, as Hendry suggests: 'if you are unsure whether a basket covered with a cloth really has a solid base, be concerned about putting all your eggs in it.'

On this point, neoclassical economists and ecologists have tended to differ; indeed Wam (2010, p. 677) argues that the precautionary principle ('in the absence of scientific consensus the burden of proof falls on those taking the actions') divides ecologists and economists, because the latter tend to focus exclusively on monetary valuations of harm. Expected utility theory is used by neoclassical economists to model risk and in this approach devastating events are treated in a probabilistic fashion. Calculations are more complex when costs and benefits occur in the future due to changes in the value of money over time, but such calculations can be made once an appropriate discount rate has been assumed, provided the probability distributions upon which they are based are known and stable. This assumption about known and stable probabilities also underpins real options theory, which is the extension of neoclassical analysis to irreversible investments.

Hendry provides a critical analysis of the relevance of this general approach in the case of uncertain catastrophic events and argues that factors such as 'deep' uncertainty, the possibility of 'mean shifts' in the underlying probability distribution, and tipping effects all undermine the very calculations upon which intertemporal evaluation relies. In addition, people's actual perceptions of, and attitudes to, risk are often at odds with those assumed by standard economic theory, with the consequence that 'behaviour may be rather different from that predicted by conventional economic analysis, absent an all knowing self-maximizer operating devoid of the social context, but facing potentially huge global externalities'. These points are picked up in the subsequent chapters by Michie and Oughton, Dawney and Shah, and Barker.

Chapter 3 by Michie and Oughton focuses on firms' behaviour and how this has been modelled using economic, managerial, institutional and evolutionary theories. Many of the social costs caused by environmental damage are the by-product of firms' economic activity. As firms are the target of numerous policy actions designed to limit environmental damage, it is important to have a clear understanding of firms' behaviour in order to predict their response to policy. This chapter explores the implications of three limitations of the standard theory of the firm: (i) the (lack of) analysis of the decision-making process and managerial discretion; (ii) the assumption of instrumental rationality; and (iii) the determinants and role of innovation and technological change. In recent years the literature on these topics has grown, providing greater understanding of firms' behaviour within a systems context and implications for the design and implementation of environmental policy.

The standard economic theory of the firm rests on the assumption of instrumental rationality (that agents have a clearly defined objective, for example, profit maximisation, and know how to achieve it) and generally focuses on price (or quantity) competition in a static equilibrium framework, assuming well-behaved cost and demand functions. Under these circumstances, firms' behaviour is reduced to calculus and, faced with the same circumstances, all firms take the same decision, so that they can be represented by a single, stylised firm (Kirman 1992). However, the strategic decision-making process is not considered in a meaningful way; firms are assumed to behave like automata and respond to price and cost signals in an identical fashion. There is no scope for managerial discretion, instead a unique equilibrium position is guaranteed/imposed courtesy of a U-shaped cost curve. Well-behaved cost curves also allow theoretical determination of the effect of taxes and subsidies on price, output and profitability.

This approach contrasts markedly with the managerial approach, whereby firms compete using price and a range of other variables including product and process innovation, organisational strategy, investment and marketing. Within the managerial literature (Nelson 1991) strategy is not confined to optimising over a single choice variable but is a more complex process that involves organising and renewing the resources of the firm to meet a range of objectives that matter alongside profit. Moreover, the possibility of increasing returns to scale makes it difficult to predict a firm's response to market-based policy instruments, thus complicating policy implementation. Increasing returns may also have the effect of creating lock-in to an inefficient technology, as it becomes difficult for a new technology to become established unless and until demand reaches minimum efficient scale of production.

Michie and Oughton explore the limitations of instrumental rationality using a game theoretic approach under different time horizons. Here, it is shown that alternative models of rationality and strategic behaviour provide more profitable outcomes for firms and society than instrumental rationality. This analysis suggests a wider range of policy instruments, including not only taxes and subsidies, but also institutional and voluntary arrangements that may be catalysed or that may evolve to govern the commons.

The penultimate section of the chapter focuses on innovation and examines the relationship between environmental outcomes, for example, lower carbon emissions, and corporate performance, including profitability. The neoclassical approach to modelling innovation, where it is possible to identify an optimal level of investment in R&D based on instrumental rationality and optimisation, is contrasted with the 'systems of innovation' approach, where innovation is determined by the interaction of interconnected institutions in the private and public sectors (Freeman 1987) as part of a process of interactive learning (Edquist 2001). Tim Foxon develops this approach in his two chapters later in the volume.

The adequacy of the standard model of rational economic man is explored further in Chapter 4 by Emma Dawnay and Hetan Shah. Their starting point is that changing consumer (and producer) behaviour is essential in order to change environmental outcomes. Therefore, a rich understanding of how individuals, firms and organisations behave is an essential building block of policy. The theoretical analysis in this chapter draws on alternative insights into rational action, including from psychology, prospect theory and social identity theory. Drawing on this interdisciplinary literature, Dawnay and Shah identify seven key principles for environmental policy:

1   Other people's behaviour matters – people do many things by observing others and copying;
2   Habits are important – people do many things without consciously thinking about them;

3   People are motivated to 'do the right thing', and there are cases when money is demotivating as it undermines people's intrinsic motivation;
4   People's self-expectations influence how they behave – they want their actions to be in line with their values and their commitments;
5   People are loss-averse and hang on to what they consider 'theirs';
6   People are bad at computation when making decisions, putting, for example, undue weight on recent events and too little weight on far-off ones;
7   People need to feel involved and effective to make a change – just giving people incentives and information is not necessarily enough.

Chapter 5 by Barker explores the whole systems approach to ecological economics that studies 'the earth as an integrated physical and social system' (Pitman 2005). The hallmark of the systems approach is that the behaviour of the system cannot be understood by analysing individual components in isolation. Environmental outcomes are produced by the interaction of natural and social systems that require a whole systems view of the Earth (Kirchner 2003). The whole systems approach is interdisciplinary, combining natural and social sciences. In part, the approach was inspired by Hardin's (1968; 1998) work which showed that in science there is a class of problem – to which the tragedy of the commons belongs – that has no technical or scientific solution. The problem may only be resolved by society. Over the past two decades this research has been consolidated within the interdisciplinary field of ecological economics, which Barker also presents.

The literature on ecological economics is beginning to shed new light on the range of policy options available. Barker argues that the traditional dichotomy between taxes and regulations is a false one as an effective policy may combine both. Moreover, these policies may be further enhanced by the use of governance structures and agreements that may evolve or be catalysed by government to manage common pool resources, such as the atmosphere or oceans.

## 2  Innovation

In Chapter 6, Tim Foxon elaborates on the 'systems of innovation' approach, covering 'national systems of innovation', 'regional systems of innovation' and 'technological systems of innovation'. The systems approach to innovation was originally developed by the late Chris Freeman, the heterodox economist who founded the Science Policy Research Unit at the University of Sussex. Professor Freeman recognised that the relative success of some countries over others in developing and adopting innovation was due not simply to their greater spending on research and development, nor indeed to any other single factor, but was due rather to a range of systemic features of the economy, including: its finance sector – and the availability of long-term, patient investment capital; its education and training system – and the proportion of scientists and engineers in the economy; its governmental and broader public policy approaches and institutions; and so on. Foxon cites Freeman's definition of a national system of innovation as 'the network of institutions in the public and private sectors whose activities and interactions initiate, import, modify and diffuse new technologies'.[3]

The systems approach to innovation was applied to the regional context by Howells (1999), who argues that Freeman's concepts are just as relevant at the regional and even local level. Howells links his analysis directly to the idea of 'technological systems of innovation' in arguing that regional systems should not be seen as an alternative proposition to national systems:

> but rather should be viewed as providing another layer or conceptual lens to the whole system of innovation. In so doing, it seeks to develop in a geographical sense at least part of Metcalfe's (1995, p. 41) view that the national unit may be too broad a category to allow a clear understanding of the complete dynamics of a technological system and instead focus should be on a 'number of distinct technology-based systems each of which is geographically and institutionally localised within the nation but with links into the supporting national and international system'.
>
> (Howells 1999, p. 67)

The policy implications of this approach are discussed in Chapter 7, again by Tim Foxon, with the clear link being that the policy measures taken to promote environmental objectives will be influenced by the understanding we have of how the economic system actually works. The systems approach encourages policy 'facilitating *systemic changes* to current technological and institutional systems; creating a *long-term, stable and consistent strategic framework* to promote a transition to more sustainable systems; and formulating clear, *long-term sustainability goals.*'

In doing so, Foxon argues that the systems approach provides a superior rationale for policy intervention in the area of environmental innovation than does the standard, neoclassical economic approach, for while the latter approach also emphasises disincentives to private firms to innovate new, clean technologies, seen as a market failure alongside the environmental externality of pollution, it does not generally allow for the two market failures to interact. The conclusion that tends to follow from this is, to paraphrase, that all that is required to solve environmental problems is a price signal reflecting the social value of pollution abatement, and that no special remedies are required in the area of innovation policy: standard, economy-wide incentives will do. The systems approach, by contrast, holds that there is indeed an interaction between the barriers to innovation and the disincentive to abate pollution, so that 'there are likely to be synergies arising from regulations that *specifically* promote environmentally beneficial innovation' (editors' own emphasis).

Foxon also discusses the 'Porter hypothesis', whereby environmental regulation need not be simply a cost or burden on business, but, through changes in managerial decisions and corporate behaviour, can simultaneously lead to improved environmental outcomes *and* increased industrial competitiveness.

Again, the possibility of a win-win outcome from the imposition of environmental regulation tends to be missed by standard economic analysis, which assumes that firms operate at their efficiency frontier prior to regulatory intervention, meaning that regulation simply imposes costs. However, Porter and his colleagues have been able to point to many case-study examples, showing that, when forced to search for efficiency improvements, firms have been able to find huge opportunities. The Porter hypothesis fits well with the innovation systems approach, Foxon argues, because both emphasise the wider social and institutional drivers of innovation, which a narrow focus on the private production costs of firms would miss.

Jonathan Köhler reports in Chapter 8 on how the different approaches to the economic modelling of climate-change mitigation seek to deal with the issue of technological change. As he observes, the politically charged debate about whether the future costs of abating greenhouse gas emissions will be manageable or prohibitive has been transformed by the recognition of how important it is to appropriately incorporate innovation of clean energy technologies. This stands to reason, since, in any feasible and remotely affordable scenario, deep cuts in emissions will require the substitution of fossil-fuel-based energy technologies with clean alternatives on a large scale.

As Köhler explains, the old economic theory of technological change, embodied in the so-called 'Solow residual', was not really much of a theory at all: technological change was simply that part of economic growth that could not actually be explained by measurable investment in capital and labour. Accordingly, the conceptual heirs to this theory in the field of energy/climate modelling simply specified innovation of clean technology as an exogenous variable ('manna from heaven'), and tended as a result to conclude that deep cuts in greenhouse gas emissions would be unaffordable. By contrast, recent theories in neoclassical economics and in other disciplines seek to model the process of technological change explicitly, including the notion that it is 'induced' by changes in government policy and private-sector investment activity. Crucially, implementation of these ideas in energy/climate modelling can lead to the conclusion that deep cuts in emissions are affordable.

Interestingly, Köhler is led to conclude that mainstream computable general equilibrium (CGE) models are limited by their inherently static nature. For instance, the assumption of diminishing returns to scale, which lies at the core of the equilibrium approach to economics, is violated in cases where learning-by-doing drives down the cost of clean technologies, in the process of deploying them at increasing scale. The idea of increasing returns to scale is linked with the notion of long waves of economic growth, which Köhler also discusses. Long-wave theory, recently made popular by the work of Carlota Perez (2002), has been developed as an attempt to explain the major technological and economic transformations of the nineteenth and twentieth centuries, including the emergence of steam power and computerisation. Given the structural change we face in decarbonising the global economy over the next half century or more, long-wave theory could be similarly insightful in helping design policy for the future.

In the final chapter (Chapter 9) of the section, Carlo Carraro, Enrica De Cian and Lea Nicita take an alternative look at how technical change can best be modelled in the context of climate-change mitigation. They point out that climate policy might well impact upon the rate and nature of economy-wide innovation, and also affect human capital formation. However, their key insight is that recent analyses in the field of energy and climate have not been able to take this fully into account, because they have neglected to model how mitigation policy affects innovation/human capital formation *outside* the energy sector. As they warn, other forms of innovation will continue to occur, and they may just as well work to increase pollution rather than decrease it.

Using a numerical economic model in the neoclassical tradition, Carraro and colleagues show that different formulations of endogenous technical change can result in climate policy having far-reaching effects on economy-wide knowledge and human capital formation. According to one of their formulations, deep cuts in greenhouse gas emissions reduce investments in research and development in the non-energy sector, which results in less technological change, and a higher cost of climate policy. But in taking an alternative approach by modelling human capital formation, Carraro and colleagues find that the opposite can obtain, provided investments in human capital indirectly reduce emissions through their positive effect on energy productivity. Clearly, more research on the linkages between climate policy and general technological change is urgently needed.

Each of these authors recognises in various ways that the impact upon the economy of economic policy interventions does not always work 'at the margin', with a rise in price (caused for example by a tax on carbon) leading to marginal changes in consumption and production. On the contrary, historically, there have been step changes in the way that economies operate, with major shifts in whole technology and productive systems. We are not talking of a marginal move towards or away from some equilibrium – were that concept to have any use, the equilibrium itself would be shifting, involving a dynamic disequilibrium. Looked at in terms of such major shifts in trajectories and long swings in economic cycles and their accompanying productive systems, it was hoped by many that just as the Great Depression of the 1930s gave rise to the New Deal, so the first global recession since the 1930s, namely the global economic downturn of 2009, following the 2007–2008 credit crunch, would give rise to a global 'Green New Deal', with government intervention leading to a major shift towards green technologies and environmentally sustainable production.[4]

At the time of writing in 2010, the opportunity appears to have been lost, with the banks returning to their pre-credit-crunch focus on short-term financial returns, and governments scaling back their spending and investments rather than promoting any major green technologies. However, provided that policy globally sets clear long-term requirements to achieve environmental improvements, there will be commercial advantage to be had by being in the lead in the new green technologies, which will need to be adopted and diffused globally. The accompanying infrastructures will most likely require public sector provision, so a Green New Deal may yet emerge in the course of the global economy recovering, within the context of having to accommodate to increasingly tough environmental standards.

## 3 Sustainability

'Policies to encourage pro-environmental behaviour', Tim Jackson observes in the concluding remarks to Chapter 10, 'have tended in the past to favour two main avenues of intervention', (i) information provision and (ii) changes to the private costs and benefits of behaviour, by means of environmental taxes, for example. Both approaches are well supported by the theory of market failure, the former being a response to imperfect information, and the latter an attempt to internalise negative environmental externalities in the tradition of Pigou's (1920) classic analysis. However, without denying the importance of information and pricing, Jackson questions whether they will by themselves be successful in promoting sustainable consumption.

They are both based, he observes, on the rational choice model of human behaviour, where individuals confront choices ranging from the everyday to the once-in-a-lifetime by carefully computing the expected net private benefits of various courses of action, with a view to choosing the alternative that is expected to maximise these benefits. This rational choice model is widely used, but is particularly notable for its central role in the economic theory of consumer preferences. Yet a number of important criticisms have over the years been levelled at rational choice theory, and the purpose of Jackson's chapter is to air these, and in doing so move towards an integrated, interdisciplinary theory of consumer behaviour. Thus Jackson develops themes introduced in Chapter 4 by Dawnay and Shah.

The first well-known critique focuses on the assumption that individuals carefully compute their expected net private benefits over a complete range of alternatives. In the face of limited resources, a rich tradition beginning with Simon (1957) and carried on by, for example, Tversky and Kahneman (1974) shows that individuals do not always (perhaps even usually) maximise expected utility, instead falling back on satisficing behaviour (i.e. selecting alternatives that are simply 'good enough'), or various rules of thumb. Another line of attack has been forged by those emphasising the role of emotion in guiding behaviour. The second critique focuses on the assumption of individuality; that is, the individual as the fundamental unit of analysis in rational choice theory. This may miss the point, some social psychologists have argued, because individuals' sense of identity is socially constructed, through interactions with others. In addition, individualism may overlook the important role played by social structures in decision making. Frequently, these social structures have much longer lifetimes than individuals, and it is possible to find many examples of institutions to which individuals belong, despite there being no obvious benefit to the individuals concerned. The third critique focuses on the assumption that individuals act in the pursuit of their own interests, instead emphasising what is rather abstractly termed 'other-regarding behaviour'. It is technically possible to incorporate such behaviour in the rational choice model, by assuming that individuals obtain utility from, for example, altruism, but for the critics this stretches the rational choice model to the point of being meaningless, tautological even.

To take these critiques seriously, Jackson argues that an integrative theory is required, which builds on the insights from social psychology, sociology and other disciplines to generate a richer model of consumer behaviour, including both internal and external drivers (i.e. to the individual), and where the internal drivers extend beyond the evaluation of expected net private benefits to embrace factors such as emotion, habits and values. Fortunately attempts to build such a theory already exist, he explains, in the work of Triandis (1977), Giddens (1984) and others.

Returning to his concluding remarks, Jackson goes further to discuss the implications of such a theory for the role of government in bringing about sustainable consumption. These implications might be profound. One interpretation of the various critiques of rational choice theory, and the integrative theory that reconciles them, is that the contemporary mantra of 'hands-off' governance is miguided. Government intervenes in the fabric of society in many ways, far beyond the direct imposition of environmental policies, which is the boundary of many conventional analyses. Jackson argues that government is partly responsible for the culture of (over-)consumption, and one might then conclude that it is widely responsible for reorienting consumer culture. Put another way, the scope of government intervention in the sustainability debate might go far beyond piecemeal regulatory intervention, to address the underlying goals of development, and the expectations and motivations people imbibe from those goals.

In Chapter 11, Lorraine Whitmarsh further develops some of these themes, looking at the social and psychological drivers of energy consumption behaviour, and the role that the public plays in the energy system more generally. The problem as things stand is that we face a 'value–action' gap: in the context of climate change, public awareness and concern have risen in recent years and have now attained a fairly high level, yet few are choosing to adopt low-carbon lifestyles, aside from domestic recycling and limited domestic energy conservation. Whitmarsh goes on to explore the reasons for this value–action gap, and concludes, in a similar vein to Jackson, that there are multiple determinants at play. These range from cultural factors, according to which some energy consumption choices result from a need to express identity and establish status (e.g. car choice and use, and domestic air conditioning), to habits and routines, whereby consumption choices quickly become automatic and essentially unconscious. Neither of these determinants, Whitmarsh points out, are afforded particular emphasis in a standard economic account, even though they have several important implications for policy. For one, policies to increase the provision of information about low-carbon energy consumption practices will need to become more targeted to points in time when individuals are reconsidering their routines, and will need at the same time to become more sensitive to the role of culture and identity in forming consumption choices. For another, the pre-eminent role of habitual behaviour points to the benefits of moving policy upstream, in effect 'editing' people's choice sets in the new tradition of libertarian paternalism (Thaler and Sunstein 2009).

Whitmarsh goes on from the analysis of energy consumption choices to consider the role of the public in the energy system more generally. For example, public support for fundamental changes in the mix of energy-supply technologies, away from power generated by fossil fuels, will be crucial, as current experience in many countries with the difficulties of building onshore wind and nuclear power plants shows. Two literatures are relevant here. First, there is the body of research on public participation and civic engagement, because there appear to be strong similarities between, on the one hand, the expressions of apathy and disengagement researchers tend to encounter in soliciting public views about climate-change policy, and, on the other hand, problems with engagement in representative democracy more widely. Participatory democracy is often touted as a solution to the wider problem, so it is natural to ask whether it would then present a potential solution to the problem of energy policy more narrowly. Second, there is the literature on socio-technical transitions, which considers the relationships between technology, infrastructure and society in the supply and demand of energy. The important insight from this approach is the co-evolution of the technological and social parts of the system, and how it leads to 'lock-in' of existing regimes. However, while this approach has been focused most frequently on technical issues, and is indeed picked up elsewhere in this volume, Whitmarsh argues that the social aspects remain underexplored. Recent work that has emphasised the social elements of the energy system has unearthed important insights into how the public might play a more active, rather than passive, role. Instead of simply soliciting public support for changes in energy technologies, might the public play a more active role in establishing the importance of decentralised, micro-generation of power, for example? The conventional economics of micro-generation might suggest a limited role for it, but wider cultural and behavioural factors paint a more optimistic picture.

We move in Chapter 12 to consider the production side of the sustainability problem, looking at the particular case of North Sea fisheries. Unusually, Prashant Vaze provides an account of the challenge of sustainable production from the perspective of the fisherman, rather than the regulator. He takes an interdisciplinary, systems-based perspective, describing the numerous dependencies between the four main actors in the fishery: fishermen at its centre; scientists responsible for quantifying fish stock levels and advising the regulator; banks as the lender to a capital-intensive and often highly leveraged sector; and the fishery manager or regulator. Fishermen in the North Sea face severe economic and regulatory pressures, Vaze explains, and these combine to generate a range of bad outcomes, from overfishing and low or even negative profits to distrust of fisheries science and of fisheries management.

Vaze argues that a broad, systems-based perspective with fishermen at its core can help overcome some of the weaknesses of the existing management regime. Two weaknesses are most pressing. The first is a lack of compliance with management rules, notably the total allowable catch or quota that fishermen are permitted. Non-compliance is widespread. Moreover his research shows that it is perceived as legitimate. Echoing Whitmarsh's discussion in Chapter 11,

Vaze proposes, alongside familiar remedies such as effective and proportional punishments for exceeding quotas, a collaborative approach to management between fishermen, scientists and managers, in order to build trust and establish the legitimacy of the management regime, rather than non-compliance with it. This is a clear example of the sort of 'thick' analysis of environmental decision making that Adger *et al.* (2003) called for. The overall success of the regime depends not only on its efficiency but also on its legitimacy. Nevertheless, the second pressing weakness does concern efficiency, namely the tendency for the fleet's killing power to grow beyond the level that can be supported by the fish stock. This is primarily a story of perverse (but rational) responses by fishermen to management measures intended precisely to reduce catch, such as subsidies for decommissioning vessels, which can reduce the cost of exit from the industry and thus make riskier investments in new fleet relatively more attractive, and restrictions on catch that apply only to large vessels, which rather obviously incentivise fishermen to switch to smaller, but crucially more powerful, boats. By putting fishermen's incentives centre stage, Vaze shows how such perverse consequences can be avoided. One important suggestion is that overfishing might be most effectively prevented not by limiting the amount of fish that can be caught but by limiting the amount of investment that can be made in the fleet.

## Notes

1 The World Bank did not consider biodiversity loss, though Dietz and Adger (2003) later showed that there was no evidence of a slowing in the rate of biodiversity loss with rising income per capita.
2 The World Resources Institute has a particularly elegant way of presenting this interdependency between emissions sources and end-use sectors (WRI 2005).
3 For detailed discussions of the national systems of innovation literature, see also Freeman's own review (Freeman 1995) and the survey by Archibugi and Michie (1997).
4 As argued, for example, in Oxford's iTunes U podcast by Michie and Yueh, *Bank Bailouts and Obama's Green New Deal*, http://itunes.ox.ac.uk.

## References

Adger, W. N. *et al.* (2003). 'Governance for sustainability: towards a "thick" analysis of environmental decisionmaking.' *Environment and Planning A* 35: 1095–1110.
Archibugi, D. and J. Michie (1997). 'Technological globalisation and national systems of innovation: an introduction.' *Technology, Globalisation and Economic Performance.* D. Archibugi and J. Michie. Cambridge, UK, Cambridge University Press.
Besley, T. (2006). *Principled Agents? The Political Economy of Good Government.* Oxford, Oxford University Press.
Dietz, S. and W. N. Adger (2003). 'Economic growth, biodiversity loss and conservation effort.' *Journal of Environmental Management* 68: 23–35.
Edquist, C. (2001). 'Systems of innovation.' *A Reader's Guide to the Social Sciences.* J. Michie. London, Fitzroy Dearbon/Routledge.
Enkvist, P.-A. *et al.* (2007). 'A cost curve for greenhouse gas reduction.' *The McKinsey Quarterly* 2007(1): 35–45.

Freeman, C. (1987). *Technology Policy and Economic Peformance: Lessons from Japan.* London, Pinter.

Freeman, C. (1995). 'The "National System of Innovation" in historical perspective.' *Cambridge Journal of Economics* 19(1): 5–24.

Giddens, A. (1984). *The Constitution of Society: Outline of the Theory of Structuration.* Berkeley and Los Angeles, University of California Press.

Goulder, L. H. and I. W. H. Parry (2008). 'Instrument choice in environmental policy.' *Review of Environmental Economics and Policy* 2(2): 152–174.

Greenspan, A. (2008). Congressional Testimony to the House Committee on Oversight and Reform.

Groenewegen, P. (2008). Political economy. *The New Palgrave Dictionary of Economics.* S. N. Durlauf and L. E. Blume. Basingstoke, Palgrave Macmillan.

Hardin, G. (1968). 'The tragedy of the commons.' *Science* 162(3859): 1243–1248.

Hardin, G. (1998). 'Extensions of "The Tragedy of the Commons".' *Science* 280(5354): 682–683.

Howells, J. (1999). 'Regional Systems of Innovation?' *Innovation Policy in a Global Economy.* D. Archibugi and J. Michie. Cambridge, UK, Cambridge University Press.

Kirchner, J. W. (2003). 'The Gaia hypothesis: conjectures and refutations.' *Climatic Change* 58(1–2): 21–45.

Kirman, A. P. (1992). 'Whom or what does the representative individual represent.' *Journal of Economic Perspectives* 6(2): 117–136.

Kuhn, T. (1962). *The Structure of Scientific Revolutions.* Chicago, University of Chicago Press.

Metcalfe, S. (1995). 'Technology systems and technology policy in an evolutionary framework.' *Cambridge Journal of Economics* 19(1): 25–46.

Nelson, R. (1991). 'The role of firm differences in evolutionary theory of technical advance.' *Science and Public Policy* 18(6): 347–352.

OECD (2008). *OECD Environmental Outlook to 2030.* Paris, OECD.

Perez, C. (2002). *Technological Revolutions and Financial Capital.* Cheltenham, UK; Northampton, MA, Edward Elgar.

Pigou, A. C. (1920). *The Economics of Welfare.* London, Macmillan.

Pitman, A. J. (2005). 'On the role of geography in earth system science.' *Geoforum* 36(2): 137–148.

Reinhardt, C. and K. Rogoff (2008). 'This time is different: a panoramic view of eight centuries of financial crises.' *NBER Working Paper No. 13882*, National Bureau of Economic Research (NBER).

Simon, H. (1957). *Models of Man.* New York, John Wiley.

Thaler, R. H. and C. R. Sunstein (2009). *Nudge: Improving Decisions about Health, Wealth and Happiness.* London, Penguin Books.

Triandis, H. (1977). *Interpersonal Behaviour.* Monterey, California, Brooks/Cole.

Tversky, A. and D. Kahneman (1974). 'Judgement under uncertainty: heuristics and biases.' *Science* 185: 1124–1131.

Wam, H. (2010). 'Economists, time to team up with ecologists!' *Ecological Economics* 69: 675–679.

World Bank (1992). *World Development Report 1992: Development and the Environment.* Washington, DC, World Bank.

World Resources Institute (2005). Navigating the Numbers: Greenhouse Gas Data and International Climate Policy. Washington, DC, World Resources Institute.

# Part I
# Foundations

# 2 Climate change

## Lessons for our future from the distant past

*David F. Hendry\**

## 1 Introduction

There seem to be potentially vital lessons from the distant past for our future, especially about how we might interpret present climate change and understand its possible impacts. By the distant past is meant from about 500 million years ago up to the present. As argued by Schmidt and Moyer (2008) and Barker (2008), interdisciplinary science is essential to understand climate change, and requires a genuinely multi-faceted approach that is all too rare in this era of deep specialization. Despite the ever present reminder that fools rush in, and conceding that the extant literature is vast (see e.g. National Academy of Science, 2008), so a summary may inadvertently distort, this chapter is an attempt to look at a wide range of scientific and economic ideas and evidence that impinge on climate change. Few in academia, government or business seem aware of all the connections between the findings across a multitude of disciplines, but combining all the results should lead to a serious rethink of the potential risks, even by current skeptics. This chapter relates climate change to past mass extinctions of life on Earth, and presents a framework of shifts in the distributions of climatic outcomes as the relevant one for policy actions.

Long-run data from earth drilling, the presence of isotopes from air trapped in rocks, fossils, and shells, evidence of repeated glaciations by the movements of rocks from their sources to present locations, and the formation of coal and oil deposits from tropical forests, all reveal a huge range of past climates from very cold to very hot (see e.g. Hoffman and Schrag, 2000). Clearly, life has survived these great changes, as many species are alive today. Moreover, life has thrived when global temperatures, and associated levels of atmospheric carbon dioxide, were much higher than today: many stable levels can support abundant life. However, *huge numbers have also become extinct in the process of change*, even if long after major climate change, new species evolve and adapt to whatever the environment happens to be: but remember, these might just be bacteria clinging to deep-sea hot vents. Currently the global climate is about 4–5 degrees Celsius above that prevailing at the end of the last ice age, when Manhattan was under a mile of ice, as were most locations at similar northern latitudes. Such a 'small' temperature rise has transformed the planet, eliminating many species in the process, including *homo neanderthalensis*. A further rise of that magnitude could effect an equally large transformation on flora and fauna, making many more species extinct, and we cannot preclude that *homo sapiens* would suffer greatly. That would especially be the case if the resulting resource strains led to mass migration, social unrest or even nuclear wars. Thus, it is essential to form as clear a view as possible of the process of climate change, and what – if anything – can be done to alleviate any potentially adverse effects.

Since most of the relevant evidence is of necessity scientific, Section 2 addresses the fallibility of scientific evidence in general, and yet its powerful contribution to our understanding of many aspects of the world. Despite the absence of certainty in the scientific approach, genuine knowledge has been acquired. Section 3 discusses the Earth's climate, leading to Section 4 on the four key greenhouse gases, how they affect climate, and how humans may affect those gases. With that background, Section 5 reviews the great extinctions over the last 500 million years, and the role of climate change in all of them. The processes behind those extinctions are often very different, yet they share many commonalities: all are due to climate change, either cooling or warming, and all are associated with high atmospheric levels of carbon dioxide, some before, some after. Section 6 discusses several of the processes leading to extinctions, and draws some implications for the present from those distant past events. Section 7 then considers seven of the entailed economic issues, and Section 8 concludes.

## 2 Science and scientific evidence

Some of the skepticism about climate change and anthropogenic influences thereon derives from the fact that science is fallible, exacerbated by the criticism that individual scientists are not 'objective', so scientific evidence is not to be trusted. We consider these two strands in turn, and show that the resulting evidence provides genuine knowledge about the world.

It is undoubtedly true that all aspects of any science are uncertain, especially in non-experimental or observational disciplines. Adam Smith might have been the first thinker to propose that even Newton's theory of universal gravitation was not an immutable truth, but a model that might be changed by future astronomers (see Stewart, 1795), a prediction that has since been vindicated, without in any way impugning Newton's great contributions. In particular, empirical knowledge is always open to revision, and is certainly not robust truth. Nevertheless, the history of the scientific enterprise manifests great progressivity, overcoming many intellectual and social obstacles to gain the huge increases in knowledge taken as given today.

Second, it must also be acknowledged that not all scientists are totally objective: excessive egos, career necessities, dogmatism blocking publication of critical results by others, and even outright fraud are far from unknown (see e.g. Waller, 2002). For example, to convince the 'establishment', Barry Marshall drank *Helicobacter pylori* to demonstrate that they caused stomach ulcers, followed by a dose of antibiotics to show he had identified the cure. That episode, humorously recounted in Marshall (2005), stresses a key attribute of the scientific process, namely that blockages and even previously undiscovered fraud are often relatively temporary, as the same human forces that create them also motivate others to overturn invalid claims. Research on climate change and the great extinctions of the past must intrinsically draw on dozens of disciplines' expertise, where few individuals can span the entire spectrum of sciences involved. That alone precludes any 'conspiracy' either of ideas, or to bolster funding, as many of the subjects will always be in direct competition for research support.[1]

The cumulative weight of evidence gained by trying to refute existing views provides an invaluable basis for current decision making, since scientific knowledge is real: from an endless list, it is obvious that electric lights work, computers calculate, planes fly, and scanners can detect cancers. These have become efficient technologies because of scientific understanding. Rosenberg (1983) showed that initial technological developments often preceded the science, and provided the incentive for the latter: for example, the first airplanes flew well before there was a scientific understanding of flight, and prompted research on aerodynamics. Nevertheless, it is now possible to accurately 'predict' what improvements will increase lumens from lights (see Fouquet and Pearson, 2006, for a fascinating history), what changes to microchips will speed up computer calculations (famously captured by 'Moore's Law'),[2] what putative aircraft will not fly well (e.g. the Spruce Goose?), and why scanners can 'see inside us'. These inferences are far beyond any local set of experiments and available evidence, are not purely inductive, and can be generalized, though doubtless within limits. Thus, despite their fallibility, scientific findings have revolutionized the world and its living standards.

In the four cases just noted, a well-based theory was developed, which was in turn both embodied in the general framework of scientific thinking and led to further advances. However, even purely empirical findings can be invaluable. For example, aspirin (acetylsalicylic acid) lowers pain, especially from headaches, and was so used for many centuries before anyone knew how or why it worked. Based initially on 'folk medicine', brewing the bark of the willow tree as a hangover remedy, the active ingredient in aspirin was first isolated in the 1760s, synthesized in the 1850s and manufactured in the 1890s, but how it operated to alleviate pain is a late twentieth century discovery (see Weissmann, 1991).

Nevertheless, even after several centuries of major scientific discoveries and brilliant theoretical insights, there remain huge uncertainties in general about what is possible, why things are the way they are, and what can happen. Such a statement applies forcefully to our knowledge and understanding of climate change, but does not entail that all views are equally valid: we now know a great deal, and some implications are all too clear, as we now discuss.

## 3 Earth's climate and its atmosphere and oceans

A complex series of interactions seems to drive the climatic process, which can make it difficult to discern the causes of climate change. We first note two possible natural drivers of change, then consider the Earth's atmosphere and its oceans.

The sun may be warming endogenously, possibly for the last few millennia, with local fluctuations manifested by sun spots, and has clearly warmed substantially over geological time. But in recent decades, that effect is not large (see UK Met Office, 2008). Also, the Earth may still be warming on a natural 'bounce' common in interglacial stadia, following the end of the last ice age, just from the removal of the factors that cause ice-age cooling (reduced albedo, changes in tilt, etc.). The temperature impacts of both factors can be inferred within reasonable bounds from ice-core drilling records extending back for half a million years.

The atmosphere itself is a complicated process exhibiting surprisingly slow mixing between layers, and even with differential warming and cooling in different layers and at different latitudes. Temperature falls with height through the Troposphere till the Tropopause (somewhat above the height of Mt. Everest at 10,000 m), stays relatively constant till the ozone layer, then rises through the Stratosphere (50,000 m), pausing before falling in the Mesosphere (to about 80,000 m), then rising in the Thermosphere (where Aurora are observed). Again, the evidence is robust, these forces are fairly well understood and can be incorporated in analyses and models.[3] Earth's gravity and its magnetic field together are essential to 'hold on to' our atmosphere against the solar wind, and our ozone layer provides protection from damaging radiation.

Atmospheric gas constituents have changed greatly over the history of the planet, especially with the exchange of carbon dioxide for oxygen through photosynthesis, and may have altered considerably over the period considered here, as discussed in Section 5. The central role of greenhouse gases and how they may affect climate is discussed in Section 4, but it is clear that an atmospheric blanket is essential to life. The National Academy of Science (2008) provides a clear explanation of why the Earth would be a frozen ball without a dense atmosphere, and provides an excellent picture of how greenhouse gases receive and radiate at different wavelengths between ultraviolet and infrared, as well as their recent relative importance.

Mars and Venus are planetary neighbours whose climates have diverged horribly, now respectively being cold with a thin atmosphere and boiling with one that suffered from a runaway greenhouse effect. Atmospheric protection needs to be 'just right', albeit within a range that has included both world wide ice ages and tropical conditions. We conclude that the physics of radiation from greenhouse gases is well understood, as is the role of the atmosphere in sustaining life on our planet.

Next, there is a worldwide ocean 'conveyor belt' system whereby cold water is mixed with warm to carry oxygen to depths and circulate nutrients. As warm water from the Gulf Stream moves north, it cools and evaporates becoming more salty and hence denser, so eventually sinks and flows south again, passing by Antarctica, then gradually warming and rising to the surface as it travels north across the Pacific Ocean. From the Pacific Ocean, warm water flows south and crosses the Indian Ocean, then moves north and cools once more. Global warming may affect and slow down these ocean conveyor belts with potentially mixed outcomes (e.g. Northern Europe may cool and North America warm). While stable over most of the Holocene era (the last 10,000 years), larger longer-term variations have occurred (see Tziperman, 1997), and must have accompanied tectonic plate movements. As seen below, altering the flows of oxygen and nutrients round the planet can disrupt many species.

Thus, the key ingredients of the climatic picture are understood. Before we can ask if climate is changing, we must consider the four main greenhouse gases in more detail.

## 4 Four greenhouse gases

Greenhouse gases are crucial to life on earth, as they are fundamental to maintaining the planet's temperature within limits supportive of life. There are four important greenhouse gases: water vapour ($H_2O$), carbon dioxide ($CO_2$), nitrous oxide ($N_2O$), and methane ($CH_4$). The last two gases have carbon dioxide equivalents, discussed below. All of these greenhouse gases are presently increasing at different rates, and are likely to alter their relative impacts in the future.

The physics of greenhouse gases are quite well understood, and date from insights starting in the late nineteenth century (see Arrhenius, 1896, who argued that atmospheric temperature change was proportional to the logarithmic change in $CO_2$). Heat enters the earth's atmosphere from the sun as radiation, warms the surface, then is re-radiated back through various atmospheric layers where greenhouse gases absorb some of the heat. This is then re-radiated, with some radiation therefore directed back towards the planet's surface. Thus, greater concentrations of greenhouse gases increase the amount of absorption and hence re-radiation. In turn, that increases convection between the surface and sequentially through atmospheric layers, raising their temperatures and water vapour content, thereby changing cloud cover. Only a sophisticated general 'equilibrium' model of the system can capture the many complicated interactions and interdependencies between all the components. We now consider the four gases in turn.

First, water vapour is currently the most important and prevalent of the greenhouse gases, and is obviously crucial to life on earth, inducing cloud cover and rainfall etc. However, increased concentrations of water vapor in upper levels of the atmosphere would reduce heat loss from radiation.

Second, carbon dioxide is also key to life, and like water vapour has been a major greenhouse gas long before the evolution of modern humans. The present half-life time of $CO_2$ in our atmosphere is 30–100 years, depending on factors like ocean absorption capacity and plant growth (see e.g. Lovelock, 2000). There is roughly a 30-year lag between emissions and their full effect on warming. Naturally, many other factors can impinge, some leading to cooling effects, such as particulate matter emissions from industrial activity and volcanoes (e.g. the 1815 AD eruption of Tambora leading to 1816 being 'the year without a summer': see Stommel and Stommel, 1979), as well as aircraft vapour trails and changing cloud cover, La Niña, etc. Other factors lead to warming, such as re-release of $CO_2$ from the oceans as they warm.

Third, nitrous oxide comprises about 7 percent of gases influencing global climate. Measures suggest it is about 300 times more potent than carbon dioxide as a greenhouse gas. In addition, following the reductions in CFCs,[4] nitrous oxide is now the most potent destructive force attacking the ozone layer (see Ravishankara *et al.*, 2009).

Fourth, methane is about 20 times as powerful as $CO_2$ as a greenhouse gas, albeit that its halflife in the upper atmosphere is about 15 years. Methane gradually gets converted to $CO_2$ in the upper atmosphere so has a second effect on climate. Present estimates of the total volume of methane already show it is vast: worldwide, the amount of methane gas hydrates alone is estimated at over 6 trillion tonnes – about twice the amount of carbon equivalent in all fossil fuels.[5]

## 4.1 How we affect the four greenhouse gases

Anthropogenic effects on climate from greenhouse gases seem to date back to the origins of agriculture around 10,000–12,000 years ago (see e.g. Bellwood, 2004), beginning at the end of what is called the Weichsel glacial period,[6] and the start of our (Holocene) era. This was followed by pottery and domestication of animals, with a rapid rise in population and land clearance, leading to increased outputs of $CO_2$. Carbon dioxide output increased greatly during the industrial revolution, and is now mainly due to power generation from fossil fuel consumption, primarily coal, gas, and oil, exacerbated by tropical deforestation.[7] As living standards rise and population growth is non-negative, 'business as usual' projections would lead to sustained growth in $CO_2$ emissions.

Nitrous oxide output has doubled since the 1970s, mainly from modern agricultural practices and burning gasoline (see Energy Information Administration, 2008, for US data). Catalytic converters in car exhaust systems break down the heavier nitrogen compounds, as well as oxidizing carbon monoxide, forming $CO_2$ and nitrous oxide in the process, producing more of the latter when the exhaust system is cold or stressed. Fertilizer overuse leads to run-off and the release of nitrous oxide: as Ravishankara *et al.* (2009) show, nitrous oxide is becoming an increasing component of greenhouse gases.

Methane is produced by living plants and animals as a by-product (e.g. cattle), and also by rotting vegetation. If warming substantially melts the Siberian permafrost, greenhouse gas output could jump.Already, at any lake in northern Siberia, drill a hole in the ice to fish, then hold a flame over the hole – but jump back to avoid being burned by the methane catching fire. That is one of several possible 'tipping points', including general release of subsea methane hydrates, and a collapse in rainforest ecology through changes in rainfall patterns.

## 4.2 Some evidence of our impact

There is a long list of evidence for a world-wide temperature trend.

Many plants flower in spring in both hemispheres about 2–3 weeks earlier than when accurate, reliable, and almost continuous, records began about 1850.

Satellite pictures confirm the melting of the Greenland and Antarctic ice shelves over the last 30 years, with concomitant rises in ocean levels of between 0.1 and 0.2 meters during the twentieth century, partly offset by increased storage in dams. Evidence of warming of many parts of the oceans is associated with bleaching of some coral beds. Most directly, global air temperatures over the last century reveal that most of the warmest records occur in the latest decades, based on data collected sufficiently far from cities to avoid contamination from 'local warming'.

The resulting world-wide temperature 'trend' is both stochastic and slow relative to fluctuations from all sources, so it is easy to be skeptical about that trend and its rate of progress. As a related example, until recently, it was believed there had been essentially no growth in English gross domestic product (GDP) per capita over 1300–1700, because real wages seemed static. However, Apostolides *et al.* (2008) have shown that real growth was 0.13 to 0.16 percent per annum. That is tiny against the huge fluctuations caused by the Black Death, famines, wars and so on, and therefore such a trend is hard to detect. Nevertheless, by nearly doubling living standards over 400 years, there was a precursor to the Industrial Revolution from the resulting high cost of labour as documented by Allen (2009). Moreover, some 'counter arguments' are invalid, including the claim in the *Australian* that there was 'little world temperature growth from 1998 to 2006' (July, 2008): an economics student who selectively joined the peak of one boom to the trough of the next slump and claimed that proved there was no economic growth would be failed.

It is change in the climate, rather than the level within bounds, that causes problems for life, because adaptation is not instantaneous, as the following discussion of 'great extinctions' emphasizes.

## 5 Climate change and great extinctions

The fossil record suggests that there were a number of major extinction events even before land life evolved. One in the pre-Cambrian era, about 600 million years ago (abbreviated to mya), was so severe that almost all micro-organisms were wiped out. A probable explanation was large scale glaciation, which is the opposite form of climate change to global warming. Next, the Cambrian seems to have witnessed four major marine extinctions, possibly due to global sea cooling leading to oxygen depletion.

There have been five other 'mass extinctions' in the past 500 million years when many of the world's life-forms ceased to exist. Of these, the first mass extinction came at the end of the Ordovician period, roughly 440 mya. The second, around 375 mya, occurred near the close of the Devonian era. The third, and worst, was at the Permian–Triassic (P/Tr) boundary, about 250 mya, and eliminated 80–90 percent of ocean dwellers and about 70 percent of plants, animals, and insects (see e.g. Erwin, 1996, 2006). The fourth extinction at the end of the Triassic, about 200 mya, opened an ecological niche for dinosaurs to emerge as a major fauna in the Jurassic. The fifth major extinction was at the well-known Cretaceous–Tertiary (K/T) boundary, roughly 60 mya, when a major lineage of dinosaurs called saurischia went extinct (all dates rounded for simplicity).

The science behind much of this dating has led to scanners, so there is no reason to doubt the occurrences of these extinctions. The key issue to which we now turn is whether, and to what extent, climate change was involved.

After a quarter century of searching for evidence, many palaeoarcheologists, paleontologists, palaeoclimatologists and palaeobiologists seem to have concluded that of these five, only the K/T boundary extinction could plausibly be attributed to extra-terrestrial forces alone, probably a meteor impact. This left two visiting cards, namely, traces of iridium in rocks separating dinosaur from mammalian eras, and the Chicxulub impact crater near the Yucatan peninsula. Even so, volcanism may also have played a role.

The remaining four 'great extinctions' seem due to global climate change from endogenous changes on earth. The first mass extinction at the end of the Ordovician is currently viewed as due to global cooling. So is the second, at the end of the Devonian, possibly due to the rapid spread of plant life on land reducing atmospheric $CO_2$ by photosynthesis.

The third, and worst, extinction event at the Permian–Triassic boundary is associated with the formation of flood basalts on a massive scale from prolonged volcanic eruptions, technically a large igneous province (LIP). These often form layered hills looking a bit like stairs, called Traps. The LIP in Siberia covered more than 2 million square kilometers. Temperatures seem to have ended about 6°C higher than today. Gas hydrates are a possible cause of this 'Great Dying', especially methane and carbonates released from relatively shallow seas by the formation of these Siberian Traps. Heydari *et al.* (2008) attribute the mass extinction to huge releases of marine gas hydrates. Direct outpourings of magma into oceans may also have perturbed their deep levels (see e.g. Ward, 2006), as undersea volcanism can lead to oceanic oxygen deficiency when LIPs disrupt the ocean conveyor belts (see Bralower, 2008). The resulting anoxia could have supported an explosion in bacteria that produce hydrogen sulfide. Ocean circulation may also have slowed or even stopped from a lack of ice at the poles. While that initially affects marine life, carbon dioxide dissolves more in cold water, so as water warms, it is released (as in sparkling water), sometimes by an overturn of water that releases huge volumes of carbon dioxide. Once released, carbon dioxide is about 1.5 times more dense than air so remains at ground level. Lake Nyos (a crater lake in the Northwest Province of Cameroon) is an example of the dreadful effects of the release of large volumes of carbon dioxide.

The fourth extinction at the end of the Triassic remains the most disputed, but is possibly also due to a massive LIP forming (the Central Atlantic Magmatic Province). The extinction may again have been due to excessive $CO_2$ from the catastrophic dissociation of gas hydrates inducing intense global warming, or possibly from sulfur dioxide leading to cooling. There is also some evidence near the Triassic–Jurassic boundary of a rise in atmospheric $CO_2$.

The fifth extinction at the K/T boundary is also associated with the formation of another LIP, called the Deccan Traps in India, where magma was extruded over a prolonged period, covering approximately 100,000 square kilometers by roughly 160 meters deep, with temperatures that were about 4°C higher than today (see Prothero, 2008, for an evaluation).

Based on the fossil record for the last 520 million years, Mayhew *et al.* (2009) show that global biodiversity for both terrestrial and marine environments was related to sea-surface temperature, with biodiversity being relatively low during warm periods (also see Clarke, 1993).

Thus, climate change is a cause in every case: excessive warming or cooling have both led to large-scale species extinction on Earth.

## 6 Possible processes causing mass extinctions

There are many possible processes causing mass extinctions and we will consider several of the most likely, before linking these to the ongoing changes in Earth's atmosphere.

One hypothesized mechanism for the warming extinctions being so drastic is that the chemocline between oxygenated water above and anoxic water below rose with temperature (see e.g. Riccardi *et al.*, 2007). When the chemocline reached the surface, archaea and anaerobic bacteria, such as green sulfur bacteria, proliferated and generated vast quantities of hydrogen sulphide ($H_2S$), with toxicity comparable to hydrogen cyanide. There is carbon isotopic evidence for the chemocline's upward excursion during the end-Permian extinction, with a large increase in phototrophic sulfur bacteria replacing algae and cyanobacteria, consistent with huge loss of ocean life. As with $CO_2$, hydrogen sulfide is heavier than air, so has a tendency to accumulate on the surface, although $H_2S$ also attacks the ozone layer if driven to the upper atmosphere by volcanism, reducing protection from solar radiation.

The recent behaviour of the Black Sea is an indication of how fast a switch in the chemocline can happen, with the anoxic layer reaching the surface, albeit that it was probably due to excess nitrogen and phosphates from run-off, not global warming per se (see Mee, 2006). Fortunately that problem is now stabilized, but the eruption of sulfur bacteria round China's southern coast just before the 2008 Olympics is another example.

A second mechanism is the growing mis-timing of annual breeding cycles of many species, especially birds and amphibians: usual birth times move increasingly out of synchrony with times at which the necessary food supplies are maximal, and some species numbers have plunged. Others, of course, do well – wasps are now found in Alaska, and some tundra is greening (see e.g. Sturm, 2010), but insects and diseases may also spread.

Since all the great extinctions seem due to global climate change, albeit from possibly different causes, and since greenhouse gases lead to temperature changes, what is the evidence for the accumulation of $CO_2$ equivalents in the atmosphere? The records collected at Mauna Loa in Hawaii by Charles Keeling,

starting in 1958, show an unequivocal upward trend, with large seasonal variations around it. For a recent graph showing the increase in $CO_2$ levels from the
low 300 parts per million (ppm) to near 400 ppm since 1958, see Scripps CO2
Program (2010). Levels of 172–300 ppm are found in deep ice-core data over
the past 800,000 years (see Lüthi *et al.*, 2008). Moreover, Loulergue *et al.* (2008)
establish that methane concentrations in the atmosphere are double relative to
the levels seen over that time scale, and also show that 'strong correlations of
methane and $CO_2$ with temperature reconstructions are consistent back 800,000
years'. Weart (2010) provides an excellent history of the discovery of global
warming.

How can we be sure human activity is responsible? Here is how. Keeling's
records match the relatively constant seasonal surge in $CO_2$ which coincides
with Northern Hemisphere winters as well as the trend increases in our use of
fossil fuels and in deforestation. Since Suess (1953) it has been known that
radioactive isotope carbon-14 is created by cosmic rays in the upper atmosphere hitting $CO_2$ molecules, after which the radioactivity gradually decays.
Since coal and oil deposits were laid down hundreds of millions of years ago,
their radioactivity has dissipated, so carbon dioxide released by their burning
lacks this radioactive isotope. The changing ratio of the isotopes of carbon
detected in the atmosphere would point directly at anthropogenic sources.
Unfortunately, atmospheric nuclear explosions have radically altered that ratio,
making it inapplicable as an indicator of human fossil fuel consumption.
However, the ratio of another heavier isotope, carbon-13, relative to carbon-12
in atmospheric $CO_2$ is also larger than its ratio in fossil fuels, and is not
affected by nuclear tests. Consequently, if additional $CO_2$ output is due to
burning fossil fuels, the ratio of carbon-13 to carbon-12 should be decreasing
– as is occurring.

Oceans can probably absorb more $CO_2$ – but with adverse effects for marine
life (see Stone, 2007): acidification slows the growth of plankton and invertebb-
rates, which are basic to the ocean food chain. Lower pH levels could prevent
diatoms and coral reefs from forming their calcium carbonate shells (e.g. just
from lowering the current pH level of 8.1 to pH of 7.9). Moreover, while oceans
rapidly absorb $CO_2$ initially, much is evaporated straight back into the atmosphere (think sparkling water left unsealed), and while later recycled, takes a long
time before much is stored in deep ocean layers.

Ward (2006) shows that the extinction at the K/T boundary began when
atmospheric $CO_2$ was just under 1,000 ppm, and the extinction at the end of the
Triassic when $CO_2$ was just above 1,000 ppm. If the Earth warms up enough to
melt the permafrost in Siberia's tundra and under the Arctic Ocean, or other
factors of which we are as yet unaware, lead to a sudden increase to the equivalent of 1,000 ppm, the jump in global temperatures could be essentially uncon-
trollable. To build on a familiar analogy, if you are unsure whether a basket
covered with a cloth really has a solid base, be concerned about putting all your
eggs in it. Which leads us to economics.

# 7  Economics of climate change

There remain uncertainties about many aspects of climate change from its long-run history, present evidence, theories of re-absorption of greenhouse gases and relevant models. Nevertheless, understanding that there may be serious risks to many life forms on earth should make us think very carefully about the economics of climate-change abatement as argued in Stern (2006) and Schneider (2008), and addressed in this section. Tol (2009) provides a relatively optimistic survey of the economics, which claims there are 'no more unknown unknowns', whereas the special issue edited by Helm (2008) is more pessimistic (e.g. p. 236): 'The science suggests that it is probably more likely than not that rapid climate change will result later in the century with potentially quite catastrophic results.'

I discern seven important issues facing economics, related by climate change externalities needing to be either priced or regulated:

1   The consequences for economic analyses of shifts in distributions;
2   risk perceptions and attitudes to anthropogenic effects on climate;
3   how to evaluate the future costs of climate changes and possible benefits from mitigation;
4   designing mechanisms, permits, and auctions to mitigate greenhouse gas emissions;
5   global negotiations about emissions abatement;
6   intellectual property rights and prizes for new technological investment; and
7   modelling and forecasting climate change and reactions to any resulting price and income changes.

These seven issues are addressed in the following sections, linked in an analysis where sudden change is not just a more rapid version of gradual change. If sudden large changes can occur, consistent with the evidence from past great extinctions, different forms of analysis are needed, as we now show.

## 7.1  Shifts in distributions

A stationary variable is one whose distribution never shifts, so it has the same mean, variance and distributional form today as in 1066 AD. There are few such processes in economics. All other processes are non-stationary, in that some aspect of their distribution has changed over time.

There are two main sources of non-stationarity. The first is called a 'stochastic trend', where many small effects cumulate over time, altering the location of a variable and leading to an increasing variance relative to an initial period as time passes. Because such variables cumulate shocks, they are called 'integrated' time series, and their changes (first differences) then become stationary. Equity prices are classically regarded as integrated, with first differences that are random.

The second form of non-stationarity is due to location shifts in the mean (or variance). GDP growth per capita has experienced many such shifts over the last millenium – fortunately mainly upwards to date, as described in Section 4.2 of this chapter.

There are important differences between a 'fat-tailed' distribution, where some very large outliers can occur, and a shift in the mean of a distribution, or its variance. A 'heavy-tailed' distribution (like a Pareto distribution) has even higher chances of very large outcomes, usually in one direction. Weitzman (2009a, 2009b) argues that: 'climate sensitivity is so uncertain at the upper end [that it] contains within itself a generic argument in favor of a very fat upper tail of temperature changes'. Dietz (2009) provides an empirical assessment of the likely economic costs from 'tail risks' to climate by perturbing integrated climate models for various parameter values, and concludes that time preferences matter even for substantial global consumption losses: Section 7.3 considers intertemporal evaluation. Katz (2010) discusses analyses of climate change, as well as their potential economic consequences, when allowing jointly for both non-stationarity and fat-tailed distributions, but favours the latter.

One cannot get too many extreme outcomes (say *25* standard deviation draws), especially in succession, as distributions must integrate to unity. However, one can have very many draws that are extreme relative to the original distribution's standard deviation if the original mean $m_0$ shifts to a new value $m_1$. Figure 2.1 illustrates this situation.

The fat-tailed distribution in Figure 2.1 is a Student's $t$ distribution with three degrees of freedom, denoted $t_3$. This distribution has a mean of zero and a variance of 3, but no other finite moments, so generates many outliers, as shown by the wide range of its distribution in Figure 2.1 (see e.g. Johnson *et al.*, 1995). Even so, there is a low probability of (say) 6 standard deviation draws, which become commonplace after the mean has shifted to 6. The combined distribution before and after the mean shift is bimodal (multi-modal after many shifts), with a much larger standard deviation, so still integrates to unity *ex post*. Climate change will not be a reversible draw that, once past, returns to the previous mean of the distribution – it will stay for millennia. The extinction of a species may be due to a large outlier, but changes the numbers of that creature forever. An appropriate method of analysis requires allowing for mean shifts of unknown magnitudes and timings, namely a non-stationary process.

Unfortunately, there also seems to be a number of potential 'tipping points' where rapid change occurs. These include ocean acidification leading to anoxia; slowing of the ocean conveyor belts; and melting of the tundra and the arctic ocean seabed releasing large volumes of methane. Thus, shifts in the mean seem likely to alter the probability of extreme events, since temperature rises lead to tipping points being reached.

Now economics faces really serious analytic problems: the very statistical theorems on which intertemporal theoretical calculations rely also fail. As shown in Hendry and Mizon (2010), conditional expectations made today of an uncertain outcome tomorrow cease to be either unbiased or the minimum mean square

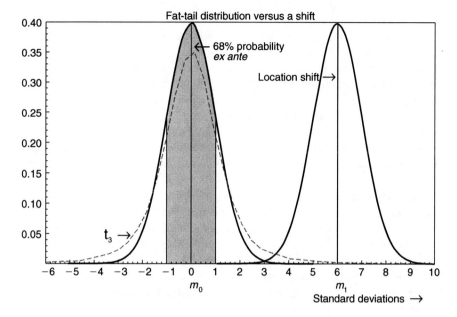

*Figure 2.1* Mean shift in a probability distribution reached.

error predictor when mean shifts occur. Moreover, the law of iterated expectations, namely that the expectation today of the conditional expectation tomorrow
equals the unconditional expectation tomorrow, does not hold.

In a sense, it is obvious that such theorems fail when means shift, because the
relevant integrals are over different distributions. However, their failure removes
the applicability of most inter-temporal theory from precisely the situation when it
is most needed, specifically when the world changes. If economists wish to make
reasoned contributions to climate change policy they must urgently address this
serious problem and develop modes of analysis that are valid despite mean shifts.

### 7.2 Risk perception and attitudes

Risk perceptions and attitudes to anthropogenic affects on climate are important
if there is a potentially serious problem looming. Since democratic policy
making requires public support, how the risks from climate change are perceived
affects policy implementation.[8]

There is considerable evidence that people cannot accurately evaluate risks in
many arenas of life (see e.g. Gigerenzer, 2002). For example, few are aware of
the relative risks of travel modes such as cars, planes, trains, ships, bicycles,
walking etc. per passenger mile travelled: most know that air travel is relatively
safe, but many wrongly believe driving and walking are also relatively safe,
and almost no one seems aware that cable cars are among the safest forms of

transport per passenger mile travelled, rather most people incorrectly believe that cable cars are highly risky.

Realistic assumptions about climate change are that individuals do not have well-defined, complete orderings over all necessary choices as a basis for utility maximization. They also have incomplete knowledge about the process, its timing and its consequences. Certainty equivalence is not a viable basis for decision taking when distributions of events are essentially unknown. Thus, one must consider recent ideas from behavioural economics such as 'cognitive dissonance' (Festinger, 1957) and 'prospect theory' (Kahneman and Tversky, 1979). Economic actors may take anticipated regret into account when making decisions as suggested by 'regret theory', leading to 'inaction' biases (Butler and Loomes, 2007).

Behavior may be rather different from that predicted by conventional economic analyses, absent an all-knowing self-maximizer operating devoid of the social context, but facing potentially huge global externalities. Brekke and Johansson-Stenman (2008) is an ambitious attempt to apply ideas from behavioral economics to understand the economics of climate change, including risk perceptions, attitudes to anthropogenic effects on climate, negotiations about climate abatement, and how to evaluate intertemporal comparisons. We next consider that last aspect.

### 7.3 Intertemporal evaluations

Money today is more valuable than money next year, but by how much? The classical answer is that a discount rate of (say) 5 percent suggests $100 next year is worth 5 percent less than $100 now, namely $95. Two years ahead, $100 would be worth only $90.25 now. Alternatively expressed, impatience entails that individuals will accept $95 today in exchange for paying $100 next year.

In the Nordhaus (2008) critique of Stern (2006), the appropriate size of the discount rate to evaluate future climate change damage played an important role in the economics discussions. However, the resulting analysis implicitly assumed that the situation was relatively stable and slowly evolving. If sudden large changes can occur, such a debate may divert attention from some key issues.

As Stern (2008) argues, analyses need a 'different discount rate for each possible sequence of outcomes.' Yet those sequences are also endogenous to the choice of discount rate (see e.g. Dietz and Hepburn, 2010). The important intertemporal evaluation problem is somewhat like a reverse 'St. Petersburg paradox'. In the original form, a fair coin is tossed until a head appears, and you receive $\$2^{n-1}$ if the head first comes on the $n$th toss. That event has a probability of $(1/2)^n$ of happening, so your expected payment, adding up the product of each event's payment times its probability, is infinite. Thus, you should pay an infinite amount to enter the game. In practice, few people would willingly pay even $50 to enter. The paradox was supposedly resolved by using the expected utility of money, rather than the expected amount of money, because marginal utility falls as the amount of money increases. When distributions shift in unknown ways, however, those expectations cannot be validly calculated. A different 'solution' is needed to evaluate what we should willingly pay to avoid a future catastrophe than 'discounting' the costs to the present.

A possible analogy is that of being in a car at the top of a road down a very long hill, with a cliff at the end, an unknown distance away and of an unknown drop.The car starts slowly down the hill, gradually accelerating, when you discover that there are no brakes to slow or stop it. Since it will be a long time before the car falls off the cliff, do you:

1    seriously 'discount the future' to decide when to jump later,
2    hope that a rescue will somehow appear (e.g. there is a 'runaway truck ramp' at some point), or
3    jump out now when you may survive given the present speed?

Here my cliff is the potential for mass extinction, which would seriously affect humanity and its present form of civilization if mitigating action is too delayed. Jumping corresponds to taking sensible action in the face of the evidence. The level of the 'discount rate' is hardly the key consideration for making this particular inter-temporal evaluation.

Portfolio diversification suggests taking some actions now not leaving – literally – all the world's eggs in one basket. Many of the first steps could actually improve living standards yet reduce greenhouse gas emissions, such as mandating more efficient car engines within already known technologies, and better house insulation. The next issue, therefore, is to create the right incentives to do so.

### 7.4 Mechanism design, permits and auctions

We briefly consider three mechanisms, namely markets, permits, and auctions, that might help create the correct incentives for mitigation.

Designing market mechanisms in general, and creating schemes to mitigate greenhouse gas emissions in particular, are both large literatures: see (e.g.) Roth (2002) for the former and Klemperer (2009) for the latter. Careful analyses are essential to ensure that incentives to reduce pollution are correctly aligned, are relatively accurately costed, do not create a 'substitution' to the least regulated or cheapest areas, nor undermine living standards, and yet protect the poorest sections of society. These are demanding, but not infeasible, requirements.

As the world economy emerges from the financial-crisis induced sharpest downturn since the Great Depression, there is a potential role for modern finance theory in designing options and permit trading, despite their reputation as 'weapons of financial mass destruction'. Given a long-run emissions target, say, McKibbin and Wilcoxen (2002) propose that a fixed number of long-term permits be issued, designed to rise in value as carbon prices rise, and so could create balance sheet value to offset current increased abatement costs.

The theory of auctions also has an important role to play in the design of effective carbon trading schemes (see e.g. Milgrom, 2004). As shown by

Klemperer (2002) and Binmore and Klemperer (2002) for the various different G3 telecom auctions, auction design can have a huge impact on the realized outcomes.

### 7.5 *Negotiations about emissions abatement*

There are many precedents of direct relevance to agreements about emissions reductions.

First, the various 'Clean Air Acts' led to consequential reductions in air pollution, especially smogs, but at the time (UK, 1956; various times in other countries) were accompanied by protests about the lack of smokeless fuels and their high costs. Garnaut (2008) argues that seeking a climate change agreement creates a 'prisoner's dilemma in international collective action' (really a free rider problem). However, that only holds for countries small enough not to affect the world's or their own climate in a way harmful to themselves. Many countries separately legislated on clean air, as well as on the next precedent, namely acid rain, for that reason. For example, Chatterji and Ghosal (2009) suggest that unilateral commitments combined with technology transfers could lead to cumulative emissions reductions.

Second, growing and high levels of acid rain due to sulfur dioxides ($SO_2$) prompted legislation for their reduction in an effort to save increasingly acid lakes and dying forests, based on a cap and trade system in the US. Even that move faced serious coordinated opposition despite the huge potential environmental benefits: see Dumanoski (1987), writing three years before the bill's passage.

Third, CFCs were initially believed to be inert, but were later found to be causing destruction of the ozone layer from release of their chlorine by solar radiation. A phased reduction and elimination of their use was agreed rapidly in the Montreal Protocol, signed in 1987, supported by a 'Multilateral Fund' to help developing countries adjust, one of the world's first global environmental funds with about $160 million to speed up the phasing out. The ozone layer appears to be recovering slowly. Unfortunately, the replacement gases, hydrochlorofluorocarbons (HCFCs), and hydrofluorocarbons (HFCs), seem to be highly problematic as greenhouse gases. Molina *et al.* (2009) propose building on the Montreal Protocol to mitigate that growing problem.

In each case, there were objections at the time of the potential high costs of abatement – yet in no case has there been a notable impact on any country's GNP from solving those problems. Indeed, there were beneficiaries in new industries as well as losers in old. The first two cases were usually domestically driven in a range of countries, but the third was explicitly an international agreement, as may be needed for climate change.

Thus, can we hope to forge the requisite international agreements? A partial answer follows.

In his *Theory of Moral Sentiments*, Adam Smith (1759) argued that humans act reciprocally and expect others to treat them likewise. In evolutionary terms, humanity may have survived because distant ancestors had a propensity to trade, barter, and share, unlike many primates. His most famous phrase, the 'invisible hand', first appeared in the *Sentiments*, and his better known *Wealth of Nations* was probably written as an attempt to reconcile his views about natural fellow feeling ('sympathy') with the apparently self-interested behaviour of economic actors:

> Man has almost constant occasion for the help of his brethren, and it is in vain for him to expect it from their benevolence only.... It is not from the benevolence of the butcher, the brewer, or the baker that we expect our dinner, but from their regard to their own interest. We address ourselves, not to their humanity but to their self-love.
>
> (Smith, 1776, chapter 2)

In practice, most bakers probably provide fresh unadulterated bread, not just from 'self-love' and a rational investment in their future business, but also taking account of how they expect others to treat them. Negotiators committed to resolving the climate change problem need to augment self-interests with fellow feeling, as reinforced by modern findings about reciprocity and trust in (e.g.) Fehr *et al.* (2005) and Gintis *et al.* (2005).

An altogether different, but related, precedent is international agreement on the United Nations Convention on the Law of the Sea, signed by most major countries (but not ratified by the US). Thus, although international climate-change negotiations will be far from simple, there is hope: see Sebenius (1991) and Barrett (2003).

## 7.6 Intellectual property rights and prizes

Intellectual property rights are one approach to creating incentives to develop ideas into outcomes. Hall and Helmers (2010) show that they often provide an incentive to produce both large and small technological innovations in response to climate change, although patent rights may also limit the diffusion of new technologies. What they term the 'double externality' problem, namely the presence of both environmental and knowledge externalities, may make the patenting solution to the R&D externality less attractive for climate policy. In any case, it may be hard to protect intellectual property rights for major advances resolving climate change.

An alternative approach is to offer a series of large prizes for achieving various pre-defined goals (on inexpensive carbon sequestration, efficient non-carbon producing energy systems, etc.), as with the 'Longitude Problem' (see Sobel, 1995, eventually solved by John Harrison developing the chronometer), or the 'Rainhill trials' won by the Stephensons' *Rocket* (see e.g. Fullerton *et al.*, 2002). There are two recent successful examples of responses to such prizes. The first is the Darpa Grand Challenge where a $1m prize was offered in 2004 for developing a self-controlled robotic vehicle that could cross the Mojave Desert in less than ten hours. The prize would double each year thereafter that it was not won. In the first race in 2004, no unmanned vehicles went more than a few miles before crashing or suffering crippling technical problems. The next year, four finished the 24 km race in less than the required time (see DARPA, 2005).

The second was the Ansari X Prize of just $10m for the first viable passenger spacecraft to accomplish two successive sub-orbital human spaceflights, which was achieved in well under a decade.

Both of these were prizes of a few million USD, small relative to the potential benefits of solutions to climate change. Bilmes and Stiglitz (2008) claim that the US will have spent around $3 trillion on the Iraq war: a small fraction of that sum could fund a vast R&D program for improved technologies. The world is not short of ideas for: direct greenhouse gas reductions or sequestration; new approaches to energy production; better catalytic converters; exploiting natural gas hydrates as a potentially vast energy resource; using nitrous oxide as a fuel; more efficient solar energy conversion; deep sea deposition of $CO_2$ in hydrates; harnessing wave power; high-temperature super-conductivity to reduce power loss in grid transmissions, etc. 'Wireless transmission', 'heavier than air flight' and many other ideas were ridiculed initially but worked. If we do not try we will not find out, albeit that anti-gravity or perpetual-motion machines look distinctly unpromising.

The above list are relatively small investments against potentially huge risks. Some dramatic 'solutions' have also been proposed, including geo-engineering with shields around the planet. However, careful evaluation of all new technologies is essential: remember supposedly 'inert' CFCs. Another warning comes from the demise of the Sumerian civilization, one of the first to develop writing and practice intensive, year-round agriculture about 7000 years ago. Although successful for over 2000 years, Sumeria faltered on a 'technological solution' to its increasingly saline soil, by *increased irrigation*. The idea was basically sensible, but flawed by retaining water, rather than having it flowing through. With poorly draining soil, day-time evaporation concentrated salts and minerals dissolved in the water, and seriously depleted agriculture output (see Crawford, 2004, p. 47).

Nevertheless, we seem to be on the threshold of a potential energy revolution that could drive a rapidly growing yet low carbon world economy. Such investments have a triple advantage (see Grubb *et al.*, 2002):

1   reducing the risk of serious climate-related problems;
2   stimulating economies when there is a great deal of slack;
3   initiating the crucial 'learning by experience' that leads to dramatic cost reductions.

### 7.7 *Modelling and forecasting*

There is still much that is uncertain about the extent and speed of climate change itself, and about plausible responses to changes in energy prices and associated income shifts. The more traditional role of the econometrician lies in evaluating models that purport to provide 'realistic' simulations about such impacts. However, my skepticism is more about the validity and reliability of any models that are built 'as if' twentieth century parameters will not change despite no action being taken. Even the concept of 'business as usual' as the baseline for model simulations becomes meaningless if a radically altered environment will occur. For example, a sudden jump in methane release, followed by a rise in temperature that triggers nuclear wars over failing water and food resources, or from trying to prevent mass migration from untenable areas, is inconsistent with the scenario supposedly being simulated.

Forecasting non-stationary processes is extremely difficult, increasingly so the further ahead the horizon: Clements and Hendry (1999) provide an extensive analysis, with an update in Clements and Hendry (2002) and a non-technical overview in Clements and Hendry (2008). Many of the implications from their analyses apply to forecasting in general.

First, integrated and near-integrated processes, typical of stochastic, slowly evolving trend-like behaviour, lead to rapidly growing interval forecasts as shown analytically in Stock (1996) for the latter. Thus, uncertainty increases rapidly, the more so the shorter the period available for model building prior to the forecast.

Second, breaks in distributions are usually not predicted – the recent gyrations in food and oil prices are a typical example, but even the massive financial crisis of 2007–2010 came as a surprise to most, including some of the world's largest financial institutions that supposedly make a living by anticipating developments. Figure 2.1 above illustrated the problem. Once a shift has occurred in the mean of a distribution, what previously seemed like 'extreme' draws or outliers become central and are all too likely to recur. A mean change in the Earth's temperature has that property, and while one ill-matched breeding season, or one year's inappropriate weather for the given flora and fauna, can be recovered from, a sequence is much harder.

Third, life is adaptable, but mass extinctions painfully reveal the limits of that adaptability. Past breaks in turn distort estimates of models that do not allow for their occurrence, inducing systematic departures between fit and outcome, all too often 'patched' to camouflage the appearance of that difficulty (e.g. differencing can 'remove' a past mean shift, but the problem reappears if levels are properly evaluated). Forecasts may be unusually uncertain but that is no argument for 'doing nothing'; rather, the possibilities of very large losses require actions both to reduce uncertainties and to lower the chances that harmful outcomes will eventuate.

## 8  Conclusions

This chapter tries to connect the paths that have been cleared by a wide range of different sciences. A multi-disciplinary approach is essential to relate the many aspects bearing on the possible causes and consequences of climate change, and to draw whatever lessons the distant past may hold for humanity. The chapter, therefore, focused on mass extinctions and mean shifts in global temperatures due to increased greenhouse gases, rather than the many other changes that may be entailed, such as rising ocean levels due to thermal expansion and ice melting, through turbulent weather to changed rainfall patterns.

First, the limitations of empirical evidence were addressed against the undeniably huge successes of science over the last millennium. Results and theories may mislead for a period, but self-interest leads to correction.

Second, the science of how greenhouse gases re-radiate energy back to the ground is clear. There are four major such gases, water vapour, carbon dioxide, nitrous oxide, and methane, augmented recently by HCFCs and HFCs as replacements for ozone-destroying CFCs. The increasing levels of carbon dioxide equivalents in the atmosphere are now established, as is their source in human activity – we know we are burning fossil fuels, deforesting, and using large quantities of fertilizer. World-wide temperatures are rising on a stochastic trend, buffeted by many high variance influences, but with obvious markers discussed by Stern (2006). For unclear reasons, this evidence seems insufficient to persuade nay sayers.

Third, the evidence from the great extinctions of the past 500 million years is a major warning from the distant past, the dramatic relevance of which has become increasingly clear the greater the knowledge gained about their causes. That research activity, and the implications therefrom, must intrinsically draw on the expertise of dozens of disciplines, where few individuals can span the entire spectrum of sciences involved. The very different approaches, types of measurements, and sources of evidence across such a range of disciplines makes for a compelling case: climate change is the main culprit of previous mass extinctions, albeit with several different triggers. Humanity is the latest trigger.

Fourth, economic analysis offers a number of ideas around the common theme that externalities need to be either priced or regulated – and climate change is one of the largest world-wide externalities ever. Seven aspects were discussed, all affected by the possibility that abrupt changes can occur. The key problem is the unknown uncertainty when distributions can shift, which makes action more urgent to avoid possible, even likely, future shifts. Most home owners wisely insure against low probability, high cost events like fire risk: humanity needs to do likewise.

Fifth, adaptation ceases to be meaningful if food, water, and land resources become inadequate following major shifts in climate. The first mitigation steps need not be costly, and a rising price of carbon could lower usage and stimulate innovation. International negotiations are more likely to succeed if some actions have already been taken at the country level – potentially creating opportunities as new technologies develop.

Planet Earth will survive whatever humanity is doing, so the crucial issues are the effects of continuing climate change on its present inhabitants, including humanity and its civilization, especially the 'threat multiplier' from unstable regions. It is a risky strategy to do nothing if that entails potentially huge costs when the costs of initial action are small. Thus, the obvious time to start is now, beginning with the many low cost implementations that will help mitigate greenhouse gases (see e.g. Stern, 2008, for a list). Just in case.

## Notes

\* I am grateful to Bob Allen, Chris Allsopp, Dennis Anderson, Tony Beatton, Alok Bhargava, Jennifer L. Castle, Simon Dietz, Neil Ericsson, Karen Florini, Paul Frijters, Bronwyn Hall, John D.R. Hendry, Vivien L. Hendry, Cameron Hepburn, Rick Katz, David King, Paul Klemperer, Katarina Juselius, Grayham Mizon, and Nick Stern for numerous helpful discussions and suggestions, and to participants in a seminar at Queensland University of Technology during a visit in 2008. This research was supported in part by grants from the Open Society Institute and the Oxford Martin School. The chapter is dedicated to the memory of Dennis Anderson, who stimulated my interest in climate change.
1 I have been quoted that 'weather forecasters get increased budgets after failing to forecast major storms, whereas economists get their budgets cut when they fail to forecast crises', so have long been in competition for those scarce funds.
2 That the 'complexity for minimum component costs has increased at a rate of roughly a factor of two per year.... Over the longer term ... there is no reason to believe it will not remain nearly constant': Moore (1965).
3 Weather is affected by many factors that are hard to forecast over weeks ahead. The jet stream appears to have changed location over the last half century, perhaps both cause and consequence of climate changes, but its location is not easily forecast. El Niño and La Niña Southern Oscillations both greatly alter weather conditions over shorter time scales, as do major storms, and volcanic eruptions, etc., with possibly more eruptions as the polar ice melts.
4 Chlorofluorocarbons, including halons and other man-made halocarbons.
5 Gas hydrates are crystalline solids similar to ice, where the building blocks are a gas molecule surrounded by a cage of water molecules, which acts as 'cement' for methane. The breakdown of one unit volume of methane hydrate at one atmosphere produces about 160 unit volumes of gas. All hydrates become unstable as the surrounding temperature rises, but most are in sediments too deep to respond rapidly at present. Conversely, finding a catalyst that inexpensively bound any of the greenhouse gases into hydrates would be invaluable.
6 Named after the Polish river Weichsel.
7 The weight ratio of $CO_2$ produced per octane molecule burned is roughly 3 to 1 – roughly a ton of gasoline produces 3 tons of $CO_2$ – as carbon atoms in hydrocarbons are mostly attached to light hydrogen atoms, and when the octane is burned, attach to oxygen which produces heavier $CO_2$.
8 Major re-insurers worrying about the changing probabilities of extreme events and catastrophes are an indication of the growing awareness of possible risks.

## References

Allen, R. C. (ed.) (2009). *The British Industrial Revolution in Global Perspective*. Cambridge: Cambridge University Press.
Apostolides, A., Broadberry, S., Campbell, B., Overton, M., and van Leeuwen, B. (2008). English Gross Domestic Product, 1300–1700: Some preliminary estimates. Discussion paper, University of Warwick, Coventry.
Arrhenius, S. A. (1896). On the influence of carbonic acid in the air upon the temperature of the ground. *London, Edinburgh, and Dublin Philosophical Magazine and Journal of*

*Science (fifth series)*, 41, 237–275. www.globalwarmingart.com/images/1/18/Arrhenius.pdf.

Barker, T. (2008). The economics of avoiding dangerous climate change. An editorial essay on the Stern Review. *Climatic Change*, 89, 173–194. DOI: 10.1007/s10584-008-9433-x.

Barrett, S. (2003). *Environment and Statecraft: the Strategy of Environmental Treaty-Making*. Oxford: Oxford University Press.

Bellwood, P. (2004). *First Farmers: The Origins of Agricultural Societies*. Oxford: Blackwell.

Bilmes, L., and Stiglitz, J. (2008). The Iraq War will cost us $3 trillion, and much more. *Washington Post*, March 9. www.washingtonpost.com/wpdyn/content/article/2008/03/07/AR2008030702846.html.

Binmore, K., and Klemperer, P. (2002). The biggest auction ever: the sale of the British 3G telecom licenses. *Economic Journal*, 112 (C74–C96).

Bralower, T. J. (2008). Earth science: Volcanic cause of catastrophe. *Nature*, 454, 285–287. DOI: 10.1038/454285a.

Brekke, K. A., and Johansson-Stenman, O. (2008). The behavioural economics of climate change, in Helm (2008), pp. 280–297.

Butler, D., and Loomes, G. (2007). Imprecision as an account of the preference reversal phenomenon. *American Economic Review*, 97, 277–297.

Chatterji, S., and Ghosal, S. (2009). Technology, unilateral commitments and cumulative emissions reduction. *CESifo Economic Studies*, 55, 286–305. DOI: 10.1093/cesifo/ifp009.

Clarke, A. (1993). Temperature and extinction in the sea: A physiologist's view. *Paleobiology*, 19, 499–518.

Clements, M. P., and Hendry, D. F. (1999). *Forecasting Non-stationary Economic Time Series*. Cambridge, MA.: MIT Press.

Clements, M. P., and Hendry, D. F. (2002). Explaining forecast failure in macroeconomics. In Clements, M. P., and Hendry, D. F. (eds), *A Companion to Economic Forecasting*, pp. 539–571. Oxford: Blackwells.

Clements, M. P., and Hendry, D. F. (2008). Economic forecasting in a changing world. *Capitalism and Society*, 3, 1–18.

Crawford, H. E. W. (2004). *Sumer and the Sumerians* 2nd edn. Cambridge: Cambridge University Press.

DARPA (2005). Grand challenge 2005. www.darpa.mil/grandchallenge05/, US Defence Advanced Research Projects Agency, Arlington, VA.

Dietz, S. (2009). High impact, low probability? An empirical analysis of risk in the economics of climate change. Working paper 9, Grantham Research Institute on Climate Change and the Environment, London School of Economics.

Dietz, S., and Hepburn, C. (2010). On non-marginal cost–benefit analysis. Working paper, 18, Grantham Research Institute on Climate Change and the Environment, London School of Economics.

Dumanoski, D. (1987). Acid rain bills again face stiff opposition. *The Boston Globe*, February 19.

Energy Information Administration (2008). Emissions of greenhouse gases report. Report doe/eia-0573(2008), www.eia.doe.gov/oiaf/1605/ggrpt/nitrous.html.

Erwin, D. H. (1996). The mother of mass extinctions. *Scientific American*, 275(1), 72–78.

Erwin, D. H. (2006). *Extinction: How Life on Earth Nearly Ended 250 Million Years Ago*. Princeton: Princeton University Press.

Fehr, E., Fischbacher, U., and Kosfeld, M. (2005). Neuroeconomic foundation of trust and social preferences. Dp.5127, CEPR, London.

Festinger, L. (1957). *A Theory of Cognitive Dissonance.* Stanford: Stanford University Press.

Fouquet, R., and Pearson, P.J.G. (2006). Seven centuries of energy services: The price and use of light in the United Kingdom (1300–2000). *Energy Journal*, 27, 139–178.

Fullerton, R. L., Linster, B. G., McKee, M., and Slate, S. (2002). Using auctions to reward tournament winners: Theory and experimental investigations. *RAND Journal of Economics*, 33, 62–84.

Garnaut, R. (2008). *The Garnaut Climate Change Review: Final Report.* Cambridge: Cambridge University Press.

Gigerenzer, G. (2002). *Reckoning with Risk: Learning to Live with Uncertainty.* London: Allen Lane.

Gintis, H., Bowles, S., Boyd, R. T., and Fehr, E. (eds) (2005). *Moral Sentiments and Material Interests: The Foundations of Cooperation in Economic Life.* Cambridge, MA.: MIT Press.

Grubb, M., Köhler, J., and Anderson, D. (2002). Induced technical change in energy and environmental modeling: Analytic approaches and policy implications. *Annual Review of Energy and the Environment*, 27, 271–308. DOI: 10.1146/annurev. energy.27.122001.0834089.

Hall, B. H., and Helmers, C. (2010). The role of patent protection in (clean/green) technology transfer. Discussion paper, forthcoming, Santa Clara High Technology Law Journal.

Helm, D. (ed.) (2008). *Oxford Review of Economic Policy: Special Issue on Climate Change.* Oxford: Oxford University Press.

Hendry, D. F., and Mizon, G. E. (2010). On the mathematical basis of inter-temporal optimization. DP. 497, Economics Department, Oxford.

Heydari, E., Arzani, N., and Hassanzadeh, J. (2008). Mantle plume: The invisible serial killer – application to the Permian-Triassic boundary mass extinction. *Palaeogeography, Palaeoclimatology, Palaeoecology*, 264, 147–162.

Hoffman, P.F., and Schrag, D. P. (2000). Snowball Earth. *Scientific American*, 282, 68–75.

Johnson, N. L., Kotz, S., and Balakrishnan, N. (1995). *Continuous Univariate Distributions.* 2nd edn. New York: John Wiley.

Kahneman, D., and Tversky, A. (1979). Prospect theory: An analysis of decision under risk. *Econometrica*, 47, 263–291.

Katz, R. W. (2010). Statistics of extremes in climate change: an editorial essay. *Climatic Change.* DOI: 18 10.1007/s10584-010-9834-5.

Klemperer, P. (2002). What really matters in auction design. *The Journal of Economic Perspectives*, 16, 169–189.

Klemperer, P. (2009). What is the top priority on climate change? In Schellnhuber, H.-J., Molina, M., Stern, N., Huber, V., and Kadner, S. (eds), *Global Sustainability: A Nobel Cause*, pp. 231–240: Lavoisier, France.

Knoll, A. H., Bambach, A. K., Canfield, D. E., and Grotzinger, J. P. (1996). Comparative Earth history and late Permian mass extinction. *Science*, 273, 452–457.

Knoll, A. H., Bambach, A. K., Payne, J. L., Pruss, S., and Fischer, W. W. (2007). Paleophysiology and end-Permian mass extinction. *Earth and Planetary Science Letters*, 256, 295–313.

Loulergue, L., Schilt, A., Spahni, R., Masson-Delmotte, V., Blunier, T., Lemieux, B.,

Barnola, J.-M., Raynaud, D., Stocker, T. F., and Chappellaz, J. (2008). Orbital and millennial-scale features of atmospheric CH4 over the past 800,000 years. *Nature*, 453. DOI: 10.1038/nature06950.

Lovelock, J. (ed.) (2000). *Gaia: a new look at life on earth*. Oxford: Oxford University Press.

Lüthi, D., Le Floch, M., Bereiter, B., Blunier, T., Barnola, J.-M., Siegenthaler, U., Raynaud, D., Jouzel, J., Fischer, H., Kawamura, K., and Stocker, T. F. (2008). High-resolution carbon dioxide concentration record 650,000–800,000 years before present. *Nature*, 453. DOI: 10.1038/nature06949.

Marshall, B. (2005). Nobel Prize Lecture. http://nobelprize.org/nobel prizes/medicine/laureates/2005/marshall-lecture.html.

Mayhew, P.J., Jenkins, G. B., and Benton, T. G. (2009). A long-term association between global temperature and biodiversity, origination and extinction in the fossil record. *Proceedings of the Royal Society, B*, 275: (1630), 47–53.

McKibbin, W. J., and Wilcoxen, P.J. (2002). Climate change after Kyoto: Blueprint for a realistic approach. Monograph, The Brookings Institution, Washington.

Mee, L. (2006). Reviving dead zones: How can we restore coastal seas ravaged by runaway plant and algae growth caused by human activities? *Scientific American*, 295, 78–85.

Met Office (2008). Climate change – the big picture. Discussion paper, Met Office, Exeter, UK.

Milgrom, P. (2004). *Putting Auction Theory to Work*. Cambridge: Cambridge University Press.

Molina, M., Zaelke, D., Sarma, K. M., Andersen, S. O., Ramanathan, V., and Kaniaru, D. (2009). Reducing abrupt climate change risk using the Montreal Protocol and other regulatory actions to complement cuts in CO2 emissions. *Proceedings of the National Academy of Sciences*, 106:49, 20616–20621.

Moore, G. E. (1965). Cramming more components onto integrated circuits. *Electronics Magazine*, 38(8). ftp://download.intel.com/museum/Moores Law/Articles-Press Releases/Gordon. Moore 1965 Article.pdf.

National Academy of Science (2008). Understanding and responding to climate change. Report, U.S. National Academy of Sciences, http://dels-old.nas.edu/climatechange/understandingclimate-change.shtml.

Nordhaus, W. D. (2008). *A Question of Balance*. New Haven: Yale University Press.

Prothero, D. R. (2008). Do impacts really cause most mass extinctions? In Seckbach, J., and Walsh, M. (eds), *From Fossils to Astrobiology*, pp. 409–423. Netherlands: Springer.

Ravishankara, A. R., Daniel, J. S., and Portmann, R. W. (2009). Nitrous oxide (N2O): The dominant ozone-depleting substance emitted in the twenty-first century. *Science*, 326, 123–125.

Riccardi, A., Kump, L. R., Arthur, M. A., and D'Hondt, S. (2007). Carbon isotopic evidence for chemocline upward excursion during the end-Permian event. *Palaeogeography, Palaeoclimatology, Palaeoecology*, 248, 263–291.

Rosenberg, N. (1983). *Inside the Black Box: Technology and Economics*. Cambridge: Cambridge University Press.

Roth, A. E. (2002). The economist as engineer: Game theory, experimentation, and computation as tools for design economics. *Econometrica*, 70, 1341–1378.

Schmidt, G., and Moyer, E. (2008). A new kind of scientist. *Nature*. www.nature.com/climate/2008/0808/full/climate.2008.76.html.

Schneider, S. H. (2008). The Stern Review debate: an editorial essay. *Climatic Change*, 89, 241–244. DOI: 10.1007/s10584-008-9432-y.

Scripps CO2 Program (2010). The Keeling curve. http://scrippsco2.ucsd.edu/program history/keeling curve lessons.html, Scripps Institution of Oceanography, La Jolla, CA.

Sebenius, J. K. (1991). Designing negotiations toward a new regime: The case of global warming. *International Security*, 15, 110–148.

Smith, A. (1759). *Theory of Moral Sentiments*. Edinburgh: A. Kincaid & J. Bell.

Smith, A. (1776). *An Inquiry into the Nature and Causes of the Wealth of Nations*. London: W. Strahan & T. Cadell.

Sobel, D. (1995). *Longitude*. New York: Penguin.

Stern, N. (2006). *The Economics of Climate Change: The Stern Review*. Cambridge: Cambridge University Press.

Stern, N. (2008). The economics of climate change. *American Economic Review*, 98:2, 1–37.

Stewart, D. (ed.) (1795). *Essays on Philosophical Subjects by Adam Smith*. Edinburgh: W. Creech. Liberty Classics edition, by I. S. Ross, 1982.

Stock, J. H. (1996). VAR, error correction and pre-test forecasts at long horizons. *Oxford Bulletin of Economics and Statistics*, 58, 685–701.

Stommel, H., and Stommel, E. (1979). The year without a summer. *Scientific American*, 240, 176–186.

Stone, R. (2007). A world without corals? *Science*, 316, 678–681.

Sturm, M. (2010). Arctic plants feel the heat. *Scientific American*, 302, 48–55.

Suess, H. E. (1953). Natural radiocarbon and the rate of exchange of carbon dioxide between the atmosphere and the sea. In On Nuclear Science, N. R. C. C. (ed.), *Nuclear Processes in Geologic Settings*, pp. 52–56: Washington, D.C.: National Academy of Sciences.

Tol, R. S. J. (2009). The economic effects of climate change. *Journal of Economic Perspectives*, 23, 29–51.

Tziperman, E. (1997). Inherently unstable climate behaviour due to weak thermohaline ocean circulation. *Nature*, 386, 592–595.

Waller, J. (2002). *Fabulous Science*. Oxford: Oxford University Press.

Ward, P.D. (2006). Impact from the deep. *Scientific American*, 295, 64–71.

Weart, S. (2010). The discovery of global warming. www.aip.org/history/climate/co2.htm.

Weissmann, G. (1991). Aspirin. *Scientific American*, January, 58–64.

Weitzman, M. L. (2009a). Additive damages, fat-tailed climate dynamics, and uncertain discounting. Working paper, Department of Economics, Harvard University.

Weitzman, M. L. (2009b). The extreme uncertainty of extreme climate change: An overview and some implications. Working paper, Department of Economics, Harvard University. 20.

# 3 Managerial, institutional and evolutionary approaches to environmental economics

## Theoretical and policy implications

*Jonathan Michie and Christine Oughton*

## 1 Introduction

Research on environmental economics and policy has been dominated by neoclassical theory. While there have been significant advances in this approach, including more sophisticated analysis of imperfect information and time, as well as the development of endogenous growth theory, neoclassical models contain a number of underlying characteristics that limit their relevance for modelling firm behaviour, especially in relation to environmental issues, innovation and change. The limitations spring fundamentally from the underlying model of rational choice or business decision making, the treatment of innovation and the lack of any meaningful analysis of the institutional environment in which business and policy decisions are taken. In this chapter we explore the implications of these restrictive assumptions and show how alternative managerial, institutional and evolutionary theories may provide richer insights into environmental problems and a broader spectrum of policy choices.

To focus the discussion we have grouped the limitations of neoclassical economics into three categories, which we outline here. First, mainstream economics assumes that corporate decisions on pricing and output are determined by costs, demand and market structure. However, the decision-making process is not explicitly modelled; managers, or rather firms, are assumed to behave as automata that respond automatically to price signals. Neoclassical assumptions regarding the objective of firms and the choice variables over which a representative firm has strategic control are simplified, normally being reduced to a single objective of profit maximisation subject to a technology constraint. In such treatments of the firm, the only choices the firm makes are how much to produce (and by implication how much capital and labour to employ). More sophisticated versions include other inputs, such as natural resources, human capital and knowledge or research and development (R&D) expenditure. Nevertheless, the term 'decisions' implies a degree of discretion that is not normally assumed to exist: once the underlying motivation (profit maximisation) and the constraints (technology, demand) are specified the decision making 'process' is reduced to calculus. This contrasts with managerial approaches where the focus is on how corporate decisions are made and how managerial discretion will be utilised and with what outcomes, given the constraints faced; and even here, constraints are rarely viewed as exogenously given as is the norm within mainstream economic modelling.

Second, the underlying model of rational choice in neoclassical economics is *instrumental rationality* based on methodological individualism. However, there is now a substantial body of empirical evidence from behavioural and experimental economics that shows that managers do not necessarily operate as predicted by the profit-maximising model of instrumental rationality. Moreover, theoretical analysis of the cost, availability and reliability of information; the ability to process information that is available (and considered to be reliable); the ways in which individuals cooperate during the production process; and the importance of cultural and institutional conventions or routines, shows that many other factors also influence managerial decisions. Perhaps more importantly, instrumental rationality provides ineffective guidance to firms making strategic choices in situations where there are multiple equilibria, that is, where two or more strategy choices offer the same expected returns to firms. The neoclassical trick of adopting a randomised or mixed strategy choice often leads to inefficient outcomes. Alternative models of rational choice (such as the use of conventions and institutions that provide focal points) offer the possibility of superior results both in terms of profitability and in terms of the impact of firms' strategic choices on other outcomes, such as environmental damage.

Third, the assumption of a representative firm rules out the possibility that the behaviour of firms differs from firm to firm, even where there appears to be no difference in exogenously 'given' determining factors. Differences in firms' behaviour may arise as a result of differences in internal organisation, strategic priorities, capabilities, and cultural and systemic factors – such as the legal system – that vary from country to country and over time. Thus, for example, the pattern and behaviour of innovation and technological advance between countries has long been recognised to depend in part at least on the system of innovation within the respective countries. To shift technological development onto a more environmentally sustainable trajectory, we need to look not only at the degree of managerial discretion, and the role that rationality plays in this, but also at the wider systems within which firms are operating. The 'systems of innovation' literature has pointed to the importance of national, regional and industrial factors, analysing 'lock in' and other 'deviations' from pure price-signal behaviour.[1] And evolutionary and institutional economics has long stressed the importance of routines, tacit knowledge and culture in making economic change a complex process.[2]

In Sections 2, 3 and 4 below, we consider the implications of relaxing each of these sets of restrictions in turn and show how managerial, institutional and evolutionary approaches to economic theorising can shed new light on environmental problems such as carbon emissions and global warming. The final section draws out the lessons for environmental policy.

## 2  Corporate behaviour and managerial discretion

This section considers the various reasons why economic 'agents' may not react to price signals, or other incentives, as might be expected. Some of the relevant factors have been discussed within the mainstream economics literature for decades – with John Maynard Keynes, for example, stressing the importance of risk and uncertainty, herd behaviour, and institutional factors in affecting economic decisions. More recent developments within economics have thrown light on the complex nature of economic rationality, through game theory and behavioural economics. The business management literature takes for granted that firms are complex organisms in which management has considerable discretionary authority over the firm's strategy and policies:

> It is presumed that firms in roughly comparable situations often will differ in what they do, and that these differences will matter in terms of how they do it. The question of what makes for good policies is what the business management field is all about.
>
> In contrast, in most of economics, firms are treated as simple entities … management chooses the policies that will 'maximize' firm profits. The 'question' that is at the centre of concern in the business management field is assumed trivial to answer. And since it is, all firms in the same economic context are presumed to have the same policies – those that are best in that context – and to do the same thing.
>
> (Nelson, 1991a, p. 347)

Most firms are not simple 'price takers', as in the world of perfect competition, but, in the language of neoclassical market structures, operate in what would be more like oligopolistic markets. Such firms are not monopolies – they do face competitors. But they face only a limited number of such competitors.[3] And crucially, the number of competitors is such as to leave them some scope and leeway for considering what prices to charge for their goods and services – rather than being forced to accept the prices determined by a Walrasian general equilibrium outcome. Pricing thus becomes a conscious act – influenced, certainly, by the expected reaction of rival firms to any change that the firm might make to its pricing strategy. But nevertheless, the pricing strategy becomes one part of the firm's overall strategy, along with decisions concerning output levels, investment, technologies, marketing (aimed at shaping preferences) and so forth. It is within these decision-making processes and strategies that environmental policy needs to impact.

As well as the idea of perfect competition generally being misleading, so is the neoclassical assumption that firms price according to a rising marginal cost of production. The assumption of 'marginalism' – with economic actors making decisions at the margin, on the basis of rising marginal cost curves – was challenged some time ago by Sraffa (1926, p. 543):

> The chief obstacle against which they have to contend when they want gradually to increase their production does not lie in the cost of production –

which, indeed, generally favours them in that direction – but in the difficulty of selling the larger output of goods...

Similarly, Kaldor (1972) argued that 'at the empirical level, nobody doubts that in any economic activity which involves the processing or transformation of basic materials – in other words, in industry – increasing returns dominate the picture'.[4]

Rather, firms tend to price according to a mark-up over normal operating costs.[5] The resulting price will thus be above the long-run marginal cost; this makes the perfect competition required by the theory of competitive equilibrium impossible. Hence while it is argued above that many markets and industries will be oligopolistic, the fact that prices are above marginal cost means that the alternative to oligopoly cannot in any case be a Walrasian competitive equilibrium. Thus Hicks (1939) admitted that 'unless we can suppose that marginal costs generally increase with output at the point of equilibrium ... the basis on which economic laws can be constructed is shorn away.'[6]

Policy decisions based on an assumption of increasing costs – which allows output and price levels to be calculated at the margin – will therefore be based on a false premise. If, as is likely, costs are not rising, there will be no intersection of the cost and revenue curves, hence no deterministic outcome for output and price levels. Rather, output will be determined by demand and the growth of the market. And prices will be determined by a mark up over normal operating costs. Increasing the degree of competition to the market may or may not bring more benefits than costs. But it will not create a world in which marginal cost curves slope upwards. Policy based on such assumptions will not, therefore, become any more appropriate just because the degree of competition increases.

Recognising that firms, especially in the two industries with the highest carbon emissions – energy and cars – operate under conditions of falling unit costs and increasing returns requires a re-think of policy measures.

Increasing returns may also provide a source of lock-in to inefficient technologies that slows down the rate of technical change. Again, the car industry provides a useful case study. Existing petrol models with an established market will enjoy economies of scale and low unit costs of production. Incumbent technologies have a first mover advantage that makes it difficult for new, low-emission models to enter the market even if production costs at minimum efficient scale match those of the older technology. The output of new, low emission models must be at least equal to minimum efficient scale of production before market entry becomes profitable.

In terms of the macro economy (as opposed to the level of individual firms), an important concept is that of cumulative causation and dynamic economies of scale. Kaldor (1972) argued that neoclassical economics focuses attention on the *'allocative* functions of markets to the exclusion of their *creative* functions – as an instrument for transmitting impulses to economic change'.[7] It is precisely the discretion that managers and firms do have that gives them the ability to take decisions to get ahead of the game, to adopt new processes and develop new markets. With increasing returns to scale, the tendency will always be for firms that manage to expand their output to thereby gain a competitive advantage, turning otherwise competitive markets into oligopolistic ones, and oligopolistic markets into monopolistic ones. A similar idea is embedded in Schumpeter's work: monopoly profits enable firms to invest in R&D and innovation to stay ahead of the market until such time as new innovations challenge and replace existing products and technologies.

This area of managerial discretion, and the ability to create new markets, relates to another key difference between mainstream neoclassical economics on the one hand, and an institutional or evolutionary approach on the other, namely, the role of tastes and preferences. Are preferences and tastes given (exogenous) or amenable to change (endogenous)? In mainstream neoclassical economics, tastes and preferences are generally taken as given. Institutional economics, on the other hand, will see them as being heavily influenced by institutional factors, pointing to the importance of routines, conventions and culture. Evolutionary economics in addition sees all these factors as evolving over time. Tastes and preferences cannot be assumed to be constant. Neither are they unimportant or trivial; they are part of the inherited institutional and cultural context that contributes to cumulative causation and path dependency in economic processes.[8] Moreover, they have implications for the design of environmental policy: 'If preferences are affected by the policies or institutional arrangements we study, we can neither accurately predict nor coherently evaluate the likely consequences of new policies or institutions without taking account of preference endogeneity.' (Bowles, 1998, p. 75).

As Bowles (1998, p. 105) has argued, endogenous preferences give rise to 'a kind of market failure' via external effects. Culturally transmitted preferences that create fads or fashions, such as the rapid growth in demand for fuel inefficient sports utility vehicles (SUVs) may impose costs and benefits on others. For example, the growth in demand for SUVs had the effect of reducing unit costs of production making these models relatively cheaper as the market grew. At the same time the fuel inefficiency of these vehicles imposed costs on consumers and society by *ceteris paribus* raising petrol prices and carbon emissions.

Preferences for environmental goods, such as recycling and less packaging, may be shaped by a mixture of cultural attitudes, conventions and policy initiatives. While there may be a loss of predictive power in the absence of a theory of preference formation, modelling the factors that shape preferences opens up a wider set of policy instruments, including the use of information and (moral) persuasion. Firms frequently attempt to influence consumer choices via advertising and marketing strategies; likewise governments may influence consumer behaviour via information provision, taxes, subsidies, laws and advertising campaigns. For example, anti drink-driving campaigns have proved extremely successful in changing attitudes and behaviour. To create environmentally sustainable behaviour amongst consumers and producers, changing routines, conventions and culture is key. There are a number of ways in which public policy can do this – and to some extent is already doing so. First, culture can be influenced by general awareness efforts, including through education and information. Second, better labelling and more detailed information on externalities, such as carbon emissions can help consumers make more informed choices; the impact of how these messages are understood may depend on consumers' experience of negative externalities. Third, firms may be unaware of the alternative routines available, and of the economics of switching to these – such alternatives could be uncovered and illustrated through 'environmental audit' work in companies, where alternatives are identified, costed and promoted. Finally, as discussed in the following section, if the behaviour of even a small group of firms can be changed, this can have wider impacts through its demonstration effect that alternative routines and conventions are not only possible, but profitable.

## 3 Strategic interaction, economic rationality, business strategy and public policy

There is a further set of reasons to avoid designing policy on the assumption that agents will respond as rational profit maximisers. There is a large literature on strategic interaction and rationality, part of which questions the degree to which profit maximising behaviour actually succeeds in delivering maximum profits. There are also questions regarding the degree of knowledge that actors will have and their ability to use such knowledge to compute the necessary actions to maximise profits or utility – hence Herb Simon's concept of 'satisficing' rather than maximising (see for example Simon, 1959). All this points to the need to act on the factors that actually influence decision making. These factors include the influence of standard policy variables, such as taxes and subsidies, but go beyond this to include the role of learning and the adaptation and evolution of firms' behaviour over time. To explore these ideas in more detail we model firms' decision making in a strategic framework.

### 3.1 Strategic interaction, environmental strategies and public policy

Hardin's (1968) analysis of the tragedy of the commons highlights the conflict between individual rationality and Pareto efficiency. For example in the case of common pool resources such as common pastureland, fish stocks and the atmosphere, each individual agent finds that it is in his or her interest to continue to exploit common resources until they are ruined. In essence there is a contradiction between the microeconomic behaviour of individual firms and macroeconomic or system-wide effects. A similar contradiction arises in the case of lock-in to inefficient technologies. A classic example is the QWERTY keyboard. This keyboard was originally designed to slow down typing in an era when fast typing caused mechanical typewriters to jam (David, 1985). However, once this technology became embedded and workers were trained to touch-type according to the QWERTY system, the costs of any one firm switching included having to retrain new and existing employees. As a result firms became locked-in to an inefficient technology. If we consider the application of this type of problem to environmental technologies we might consider the choice between two strategies: (i) adopt the new environmentally friendly technology or (ii) stick with the existing technology. There are advantages to sticking with existing technology in terms of having pools of skilled labour to draw on and thus saving on training costs. Any firm that chooses to switch will incur additional training costs. If a firm switches while rival firms stick, that firm will have higher training and labour costs and lower profitability. If all firms switch, these costs are reduced as firms are able to draw on a bigger pool of trained managers and employees. But such a switch would require collective rather than individual action.

Lock-in effects are not uncommon and they arise for a variety of reasons (Arthur, 1996; Foxon, 2002; Page, 2006). In the example above there are systems effects or externalities that favour existing technology. Similar effects have been highlighted in the car and transport industries, for example Krugman (1998) has argued that cars are not much use without petrol stations and the lack of good infrastructure for vehicles powered by alternative energy sources places these new technologies at a disadvantage. Firms and consumers get locked in to inefficient technologies. Increasing returns in production can also act as a lock-in mechanism making it difficult for new technologies to break into a market.

In the case of lock-in effects associated with systems effects, such as the availability of skilled labour, an obvious policy implication is that some mechanism to provide collective or subsidised training in the use of environmentally friendly technologies would change the structure of the payoffs and resolve the dilemma. In the absence of such provision, firms will free-ride on existing pools of labour and will be unwilling to incur the training costs associated with switching to the new technology.

The example of the tragedy of the commons describes a situation where there are negative externalities associated with the actions of individual firms and a conflict between private and public interest, such as over-fishing that destroys or reduces future stocks. However, in a repeated game it might be reasonable to expect that inefficient outcomes would be avoided, and firms would reach a Pareto optimal, environmentally friendly outcome if the game were repeated. For example, suppose the game was repeated 20 times; after some experience of playing the game surely agents would realise that they could be better off if they each chose the production strategy without externalities that destroy their common resource. Can firms learn that cooperation pays dividends? Under the assumption of common knowledge rationality, the strict answer is 'no'. The problem is that any known finite repetition has a final play or terminating game. This final play will be played as if it were a one-shot game. Hence in the last period players will revert to the dominant strategy: production with negative externalities. But once firms recognise that this is the inevitable outcome in the last play of the game, they will see little point in cooperating in the penultimate play, since there are no future plays where having a reputation for cooperation might count. Thus, cooperation in the penultimate play is ruled out. This 'backward induction' argument continues unravelling throughout the entire 20 plays.

The fact that there is a final play, and that both players are known to be profit maximisers, means that it is impossible to build up interdependence between successive plays of the game: each play is played as if it were a one-shot game and free-riding rules the day.

There are, however, a variety of ways of resolving the conflict between private and public interest and associated market failure. The first is to use policy instruments, such as taxes, subsidies or standards and regulations. The second is to change the time horizon from a one-shot or finitely repeated game to an indefinitely or infinitely repeated game whilst preserving the assumption of common knowledge rationality. The third is to change the underlying model of business rationality and allow firms to learn and to be influenced by their institutional environment (Ostrom, 1990, 2000). We consider each of these three possibilities in turn.

### 3.2 Market-based instruments, standards and regulations, and voluntary measures

The literature on environmental policy has traditionally distinguished three types of policy instrument: (i) market-based instruments; (ii) standards and regulations; and (iii) voluntary instruments (Jaffe *et al.*, 2001; IPCC, 2007a). The theoretical foundation for market-based approaches to policy instruments is grounded in the identification of market failures arising from externalities and public goods. Market-based instruments, such as taxes and subsidies attempt to correct for market failures by changing the private incentives faced by firms and individuals – that is, by changing the payoffs. The effectiveness of these instruments depends not just on imposing the right taxes and subsidies in terms of qualitative direction, but also on setting the taxes at the right quantitative level. Given that there are discontinuities in payoff structures, this requires detailed knowledge of the 'tipping points' that make environmentally friendly strategies more profitable than free-riding strategies.

In contrast, standards work directly by regulating firms' strategic options, for example, by setting a limit on emissions or preventing over-fishing via the use of quotas. The success of these types of policies depends crucially on the degree of compliance with the regulations (and hence on the detection and punishment of non-compliance). A number of structural, institutional and cultural factors are important in determining how easy it is to detect and punish non-compliance, and perhaps, more importantly, how likely it is that firms will choose strategies of non-compliance in the first place. For example, the structure of an industry, as measured by the number and size distribution of firms will determine how difficult it is to monitor compliance. As Vogel and Kessler (1998) point out:

> In Europe, the difficulty of administering a uniform system of waste disposal has been increased significantly by the large disparities in the institutional structures underlying most national waste management programs, ranging from a few large, centralized public companies in Denmark, to dozens of

small private firms in Great Britain (Brand, 1993, pp. 242–244). Not surprisingly the latter have proven much more difficult to monitor.

(Vogel and Kessler, 1998, p. 25)

Institutional factors, such as the frequency of use of legal action by residents
living next to land fill sites and the decisions of the courts regarding the imposition and extent of penalties under 'nuisance laws' also shape the strategies used
by waste disposal firms (Tromans, 2001). Plainly, the use of litigation differs
across countries, regions and type of actor (firm, local authority, individual), and
as Tromans (2001) and Kellet (2002) point out, both the structure and use of the
legal system are significant in shaping environmental outcomes.

It is important to recognise that the extent of non-compliance is determined
not only by the probability of detection and the extent of penalties but also by
cultural factors, including firms' attitudes to adopting environmentally damaging
or environmentally friendly strategies. Under the standard economic assumption
of instrumentally rational behaviour,[9] this factor is ruled out since firms do not
care about their actions other than in terms of the payoffs associated with them.
However, as North (1990) has pointed out it is impossible to understand major
changes in our system of production without taking into account cultural factors.
The example that he famously cited was the shift from a slave based system of
agricultural production in the US to a paid system. North argued that this socio-
economic shift cannot be explained purely in terms of the payoffs from one
system compared to another, as the slave system had lower costs and higher
profits. Other cultural factors played a key part. Likewise, in the field of environmental management, the extent to which firms accept and internalise the values
of environmentalism, will determine whether they are likely to break environmental regulations when doing so would bring them private gain.

In the rationality literature this type of behaviour has been explained by the
models of 'expressive rationality' (Hargreaves Heap, 1989) and 'social man'
(Vatn, 2005). According to these alternative behavioural theories, actions are
determined not only by the payoffs associated with them but also by the 'expression', 'signal' or 'value' of the actions themselves and by the institutional and
cultural environment. Thus, firms may choose not to violate environmental regulations even when the private benefit of doing so is positive, because they value
the action of compliance. Expressive rationality is grounded in an existentialist
view of economic interaction. Agents reflect on their actions and have a desire
for self-respect that may be enhanced or diminished by those actions. It may be
argued that this desire could be incorporated into the standard model of instrumental rationality by including the desire for self-reflection and self-respect in
the utility function.[10] However, such an approach would reduce the analysis of
rational choice to an ends driven framework and this would be at odds with
valuing actions as an expression of what individuals stand for and believe, which
is the hallmark of expressive rationality.

Expressive rationality or models of choice based on 'social man' as opposed
to 'economic man' lend themselves to the third type of policy instrument,

namely voluntary measures (see IPCC, 2007a for a review). Under instrumental rationality and conventional market-based analysis, non-mandatory measures will fail because they have no impact on the price system and impose no penalties for violation. As a result they do not change the financial incentives facing firms or individuals. However, within the broader context of institutional and evolutionary economics, non-mandatory measures can work by changing the institutional context and the value system within which firms operate. Non-mandatory measures include: (1) voluntary initiatives encouraged by regulatory agencies; (2) bi-lateral initiatives that involve negotiation between government and firms on non-mandatory regulations; and (3) unilateral undertakings by individual firms to adopt environmentally friendly strategies (Khanna, 2002, p. 46). Non-mandatory measures may also include voluntary negotiations with groups or networks of firms, trade associations or industries. Other non-mandatory measures include information disclosure and improved corporate governance via increasing the influence of stakeholders (Khanna, 2002, p. 47 and p. 55).

Some non-mandatory measures clearly impose costs on firms, for example voluntary abatement agreements, yet there is empirical evidence to suggest that firms choose to follow them (see Khanna, 2002 and IPPC, 2007a and 2007b, for a review of the empirical evidence). Other non-mandatory measures may bring both increased costs and benefits. For example, adopting environmentally friendly strategies in order to improve relations with stakeholders, such as consumers, may be costly in the short run but may bring improved consumer loyalty and increased demand in the long run. Likewise the adoption of environmentally friendly technologies that enhance resource productivity and lower externalities may bring private gains in the long term even though the switching costs are considerable.

At the same time, it is evident that the effectiveness of non-mandatory measures may be greatest when there is a credible threat of mandatory measures in the absence of voluntary compliance. What is clear is that we need to understand the institutional and evolutionary context if we are to understand how these policies work and how they might best be integrated with market based measures on the one hand, and mandatory standards and regulations on the other.

### 3.3 Game theory and the time horizon

Consider the following payoff matrix which is a variant of the tragedy of the commons where two firms are deciding between strategies – one that produces externalities that impose costs on other firms (such as fish stock depletion due to over fishing, or environmental damage that at some point reduces farm yields, or land fill that depletes the available land for disposal of rubbish) and another more expensive production strategy that avoids external effects. Following the standard convention, the first number in each pair represents the payoff (profit) to Firm 1, and the second number represents the payoff (profit) to Firm 2. Under the assumption of common knowledge rationality – which implies that both firms are profit maximisers and know each other to be so – it is straightforward to find the equilibrium solution to a one-shot play of this game. Firm 1 attains a payoff of £0m or £3m if it adopts the environmentally friendly strategy, and a payoff of £1 or £5m if it adopts the strategy with externalities. The same applies to Firm 2. Given that both firms are profit maximisers, both will choose the strategy with externalities, since this strategy offers maximum profits given the profit maximising strategy of the other firm. The Nash equilibrium is therefore (£1m, £1m) which is Pareto sub-optimal. Clearly the preferred outcome would be for both firms to produce without creating any externalities. They would then receive profits of £3 million a year each. However, common knowledge instrumental rationality rules out this possibility in a one shot play or a finite repetition.

Thus, under perfect information and common knowledge rationality, the dominant strategy is for both firms to adopt the production strategy with negative externalities. Under this Nash equilibrium, each player's strategy is a best response to its rival's strategy. The Nash equilibrium also describes a situation of fulfilled expectations by players: each player, knowing that the other is instrumentally rational, expects their rival to adopt the environmentally unfriendly strategy, and in Nash Equilibrium (£1m, £1m) these expectations are fulfilled. Collectively, both firms would be better off if they could adopt the cooperative strategy that avoids the production of negative externalities, but instrumental rationality rules this out, leading firms to adopt the strategy that produces externalities and leaving them with a lower payoff. Paradoxically, two 'irrational' players could attain higher profits than two instrumentally rational maximisers.

In the absence of policy measures that change the payoffs (taxes and subsidies) or that rule out certain strategy choices (standards and regulations), inefficient outcomes may be avoided by changing the time horizon over which the game is played. In an indefinite repetition of the game it can be shown that firms may adopt the cooperative strategy if they attach sufficient weight to future payoffs and are prepared to use punishment strategies, such as the trigger strategy or the tit-for-tat strategy. The trigger strategy starts by choosing cooperation but will punish any move of non-cooperation by rivals with non-cooperation in all future plays. The tit-for-tat strategy starts by choosing cooperation and then follows the strategy that the other player adopted in the previous period. It is

*Table 3.1* A tragedy of the commons-type game

|  |  | Firm 2 | |
|---|---|---|---|
|  |  | Strategy with negative externalities | Strategy without externalities |
| *Firm 1* | Strategy with negative externalities | (1, 1) | (5, 0) |
|  | Strategy without externalities | (0, 5) | (3, 3) |

more sophisticated than the trigger strategy as it punishes non-cooperation with non-cooperation but is prepared to follow a move back to cooperation. Hence, the tit-for-tat strategy is 'nice', 'provacable' and 'forgiving' (Axelrod, 1981).

With the use of simple punishment strategies such as these it can be shown that private profit-maximising firms may reach and follow an equilibrium path characterised by cooperation in all plays of the game. The key factor that determines whether, with the use of threats and punishments, firms are prepared to cooperate now for the sake of a better future is the weight that players attach to future profitability (or the discount factor). This suggests that policies that encourage firms to take a longer time horizon may be important in encouraging environmentally friendly strategies. Such policies might include changes in the corporate governance structure of firms that increase the influence of long-term stakeholders vis-à-vis shareholders that tend to favour short-run profits.

While indefinite repetitions can generate environmentally superior outcomes, assuming individual instrumental rationality, there are two limitations of this approach. The first is that solutions to indefinite games rely on the fact that players must believe that there is a chance that the game will last forever. As Hargreaves Heap (1989) has pointed out, players must believe in their own immortality and this assumption does not sit comfortably with the assumption of rationality that underlies the game.[11]

The second limitation is that any strategy that yields a higher payoff than adopting the non-cooperative move in each play of the game, can form part of an equilibrium strategy. This finding – known as the Folk Theorem – shows that there are multiple Nash equilibria, and that as a consequence it is difficult to predict what will happen in games played over an indefinite time horizon.

Evolutionary game theory has attempted to discover which strategies are most likely to survive and dominate in order to regain determinacy and predictability. The idea behind evolutionary game theory is Darwinian: certain strategies do better than others and firms that adopt those strategies survive. Such strategies may be regarded as evolutionary (or collectively) stable. Axelrod (1981) has shown that tit-for-tat is an evolutionary stable strategy. While the number of evolutionary stable strategies is less than the number of Nash strategies, multiple equilibria remain. For example, the non-cooperative strategy – producing externalities – is also an evolutionary stable strategy. Thus, it is still difficult to determine what conditions might make firms adopt environmentally friendly strategies.

However, Axelrod's work on clustering does shed some light on this question that can be of help to policy makers. Using evolutionary game theory it can be shown that for a given population of firms, cooperative strategies may be spread throughout the population of firms that make up the industry by a small group of firms that adopt environmentally friendly strategies (Axelrod, 1981). The reason is that when the group of cooperative tit-for-tat players interact with each other they do very well and pick up the payoff (of £3m in Table 3.1). Provided they are of sufficient number, the positive payoff from mutual cooperation outweighs losses suffered by encounters with opportunistic firms. Axelrod's clustering result is powerful since it shows that an industry in an equilibrium characterised by all firms playing the non-cooperative strategy can be shifted to a cooperative equilibrium by a small group of firms adopting the cooperative tit-for-tat strategy. The size of the group relative to the population depends on the relative payoff structure and the discount factor but for the payoffs shown in Table 3.1, and a discount factor of 0.1, environmentally friendly outcomes can be attained in an industry of 21 firms by the entry of just 2 environmentally friendly firms adopting the cooperative strategy.[12]

This suggests that policy makers might be best placed to focus their efforts on encouraging a small number of firms to adopt environmentally friendly strategies through targeted technology transfer programmes rather than introducing a blanket tax/subsidy policy.

### 3.4  Rationality and economic behaviour

The game-theoretic approaches outlined above explain both why firms end up adopting environmentally unfriendly strategies that are Pareto sub-optimal and how such sub-optimality may be overcome whilst preserving the assumption of instrumental rationality. The third approach to resolving the tragedy of the commons and other games that capture features of environmental problems is to abandon as unrealistic the assumption of instrumental rationality. This approach does not rely on the unrealistic assumption that the game may last forever. Alternative models of rationality include bounded rationality, procedural rationality, expressive rationality and Kantian rationality. All of these models share a view of economic behaviour that is shaped by agents' cultural and institutional environment, where strategies are the outcome of an adaptive, evolutionary process (Veblen, 1898) rather than strict profit maximisation, but paradoxically all of them are capable of yielding higher profits compared to instrumentally rational choices grounded in simple profit maximisation.

Early work on evolutionary economics and economic behaviour was set forth by Veblen (1898, pp. 394–395) in his paper 'Why Is Economics Not an Evolutionary Science?':

> evolutionary economics must be the theory of a process of cultural growth as determined by the economic interest ... Like other men, the economist is an individual with but one intelligence. He is a creature of habits and propensities given through antecedents, hereditary and cultural, of which he is an outcome; and the habits of thought formed in any one line of experience affect his thinking in any other.

This approach has been influential in the literature on procedural rationality which (as with Veblen's work) is distinct from Simon's (1959) model of bounded rationality. Simon's model deals with complexity but ignores the shared cultural and institutional determinants of choice. Rather, Simon's model focuses on situations where agents' rationality is bounded by informational and computational limitations. As a result, outcomes differ from those that would be attained by unbounded maximising behaviour. However, the model does not break fundamentally with the neoclassical model of instrumental rationality, as agents would like to be instrumentally rational if only computational and information constraints could be overcome.

Instead under procedural rationality, agents, faced with complexity and informational limitations, follow well-established procedures or norms rather than pursuing strict profit maximising behaviour. Procedural rationality is consistent with evolutionary and institutional approaches and is especially relevant in games with multiple equilibria where no additional amount of computational power will help agents ascertain which equilibrium will actually prevail. Here, procedural rationality helps by showing how agents use historical norms and customs in a deterministic way to provide focal points that result in equilibrium selection (Schelling, 1960; Hargreaves Heap, 1989, 1992). In this way procedural rationality is distinct from bounded rationality because it shows how *shared* norms and beliefs are functional in resolving indeterminacy. This adds a clear historical and social dimension to the theory of rational choice and equilibrium selection. By contrast, Simon's (1959) account of bounded rationality places emphasis on norms that provide short-cuts in situations where computational ability is found lacking but the *commonality* of these norms and procedures does not feature as an integral part of his theory (Hargreaves Heap, 1989).

The significance of procedural rationality is that it provides a common foundation for coordinating activity. It is because the social, historical and institutional context provides common conventions, procedures and norms that procedural rationality or models of 'social man' are useful in determining outcomes in games with multiple equilibria. The approach also implies that changes in norms and procedures lead to changes in equilibrium outcomes. This opens up the possibility of a new set of policy instruments designed to change norms, institutions, conventions and procedures. In particular the establishment of new standards and changes in system regulation can act as powerful policy instruments for environmental change.

A similar idea is expressed in Kantian rationality which is based on the notion that as human beings we are creatures of 'reason' as well as 'instinct'. While our instinct may be to selfishly pursue our preferences, as creatures of reason we are able to avoid this instinctive behaviour and reason that cooperation will bring higher rewards. 'Kantian man' is able to distance himself from his preferences and value 'means' as well as 'ends'. Kant identified universalisable principles and argued that agents adopt these principles via a process of reason. Hence two Kantian reasoners playing the above 'tragedy of the commons' can attain the superior outcome (£3m, £3m). Hollis (1992) has argued that Kantian agents may punish opportunistic behaviour but will seek to restore cooperation for the sake of the common good. The Kantians are able to do better at maximising returns than their instrumentally rational counterparts because they are guided by universalisable principles and value actions on their merits in addition to the individual incentives that they face. Moreover, these actions provide signals to other players that convey information about the type of player they are dealing with.

This is similar to the use of norms, conventions and rules that players follow under procedural rationality which generate information about the values of players and therefore about the type of player(s) one faces. Given the existence of shared value systems or universalisable principles, players can associate themselves with different value systems by virtue of their strategy choice. This insight is reinforced by the empirical evidence from game-theoretic experiments which shows that many players adopt cooperative strategies even in finite repetitions of the game.[13]

Empirical evidence on theories of rationality suggests that instrumental rationality has been found lacking as a basis for an explanatory model of economic behaviour, in that many of its predictions are not verified by experimental data or even casual empiricism (see Andreoni and Miller, 1993, or Hough and White, 2003). For example, under a finite time horizon, choice based on instrumentally rational behaviour rules out cooperative or collective action such as trade union membership or individual participation in recycling of waste, and yet, in practice, such behaviour is commonplace. The results from experiments based on the finitely repeated prisoners' dilemma indicate that cooperation is likely and that there are some players who cooperate throughout finite games. Moreover, in their experiments where players played finitely repeated prisoners' dilemma type games for cash payoffs, Andreoni and Miller (1993) found that the proportion of cooperative outcomes increased as the games progressed, a result that is broadly consistent with evolutionary theory. Hence, the experimental evidence provides support for the view that some players, contrary to the instrumental model of rational choice, are genuinely cooperative and that others learn to be more cooperative as the game progresses.

Expressive, Kantian and procedural models of rational choice show that even in the case of finitely repeated prisoners' dilemma type games it is possible to overcome negative externalities. These models of rationality also demonstrate the importance of cultural, informational and 'learning' policies. It follows that policies designed to change the underlying behaviour of firms (and consumers) from non-cooperative to cooperative can be beneficial. There is evidence for this in the case of both firms and consumers; the work of Teisl *et al.* (2002) for example shows how information policies can be used to favour environmentally friendly production even when there are private costs to firms and consumers.

### 3.5  *Standards, regulation and strategic environmental management*

Porter and van der Linde (1995) questioned the conventional wisdom – that imposing controls on firms with the aim of reducing negative externalities will necessarily impose costs, which in turn will diminish profitability. Rather, the introduction of regulatory standards can act as a catalyst for innovation that both reduces emissions and increases profitability. The so-called Porter hypothesis –

that tougher environmental standards may enhance competitiveness – has gained widespread recognition. For example, speaking in 2007, Barack Obama said:

> It's all part of the US auto industry taking necessary steps to help its own turnaround. Here in Detroit, three giants of American industry are haemorrhaging jobs and profits as foreign competitors answer the rising global demand for fuel-efficient cars. The need to drastically change our energy policy is no longer a debatable proposition. It is not a question of whether, but how; not a question of if, but when. For the sake of our security, our economy, our jobs and our planet, the age of oil must end.
>
> (Barack Obama, 7 May 2007, cited in an article by Corey Williams, Associated Press)

The Porter hypothesis has been developed further in the strategic management literature. In particular, bounded rationality and procedural rationality have been employed to explain why firms do not adopt environmentally beneficial strategies, even when those strategies would enhance their profitability. Goldstein (2002) describes how the growth of strategic environmental management (SEM) has reduced costs and raised profits, in contrast to the standard view that there are trade-offs between environmental protection and firms' profitability. Goldstein's analysis raises the question of why, if SEM offers opportunities to increase profits, do all firms not adopt it? The answer may lie in bounded and procedural rationality, with managers stuck in existing routines and procedures that cloud strategy formation. Firms that are able to break through this *malaise* and use SEM will be able to reap the rewards:

> The opportunities for this kind of strategic repositioning are thought to originate in broad social and environmental trends. Hart (1997) argues that while 'bottom-up pollution-prevention programs have saved companies millions of dollars' (67–68) – with increased cost savings and hence profits coming from reduced waste and energy use – the best is yet to come. He points to the smaller number of firms that have begun reorienting their long term strategies, and plans for revenue growth, around solving sustainable development problems where their basic capabilities give them expertise.
>
> (Goldstein, 2002, p. 497)

This approach suggests that overcoming bounded rationality and historic norms and procedures that tie companies into inefficient and environmentally unfriendly production techniques is essential if the full benefits of SEM are to be realised. It therefore opens up a new branch of policy based on effective training in SEM, plus better corporate governance with greater involvement of stakeholders – customers, employees and local communities – to bring pressure to bear on companies to exploit and develop SEM to both improve environmental outcomes and enhance profitability.[14]

Goldstein's study presents empirical evidence from seventeen companies that were active members of a Regional Pollution Roundtable. Of these companies, fourteen introduced SEM projects as a means of enhancing profitability, two companies introduced projects on standard business criteria that turned out to have positive environmental effects although these were not considered at the initiation of the projects, and one company initiated a new project for environmental reasons alone (and not for financial returns). While more empirical evidence would be desirable, Goldstein's case studies do show that environmental protection and increased profitability *can* go hand in hand.

A further study by Cambridge Econometrics and AEA Technology undertook 65 case studies to calculate the cost savings associated with adopting new processes of production that increase resource productivity (Cambridge Econometrics, 2003). The study also calculated the potential economic gains that could be realised if these processes were diffused throughout the UK manufacturing sector. Their results indicate potential cost savings equivalent to somewhere between 4.5–6.0 per cent of manufacturing value added and 17–21 per cent of UK manufacturing profits.

These two studies are significant because they show that contrary to the standard view of environmental economics which assumes a central conflict between the private self interest of individual firms and the public interest (for example, the ubiquitous externality problem), there are classes of environmental problems where there is no such conflict, but nonetheless, firms are 'trapped' by inefficient technology even when individual firms could increase their profitability by adopting environmentally friendly strategies. The SEM approach suggests there is a clear role for policy to provide practical and far-reaching training in strategic environmental management techniques.

## 4  Systems of innovation

Richard Nelson argues that the fact that firms differ in their behaviour, and would be expected to differ in their responses to price signals, follows of necessity from the central importance of innovation:

> The developing theory of dynamic firm capabilities I am discussing here starts from the premise that ... firms are in a Schumpeterian or evolutionary context. Simply producing a given set of products with a given set of processes well, will not enable a firm to survive for long. To be successful for any length of time a firm must innovate...
>
> To be successful in a world that requires that firms innovate and change, a firm must have a coherent strategy that enables it to decide what new ventures to go into and what to stay out of. And it needs a structure, in the sense of mode of organization and governance, that guides and supports the building and sustaining of the core capabilities needed to carry out that strategy effectively.
>
> If one thinks within the frame of evolutionary theory, it is nonsense to presume that a firm can calculate an actual 'best' strategy. A basic premise

of evolutionary theory is that the world is too complicated for a firm to comprehend, in the sense that a firm understands its world in neoclassical theory.

(Nelson, 1991b, pp. 68–69)[15]

Likewise, Giovanni Dosi argues that,

A major implication of the characteristics of cumulativeness, tacitness, and partial appropriability of innovation is the permanent existence of *asymmetries* among firms, in terms of their process technologies and quality of output. That is, firms can be ranked as 'better' or 'worse' according to their distance from the technological frontier.

(Dosi, 1988, pp. 1155–1156)[16]

Technological innovation is a key driver of economic change. Indeed, for Schumpeter, innovation was the most distinctive feature of a capitalist economy, and this is why the use of equilibrium analysis was, in his view, quite inappropriate for analysing such an economy: 'In appraising the performance of competitive enterprise, the question whether it would or would not tend to maximise production in a perfectly equilibrated stationary condition of the economic process is ... almost, though not quite, irrelevant' (Schumpeter, 1943, p. 77).[17]

An evolutionary and institutional approach to understanding technical change suggests that *systems* of innovation play a key role – national systems, regional systems, and industrial systems (Mowery and Rosenberg, 1989; Archibugi and Michie, 1998; Michie *et al.*, 2002):

Some institutional economists in the tradition of evolutionary economics refer to 'systems of innovation' in which they point to the existence of 'collective entrepreneurship' (Lundvall 1992, pp. 9–10), while other institutional economists focus on technological trajectories and paradigms as special kinds of institutions (Dosi 1982, 1988; Perez 1983; Freeman, Clark and Soete 1982; Freeman and Perez 1988).

(Andersen, 2001, p. 37)

By a 'national system of innovation' is meant 'the network of institutions in the public and private sectors whose activities and interactions initiate, import, and diffuse new technologies' (Freeman, 1987, p. 1). The concept has since been developed more generally for 'systems of innovation', including national, regional or sectoral, and encompasses all the important factors that influence the development, diffusion and use of innovations, as well as the relations between these factors.

A central insight provided by the systems-of-innovation approach is that firms do not generally innovate in isolation, but do so in interaction with other organizational actors (such as other firms, universities, or standard-setting agencies) and that this interaction is shaped by (and shapes) the framework of existing institutional rules (laws, norms, technical standards). The approach takes into consideration the actions of both firms and governments. In short, this conceptual approach regards innovation as a process of interactive learning.

(Edquist, 2001, p. 1623)

Adopting a systems approach for considering environmental issues should point policy makers towards considering the whole system of taxation, regulation, innovation and so on. This in turn should prevent unrealistic expectations as to the impact that a single tax or regulatory change, on its own, may have. Changes need to be brought about, for example, in the design stage of new technologies, so the system needs to be viewed as a dynamic one, over time. Economic outcomes depend partly on competition but also on their own past evolution (North, 1990).[18] And technological change does not occur simply in response to price signals (Dosi, 1984).

Freeman stressed the importance of not only combining economic incentives with legal regulation, but also, first, of mobilising public opinion and second, encouraging appropriate technical change:

In practice most countries have begun to use a combination of economic incentives and legal regulations. However, the effectiveness of most of these methods depend on:

1.  the degree of public support for the policies. Consequently methods of public persuasion and mobilisation of public opinion also play an important role. Historically, voluntary groups and organisations have made the major contribution to this mobilisation ... The success of the environmentalist movement in the 1970s and 1980s has meant that now governmental agencies also often participate in public advocacy and persuasion, albeit not to the extent nor with the same degree of conviction as some 'Greens' might wish.
2.  a continuing high rate of technical change.

(Freeman, 1992, pp. 191–192)

This mix of policy measures may be essential in cases where there is lock-in to an existing technology. In the case of the car industry, for example, the switch to low emission vehicles requires changes in technology and demand. One difficulty is that car production is subject to increasing returns to scale and producers are operating on the downward sloping part of their average cost curves. This makes it very difficult for firms to introduce new products or technologies into the industry as they will operate at a cost disadvantage until they reach output levels close to minimum efficient scale of production. Hence, even in the case where a new technology exists and has the potential to compete with existing technologies in terms of cost (that is, there are similar production costs for both types of vehicle at minimum efficient scale), the technology will not be adopted unless there is adequate demand. The problem is a classic collective action problem that we have termed the sustainable consumption paradox (Whitmarsh *et al.*, 2008). If a new low emissions technology is developed, producers will only find switching to it profitable if there is sufficient demand to allow them to operate at or near minimum efficient scale. For this to happen, a large enough number of consumers must switch their demand to low emission models simultaneously; only then will the low emission vehicles be available at prices close to high emission vehicles. Thus, the consumption choices of consumers are interdependent: whether or not producers find it profitable to switch to low emission models, and therefore whether or not consumers get to choose between low and high emission vehicles, depends on a sufficient number of consumers switching their demand. The choice set that an individual consumer faces depends on the choices of other consumers.

In this case, taxes and subsidies are unlikely to be effective, or efficient, in isolation. This is because cost curves are downward sloping, firms face uncertainty over their costs of production, and there are 'lumpy' effects in consumption (as discussed in Section 5 below). What is required is a combination of policies designed not to just influence decisions at the margin, but to create the necessary step change, for example by: (i) developing and diffusing low carbon technologies; (ii) setting standards for emissions; (iii) taxing the production of high emission vehicles and subsidising the production of low emission vehicles; and (iv) influencing consumer preferences via information and persuasion (for example requiring producers to display clear information on carbon emissions, such as through a colour coded index scheme). The need to combine market and non-market measures leads us to a discussion of the policy implications of managerial, institutional and systems approaches.

## 5 Implications for the design of policy measures

Theorising requires abstraction and must make simplifying assumptions. Using equilibrium concepts may be a useful analytical tool to conceptualise the interactions between various elements in a system. But when it comes to policy design, it is vital that any unrealistic assumptions that have been made for conceptual purposes are replaced with ones that accurately describe how actors will actually respond to changes in prices, incentives, regulation and other factors. In trying to uncover how agents actually respond, it is important to understand the complex relation between a whole range of economic and non-economic factors. These include the role of corporate and consumer culture. They also require an understanding of how systems operate – and hence change – over time.

History matters in economic processes. Firms and industries can get 'locked in' to particular technologies.[19] Routines and corporate culture are important factors in the way firms behave, and are not easily altered. When analysing the dynamics of economic development and the design of packages of measures – including economic instruments – to achieve environmental outcomes, it is therefore important to draw on those traditions within economics that have developed these concepts and have analysed the various issues involved.

The key implications from the discussion in this chapter for the design of policy measures are as follows.

### 5.1  Corporate behaviour and managerial discretion

Governments throughout the world have for some time now been attempting to influence the behaviour of firms to make them act in more environmentally sustainable ways. However, using mainstream economic models as the basis for policy design has resulted in anomalies. For example, the reaction of firms to policy initiatives has not always been as expected, given the economic incentives that those firms face, and the changes in those incentives that governments have engineered in order to alter corporate behaviour. This is perhaps most clearly illustrated where there are a large number of firms that face seemingly similar constraints and market opportunities, but that then react differently to a change in government policy, whether affecting taxation or some other instrument. If we could understand why the reaction of firms to policy initiatives are not as expected, given the economic incentives, this would clearly be helpful in informing policy design.

Since firms price according to a mark-up over normal operating costs, policy aimed at altering decisions at the margin may fail to have the desired effect. With oligopolistic industrial structures, tax rises may squeeze profits rather than, as intended, leading to increased prices and a consequent reduction in both consumption and production of the good with the negative externality. Policy designed to alter consumer and producer decisions at the margin may prove to have much more 'lumpy' effects. In addition, the speed at which such processes work through will depend on a range of factors, one of which is the remaining lifetime of assets. Risk and uncertainty play a key role. For example, what matters is not just the effect of a tax change on relative prices, but what the *expectations* will be of price and tax changes in the future. More generally, firms' decisions to invest are shaped by factors other than short-run financial criteria. Institutional and regulatory changes – laws and codes on corporate governance, policies on corporate social responsibility, and so on – will all play a role.

Many standard models fail to recognise the political constraints imposed on policy. There has been a reluctance on the part of some governments to introduce policies designed to control carbon emissions on the basis that they impose costs on firms that are not affordable or that such policies will reduce the competitive advantage of domestically-based producers vis-à-vis competitors based in countries that do not have such stringent regulations. However, the view that the control of externalities always implies a trade-off between environmental protection and profitability has been questioned by various bodies of economic research including the strategic management literature, evolutionary economics, and the systems of innovation approaches. These literatures point to the use of standards and regulations as a way to stimulate innovation, reduce environmental damage and create competitive advantage.

## 5.2 The nature of rationality

Mainstream economic theory is founded on a model of rational choice that is problematic in a number of respects. First, the assumed information set and computational ability of firms and consumers are rarely found in practice. On the one hand, firms do not have all the available information to carry out the kinds of calculations that neoclassical analysis requires. On the other hand, the information set assumed by neoclassical economics is actually very limited and as a result there is no uncertainty (as opposed to risk). In reality firms face genuine uncertainty over many variables that are normally taken as exogenous or assumed to be calculable. For example, firms do not know the demand curve they face, the strategies of rival firms or the impact of new technology. Firms and consumers grapple with these uncertainties by relying on norms, procedures and conventions shaped by the institutional and cultural environment in which they operate. Understanding how social rules and institutions are formed and how they influence business choice leads us to a larger set of policy instruments. For example, the impact of introducing environmental reporting for firms, the construction of easily understood indices of environmental responsibility, the use of corporate governance structures that include a role for stakeholders with a long-term perspective, such as employees and local community representatives, or the mandatory use of independent non-executive directors with responsibility for company policy on environmental matters and sustainable development. All of these policy actions may engender cultural change and set new norms and standards in environmental management and corporate social responsibility.

Second, application of dynamic game theory to standard economic problems, such as the selection of standards in technology, shows that many economic games have multiple equilibria. Under multiple equilibria, no additional amount of information or computational power will provide firms with the answer as to which equilibrium path will be followed. Norms and conventions, however, can provide focal points and looking at how such social rules or institutions are formed and changed provides new policy insights. In this, it is important to recognise that environmental policy is often the outcome of inter-action between firms, government and international organisations. For example, industry standards and regulations on new technology or emissions are negotiated between firms (often via their industry representatives) and government. National governments (or unions, such as the EU) in turn negotiate with their counterparts to broker international agreements. The policy making process is part economic, part political, with firms and government as key players. Certain events may change the economic and political climate, for example, the impact of the 2009 global recession on the technology choices of car manufacturers may significantly influence policy and environmental outcomes over subsequent years.

Third, there are many cases where instrumental rationality and profit maximisation yield inefficient outcomes, as for example with the tragedy of the commons. Insights from dynamic game theory can provide solutions under instrumental and *other* models of rationality. If we stick with the standard model of rational choice, policy instruments such as taxes, subsidies or tradable permits will be required to change the payoffs that firms face. Such policies are designed to internalise externalities and resolve the tragedy of the commons. We have also seen that other instruments – such as public provision of training in environmental management or skills required for new technology – may also resolve the free-rider problem. For example, where the introduction of new, environmentally efficient technology requires significant retraining of employees in the use of new technology, individual firms will be deterred from the adoption of new technology by training costs. There is a role for public policy to internalise the free-rider problem that characterises business investment in training either by subsidising education and training in environmental technologies and management or by encouraging firms – that would otherwise free-ride – to make joint investments in training programmes.

Using evolutionary game theory and sticking with the assumption of instrumental rationality, we have applied Axelrod's analysis of 'cooperation among egoists' to show that in an evolutionary setting it is possible to switch the equilibrium outcome for a whole industry by changing the behaviour of just a small number of firms. This application provides an important insight into policies to shift an industry from its existing technology to new low emissions technologies: it suggests that governments might productively target or work with just a few firms in an industry to encourage them to switch. Government might take ownership stakes in a small number of firms, or make loans to them on condition that new environmentally friendly technologies are adopted. This will result in wider adoption throughout the industry.

### 5.3 New technology and innovation: a systems approach

A systems approach is quite different from the approach often adopted in the literature on environmental issues, of looking for market failure, and then attempting to calculate what tax or regulatory changes would be needed to overcome such failure. The differences between countries in technological progress over time cannot be explained simply by different incentives derived from their firms facing different relative prices; rather, they are influenced by a range of *systemic* factors including the countries' education and training policies, public and corporate research and development arrangements, availability of long-term finance, and so on. In seeking to move firms towards more environmentally sustainable technologies, policy needs to act on all aspects of the innovation system.

A systems approach points to the need to act on other (non-price) factors to influence decision making. As Douglas North argues:

> That institutions affect the performance of economies is hardly controversial. That the differential performance of economies over time is fundamentally influenced by the way the institutions evolve is also not controversial ... the institutional framework (of rules, norms, and enforcement characteristics)

together with the traditional constraints (budget, technology) of economic theory determine the opportunities available at any moment in time.

(North, 1993, pp. 242–243)

It is important to appreciate the power of cultural, informational and 'learning' policies. It may be that *packages* of policies will be more effective than a series of individual policy initiatives.

In summary, the variety of policy instruments that could usefully be developed is far wider than much of the standard literature suggests. At the same time, it is evident that packages of policies may be more effective than individual policies operating in a single dimension. This was clearly recognised by the Intergovernmental Panel on Climate Control (IPCC, 2007b) and the Stern Review (Stern, 2006/2007; Barker, 2008; Dietz et al., 2007 and Dietz and Stern, 2008). There is therefore a need to explore both theoretically and empirically, how, and to what extent, different policies work, both individually and in combination. In particular, there is a need for more analysis of detailed case studies to uncover the complexity of effects, as was done, for example, in applying these ideas to the car industry (see Whitmarsh et al., 2008).

## Appendix

The tragedy of the commons game illustrated in Table 3.1 can be re-expressed in general terms as shown in Table 3A.1 below (see Oughton and Whittam, 1997).

The tit-for-tat (TFT) strategy is collectively stable provided the $w$ – the discount factor, $w = 1/(1 + r)$ – is greater than:

$$\text{Max } [(\pi_1 - \pi_2/(\pi_1 - \pi_3), (\pi_4 - \pi_2)/(\pi_2 - \pi_4)]$$

For the values of the payoffs shown in Table 3.A1 it can be sent that the TFT strategy is collectively stable if $w > 2/3$. Hence, as Axelrod notes,

> The significance of this theorem is that it demonstrates that if everyone in a population is cooperating with everyone else [not producing externalities] because each is using the TFT strategy, no one can do better using any other strategy provided the discount parameter is high enough.

(Axelrod, 1981, p. 312)

As discussed above, TFT is not the only collectively (or evolutionary) stable strategy. The free-riding, environmentally unfriendly strategy is also collectively stable. Axelrod has shown that the number of collectively stable strategies is less than the number of Nash strategies and that some collectively stable strategies can be invaded by groups of players adopting other collectively stable strategies. More precisely, consider the situation where an industry is characterised by firms playing the free-riding, environmentally unfriendly strategy that produces externalities. This strategy is collectively stable and cannot be invaded by a single

*Table 3A.1* Tragedy of the commons expressed in generic terms

|  |  | Firm 2 | |
| --- | --- | --- | --- |
|  |  | Production strategy creating negative externalities | Production strategy without externalities |
| *Firm 1* | Production strategy creating negative externalities | $(\pi_3, \pi_3)$ | $(\pi_1, \pi_4)$ |
|  | Production strategy without externalities | $(\pi_4, \pi_1)$ | $(\pi_2, \pi_2)$ |

Notes
Where $\pi_1 > \pi_2 > \pi_3 > \pi_4$

player arriving and trying to play the cooperative, environmentally friendly strategy (with no externalities). However, if a small cluster of environmentally friendly firms adopt the environmentally friendly strategy then TFT can evolve as a stable strategy provided that for the proportion of environmentally friendly firms, $p$, the following holds:

$$p > [(\pi_3/\delta) - (\pi_4 + (1 - \delta)\pi_3/\delta)]/[\pi_2/2\delta - (\pi_4 + (1 - \delta)\pi_3/\delta)]$$

Given the values of the payoffs shown in Table 1 and setting $\delta = 0.1$ (which implies that two interacting players have a 90 per cent chance of meeting again) then environmentally friendly strategies can evolve as collectively stable in an industry of 21 firms provided at least two firms adopt the environmentally friendly production technique. Clearly this is a very powerful result. The intuition behind this result is that TFT does as well against free-riders as the free-riding strategy, but better than free-ridering against a like minded TFT player. It follows that the widespread adoption of environmentally friendly production strategies can emerge via the establishment of a small cluster of firms in the industry that adopt environmentally friendly techniques. This suggests that policy efforts that are targeted and that might appear expensive if the cost-per-firm were aggregated across all firms, may in fact prove to be both successful and cost effective, since only a small number of firms need to have that targeted effort, with the effect being subsequently diffused through the population of firms with no further policy effort required.

## Notes

1 For a discussion of national and regional systems of innovation, see respectively Freeman (1997) and Howells (1999).
2 For a discussion of the literature on evolutionary and institutional economics, see respectively Mitchell (2001) and Hodgson (2001).
3 In a 1995 survey of almost 1000 companies in the UK, nearly two-thirds had fewer than ten serious competitors; see Kitson and Michie (2000, p. 146) for further detail

and discussion. This paper also discusses the relationship between competition and cooperation, pointing to the importance of productive cooperation between firms, which is not necessarily anti-competitive collusion.

4 This has been confirmed by more recent studies, for example, Fingleton and McCombie (1998) though Basu and Fernald (1997) found equivocal evidence of increasing, constant and deceasing returns at the industry level, but part of this ambiguity is caused by aggregation effects. Controlling for economy wide effects the authors find that 'a typical firm produces with approximately constant returns to scale, although we cannot rule out increasing returns' Basu and Fernald (1997, p. 276).

5 For an empirical investigation of this, see Coutts *et al.* (1978).

6 This is quoted by Thirlwall (1987), which also discusses the various objections made by Lord Kaldor to neoclassical equilibrium theory.

7 Emphasis in the original.

8 See Hodgson (2003) who points out that preferences and values are changed through learning, yet for much of mainstream economics, there is no role for 'persuaders', only for transmitters of information (p. 160).

9 The different types of rationality are defined and discussed in Section 3.4 below.

10 Boland (1981) points out that utility theory cannot be disproved, since we cannot know for sure that firms and people aren't always attempting to maximise something or other.

11 A further means of escaping the Prisoners' Dilemma is to assume a finite time horizon and imperfect information about the type of player one faces, in particular, uncertainty as to whether they are instrumentally rational. This approach requires either that non-instrumentally rational players exist, or that instrumentally rational players believe they exist even though they do not. The first option paves the way for alternative models of rational choice since we need to say something about what motivates non-instrumentally rational players. The second option, which has been referred to in the literature as the 'strong rationality assumption' is unsatisfactory because it leads to the contradiction that 'rational' players hold irrational beliefs. As suggested below, policy might usefully introduce such players – namely, firms that would follow the environmentally friendly strategies.

12 See the Appendix for further detail.

13 See for example Andreoni and Miller (1993).

14 Such an approach would be consistent with the Higgs report which called for non-executive directors to be drawn from a wider pool than at present (Higgs, 2003).

15 Nelson acknowledged that he is largely 'restating what Chandler, Lazonick, Williamson, and other scholars of the modern corporation, have been saying for some time'. See for example Chandler (1966, 1990), Lazonick (1990), and Williamson (1979).

16 Emphasis in the original.

17 Cited in Rosenberg, 1994, which contains an excellent discussion of Schumpeter's work on economic growth and innovation. See also the proceedings of the International Joseph A. Schumpeter Society Conference, Vienna, 1988, published in the *Journal of Evolutionary Economics*, Volume 10, number 3, 2000.

18 Rosenberg (1994) argues that technological changes are often 'path dependent':

> Additional knowledge of new production possibilities is not costless, nor is the rate and direction of technological change exogenous. Consequently, understanding the particular sequence of events that has shaped the knowledge of the technological frontier is crucial, not only to the historian, but to the economist as well. Technology and science, which are now generally acknowledged to be central to the achievement of economic growth, need to be understood as path-dependent phenomena.
>
> (p. 23)

19 For a discussion of which, see for example David (1985).

## References

Andersen, E.S. (1994) *Evolutionary Economics: Post-Schumpeterian Contributions*, Pinter, London.

Andersen, B. (2001) *Technological Change and the Evolution of Corporate Innovation*, Edward Elgar, Cheltenham.

Andreoni, J. and Miller, J. (1993) Cooperation in the Finitely Repeated Prisoners' Dilemma, *Economic Journal*, 103:418, pp. 570–585.

Arthur, W. Brian (1988a) Self-reinforcing Mechanisms in Economics, in Anderson, Philip W., Kenneth J. Arrow and David Pines (eds) (1988), *The Economy As An Evolving Complex System*, Redwood City, California: Addison-Wesley, pp. 9–31.

Arthur, W. Brian (1988b) Competing Technologies: An Overview, in Dosi *et al.* (eds) (1988), pp. 590–607.

Arthur, W. Brian (1989) Competing Technologies, Increasing Returns, and Lock-in by Historical Events, *Economic Journal*, 99, pp. 116–31.

Arthur, B. (1996) Increasing Returns and the New World of Business, *Harvard Business Review*, July–August.

Archibugi, D. and Michie, J. (1998) Technical Change, Growth and Trade: New Departures in Institutional Economics, *Journal of Economic Surveys*, 12:3, pp. 313–32.

Axelrod, R. (1981) The Emergence of Cooperation Among Egoists, *American Review of Political Science*, 75, pp. 306–318.

Barker, T. (2008) The Economics of Avoiding Dangerous Climate Change. An Editorial Essay on The Stern Review, *Climate Change*, 89, pp. 173–194.

Basu, S. and Fernald, J. (1997) Returns to Scale in US Production: Estimates and Implications, *Journal of Political Economy*, 105:2, pp. 249–283.

Boland, L.A. (1981) On the Futility of Criticizing the Neoclassical Maximization Hypothesis, *American Economic Review*, 71:5, pp. 1031–1036.

Bowles, S. (1998) Endogenous Preferences: The Cultural Consequences of Markets and other Economic Institutions, *Journal of Economic Literature*, XXXVI, March, pp. 75–111.

Brand, E.C. (1993) Hazardous Waste Management in the European Community: Implications of 1992, *The Science of The Total Environment*, 129, February, pp. 241–251.

Chandler, A.D., Jr. (1996) *Strategy and Structure*, Doubleday & Co., Anchor Books Edition, New York.

Chandler, A.D., Jr. (1990) *Scale and Scope: The Dynamics of Industrial Capitalism*, Harvard University Press, Cambridge, MA.

Cook, J., S. Deakin, J. Michie and D. Nash (2003) *Honest Business: Realising a Mutual Advantage?*, Mutuo, London.

Coutts, K., Godley, W. and Nordhaus, W. (1978) *Industrial Pricing in the United Kingdom*, Cambridge University Press, Cambridge.

David, P.A. (1985) Clio and the Economics of QWERTY, *Economic History*, 75:1, pp. 332–337.

Dietz, S., Anderson, D. and Stern, N. (2007) Right for the Right Reasons: A Final Rejoinder on the Stern Review, *World Economics*, 2, pp. 229–258.

Dietz, S. and Stern, N. (2008) Why Economic Analysis Supports Strong Action on Climate Change: A Response to the Stern Review's Critics, *Review of Environmental Economics and Policy*, Winter: 2, pp. 94–113.

Dosi, G. (1982) Technological Paradigms and Technological Trajectories: A Suggested Interpretation of the Determinants and Directions of Technical Change, *Research Policy*, 11:3, pp. 47–162.

Dosi, G. (1984) Technological Paradigms and Technological Trajectories: The Determinants and Directions of Technical Change and the Transformation of the Economy, in C. Freeman (ed.), *Long Waves in the World Economy*, Pinter, London.

Dosi, G. (1988) Sources, Procedures, and Microeconomic Effects of Innovation, *Journal of Economic Literature*, 26, pp. 1120–1171.

Dosi, G., Freeman, C., Nelson, R., Silverberg, G., and Soete, L. (eds) (1988) *Technical Change and Economic Theory*, Pinter, London.

Edquist, C. (2001) Systems of Innovation, in J. Michie (ed.), *A Reader's Guide to the Social Sciences*, Fitzroy Dearborn/Routledge, London.

Fingleton, B. and McCombie, J. (1998) Increasing Returns and Economic Growth: Some Evidence for Manufacturing from the European Regions, *Oxford Economic Papers*, 50, pp. 89–105.

Foxon, T. (2002) Technological and Institutional 'Lock-in' as a Barrier to Sustainable innovation. ICCEPT Working Paper, November, downloaded from http://iccept.ic.ac.uk/public.html.

Freeman, C. (1992) *The Economics of Hope: Essays on Technical Change, Economic Growth and the Environment*, Pinter, London.

Freeman, C. (1997) The 'National System of Innovation' in Historical Perspective, in D. Archibugi and J. Michie (eds), *Technology, Globalisation and Economic Performance*, Cambridge University Press, Cambridge and New York.

Freeman, C., Clarke, J. and Soete, L. (1982) New Technological Systems: An Alternative Approach to The Clustering of Innovation and the Growth of Industries, in Freeman, Clarke and Soete (eds), *Unemployment and Technical Innovation*, Pinter, London.

Freeman, C. and Perez, C. (1988) Structural Crises of Adjustment: Business Cycles and Investment Behaviour, in G. Dosi, C. Freeman, R. Nelson, G. Silverberg and L. Soete (eds), *Technical Change and Economic Theory*, Pinter, London.

Goldstein, D. (2002) Theoretical Perspectives on Strategic Environmental Management, *Journal of Evolutionary Economics*, 12:5, pp. 495–524.

Hardin, G. (1968) The Tragedy of the Commons, *Science*, 162:3859 (13 December, 1968), pp. 1243–1248.

Hargreaves Heap, S. (1989) *Rationality in Economics*, Basil Blackwell, Oxford.

Hart, S. (1997) Beyond Greening: Strategies for a Sustainable World, *Harvard Business Review*, 75, pp. 67–76.

Hicks, J. (1939) *Value and Capital*, Oxford University Press, Oxford.

Higgs, D. (2003) *Review of the Role and Effectiveness of Non-executive Directors*. The Stationery Office, London.

Hodgson, G.M. (2001) Institutional economics, in J. Michie (ed.), *Reader's Guide to the Social Sciences*, Fitzroy Dearborn & Routledge, London.

Hodgson, G.M. (2003) The Hidden Persuaders: Institutions and Individuals in Economic Theory, *Cambridge Journal of Economics*, 27:1, pp. 159–175.

Howells, J. (1999) Regional Systems of Innovation?, in D. Archibugi, J. Howells and J. Michie (eds), *Innovation Policy in a Global Economy*, Cambridge University Press.

Hollis, M. (1992) A Rational Agent's Gotta Do what a Rational Agent's Gotta Do, *Royal Economic Society Newsletter*, January.

Hough, J.R. and White, A.A. (2003) Environmental Dynamism and Strategic Decision-making Rationality: An Examination at the Decision Level, *Strategic Management Journal*, 24, pp. 481–489.

IPCC (2007a) Gupta, S. *et al.*, *Policies, Instruments and Co-operative Arrangements*, Chapter 13 in *Climate Change 2007: Mitigation. Contribution of Working Group III to the Fourth Assessment Report of the Intergovernmental Panel on Climate Change* (B. Metz, O. R. Davidson, P.R. Bosch, R. Dave, L. A. Meyer, [eds]) Cambridge University Press, Cambridge.

IPCC (2007b) Summary for Policymakers, in *Climate Change 2007: Mitigation. Contribution of Working Group III to the Fourth Assessment Report of the Intergovernmental Panel on Climate Change* (B. Metz, O. R. Davidson, P.R. Bosch, R. Dave, L. A. Meyer [eds]) Cambridge University Press, Cambridge.

Jaffe, A.B., Newell, R.G. and Stavins, R.N. (2001) *Technological Change and the Environment, Resources for the Future*, Washington, DC.

Jaffe, Adam B., and Robert N. Stavins (1995) Dynamic Incentives of Environmental regulations: The Effects of Alternative Policy Instruments on Technology Diffusion, *Journal of Environmental Economics and Management*, 29:3, pp.S-43–S-63.

Juma, C. (1989) *The Gene Hunters: Biotechnology and the Scramble for Seeds*, African Centre for Technology Studies, Research Series, No. 1. London: Zed Press.

Kaldor, N. (1934) The Equilibrium of the Firm, *The Economic Journal*, 44, pp. 60–76, reprinted in Buckley and Michie (eds), *Firms, Organizations and Contracts: A Reader in Industrial Organization*, Oxford University Press, Oxford

Kaldor, N. (1972) The Irrelevance of Equilibrium Economics, *The Economic Journal*, 82.

Kant, I. (1981/1896) *Critique of Pure Reason*, translated by F. Max Müller, London, Macmillan.

Kant, I. (1785/1949) *Foundations of the Metaphysics of Morals*, translated by Lewis White Beck. Chicago, University of Chicago Press.

Katz, M. and Shapiro, C. (1985) Network Externalities, Competition and Compatibility, *American Economic Review*, 75, pp. 424–40.

Katz, M. and Shapiro, C. (1986) Technology Adoption in the Presence of Network Externalities, *Journal of Political Economy*, 94, pp. 822–41.

Kellet, P. (2002) Implementing the landfill directive through the PPC regime in England and Wales, in Boswell, J. and R. Lee (eds) (2002), *Economics Ethics and the Environment*, Cavendish Publishing, London and Sydney.

Khanna, M. (2002) Non-mandatory Approaches to Environmental Protection, in Hanley, N. and Roberts, C. (eds) *Issues in Environmental Economics*. Oxford, Blackwell.

Kitson, M. and Michie, J. (2000) Markets, competition and innovation, Chapter 9 of Kitson and Michie, *The Political Economy of Competitiveness: Essays on employment, public policy and corporate performance*, Routledge, London.

Krugman, P. (1998) Will Capitalism go to Hollywood? Downloaded from www.pkarchive.org/new/values.html.

Lazonick, W. (1990) *Competitive Advantage on the Shop Floor*, Harvard University Press, Cambridge, MA

Lundvall, B.-A. (ed.) (1992) *National Systems of Innovation: Towards a Theory of Innovation and Interactive Learning*, Pinter, London.

Michie, J., Oughton, C. and Pianta, M. (2002) Innovation and the Economy, *International Review of Applied Economics*, 16:3, pp. 253–264.

Michie, J., Oughton C. and Wilkinson, F. (2002) Against the New Economic Imperialism: Some Reflections, *The American Journal of Economics and Sociology*, 61:1, pp. 347–361.

Mitchell, L.S. (2001) Economics and Evolution, in J. Michie (ed.), *Reader's Guide to the Social Sciences*, Fitzroy Dearborn & Routledge, London.

Mowery, D.C. and Rosenberg, N. (1989) Technology and the Pursuit of Economic Growth, Cambridge University Press, Cambridge.

Nelson, R.R. and Winter, S.G. (1982) *An Evolutionary Theory of Economic Change*, Cambridge, MA: Harvard University Press.

Nelson, R.R. (1991a) The Role of Firm Differences in an Evolutionary Theory of Technical Advance, *Science and Public Policy*, 18:6, pp. 347–352.

Nelson, R.R. (1991b) Why do Firms Differ, and How Does it Matter?, *Strategic Management Journal*, 12, pp. 61–74.

North, D.C. (1990) *Institutions, Institutional Change and Economic Performance*, Cambridge University Press, Cambridge and New York.

North, D.C. (1993) Institutions and Economic Performance, in Maki, U., Gustafsson, B. and Knudsen, C. (eds) *Rationality, Institutions and Economic Methodology*. London, Routledge.

Ostrom, E. (1990), *Governing the Commons: The Evolution of Institutions for Collective Action*, Cambridge University Press.

Ostrom, E. (2000) Collective Action and the Evolution of Social Norms, *The Journal of Economic Perspectives*, 14:3, pp. 137–158.

Oughton, C. and Whittam, G. (1997) Competition and Cooperation in the Small Firm Sector, *Scottish Journal of Political Economy*, 44:1, pp. 1–30.

Page, S. (2006) Path Dependence, *Quarterly Journal of Political Science*, 1, pp. 87–115.

Perez, C. (1983) Structural Change and Assimilation of New Technologies in the Economic and Social Systems, *Futures*, 15:5, pp. 357–375.

Rosenberg, N. (1982) *Inside the Black Box: Technology and Economics*, Cambridge: Cambridge University Press.

Rosenberg, N. (1994) *Exploring the Black Box: Technology, Economics, and History*, Cambridge, Cambridge University Press.

Schelling, T. (1960) *The Strategy of Conflict*, Harvard University Press, Cambridge, MA.

Schumpeter, J. (1943) *Capitalism, Socialism and Democracy*, 2nd edn, George Allen & Unwin, Ltd, London.

Simon, H.A. (1959) Theories of Decision-making in Economics and Behavioural Science, *American Economic Review*, 49, pp. 253–283.

Sraffa, P. (1926) The Laws of Returns under Competitive Conditions, *Economic Journal*, 36, December, pp. 535–550.

Teisl, M.F., Roe, B. and Hicks, R.L. (2002) Can Eco-Labels Tune a Market?, *Journal of Environmental Economics and Management*, 43, pp. 339–359.

Thirlwall, T. (1987) *Nicholas Kaldor*, Wheatsheaf Books Ltd, Brighton.

Tromans, S. (2001) Civil Liability for Landfill Sites, in Boswall, J. and Lee, R. *Economic, Ethics and the Environment*, Routledge-Cavendish.

Vatn, A. (2005) Rationality, Institutions and Environmental Policy, *Ecological Economics*, 55, pp. 203–217.

Veblen, T. (1898) Why Is Economics Not an Evolutionary Science? *Quarterly Journal of Economics*, July, pp. 374–397.

Whitmarsh, L., Köhler, J., Michie, J. and Oughton, C. (2008) Can the Car Makers Save the Planet? in Foxon, T., Köhler, J. and Oughton, C. (eds) *Innovation for a Low Carbon Economy*, Routledge.

Williams, C. (2007) *Obama Outlines Reforms for Energy Policy*, ABC News, 18 May 2007. Downloaded from: http://actrees.org/files/Newsroom/ABC%20News_Obama%20Energy%20Plan.pdf.

Williamson, O. (1979) Transaction-Cost Economics: The Governance of Contractual Relations, *Journal of Law and Economics*, 22:2, pp. 233–261, reprinted in P. Buckley and J. Michie (eds), *Firms, Organizations and Contracts: A Reader in Industrial Organization*, Oxford University Press, Oxford.

# 4   Behavioural economics

## Seven key principles for environmental policy[1]

*Emma Dawnay and Hetan Shah*

## Introduction

An important part of any notion of political economy is an exploration of the theoretical paradigm(s) within which discussions take place. This chapter is an exercise in shifting the political economy of the environment, in particular of environmental policy. We aim to do this through providing an alternative economic paradigm for understanding how to approach issues of environmental policy.

Environmental policy is a difficult area for economics. Many relevant factors have no market prices, and there are many market failures and externalities. Much of the aim of environmental policy is to try to change people's or organisations' behaviour so they act in more environmentally sustainable ways. One approach to thinking about environmental policy making which has perhaps been dominant in environmental policy is to apply what is known as 'neoclassical' economics. In the narrow definition of this theory, people are assumed to be fully rational and to behave in a way to maximise their opportunities given their preferences. In this chapter this is referred to as 'rational-man' economics. The typical rational-man policy is to internalise externalities through the mechanism of price. Whilst this rational-man approach yields a powerful tool for analysis, it has shortcomings that can lead to unrealistic policy, especially where policy is concerned with human behaviour change – which is often the case for environmental policy. An alternative (and sometimes complementary) paradigm is that of behavioural economics. There is a large academic literature on behavioural economics. This chapter distils many concepts from behavioural economics and psychology down to seven key principles, which highlight the main shortfalls in the rational-man model of human behaviour. Many of the examples are taken from situations outside environmental policy, either where examples from environmental policy are not available, or where the examples chosen best illustrate the principle. We have fully referenced the supporting literature thereby enabling the reader to find all source texts if necessary.

The seven principles are:

1   Other people's behaviour matters
2   Habits are important

3    People are motivated to 'do the right thing'
4    People's self-expectations influence how they behave
5    People are loss-averse
6    People are bad at computation
7    People need to feel involved and effective to make a change.

The principles complement other policy approaches that emerge from mainstream economics.

It is important to note that although most of the work in the literature relates to individuals, it is applicable to small groups, businesses or organisations where there are no formal processes to counteract these behavioural tendencies as these organisations are essentially composites of individuals whose behaviour is subject to these principles.

### *Structure of this chapter*

In the following sections each of the principles is presented in a uniform way:

•    Introduction – an overall introduction to the idea.
•    Theory – how rational-man economics would approach this issue, and how a behavioural economics approach can broaden and develop the perspective.
•    Examples – specific examples that illustrate the principle.
•    Policy relevance – an initial discussion on how the principle might relate to policy.

The final section discusses what the gaps in the research are, and how future research projects might address them.

## Principle 1: Other people's behaviour matters

### *Introduction*

Much of our behaviour is strongly influenced by other people's behaviour – for example the clothes we wear or whether we haggle when shopping. Social learning is a process by which we subconsciously take in the behaviour of others to learn how to behave. In more complex situations with which we are unfamiliar we consciously watch and learn from the behaviour of others (which is known as 'social proof') – for example when using a new library for the first time. When we must make a conscious decision on how to behave, our sense of social identity is important – we think: how would other people from 'my group' behave in this situation? In situations where there is high social capital (i.e. where there are strong networks between people and a high level of mutual trust), other people's behaviour and our sense of social identity may be extremely important in influencing our behaviour. We are particularly open to influence from people in authority or from people whom we respect or like. The influence of people's behaviour on social norms – which themselves influence yet more people's behaviour – gives rise to the ever-evolving system of shifting social norms. Illustrations of the importance of other people's behaviour abound, including fashion, the films we watch, stock market prices and the pursuit of status, which is always socially defined and changes through time (de Botton 2004).

## *Theory*

The rational-man economic theory stops short of trying to explain where people's preferences come from, so it does not take account of the direct influence of other people's behaviour and social norms. People's preferences are exogenous to the economic model (i.e. they are taken as given and are outside of the model). The theory assumes we independently know what we want and that our preferences are fixed. This rational-man theory is very good at explaining short-term decision making (I want a green vegetable and choose beans as they are on special offer) but cannot explain longer-term changes in preferences (I now only choose organic food). Along the same lines the importance of institutions – both formal institutions such as regulations, and informal ones, for example, how people organise markets – and the evolution of the whole economic system are not subjects of rational-man economic analysis. This has significant implications for policy design (see for instance Levett *et al.* 2003).

The rational-man model also assumes that people carry out a full rational 'analysis' of all their available options. This requires a lot of brainpower, which can also be considered a scarce resource. Therefore, 'copying' can be thought of as a type of 'procedural rationality' (Simon 1957). It would require too much effort to, for example, look up all the rules when driving in a new country, find out all the fines/punishments for failing to meet the rules, work out the probability of being caught and the possible costs, before deciding how to drive there. Instead we just copy other people, and perhaps adjust our behaviour according to the feedback we receive (if someone hoots when I pull out of a junction, next time I might give way at a similar junction). Procedural rationality is not usually taken into account in rational-man economics.

In contrast to rational-man economics, many models from psychology attempt to show how social norms influence us, for example see Fishbein and Ajzen's *Theory of Reasoned Action* (1975). For a comprehensive review of such models see Tim Jackson's (2005) report Motivating Sustainable Consumption. Related topics from the psychology literature include:

- *Social learning*: Psychologist Bandura (1977a) showed that people learn by observing what others do. His first experiment showed that kindergarten children were likely to violently attack a 'bobo' doll after having been shown a film of someone attacking a bobo doll. Experiments have been repeated with adults in a wide variety of settings with similar results.
- *Social proof*: Social psychologist Cialdini (1993) has shown that we look to others to see how to behave, especially in ambiguous situations, in crises

and when others are experts. He had some accomplices stare upwards on a street pavement as if looking at something – other people quickly joined in and a large group stayed long after the accomplices had left. Another example of how we look to other people to know how to behave comes from an experiment where people who didn't know each other were sitting in a waiting room where it was arranged that smoke would pour in through a vent. It was found that the more people sitting in the room, the less likely was anyone to raise the alarm – the people all just looked at each other to try to work out what to do (Darley and Latane 1968).

* *Social identity theory*: Psychologists Tajfel *et al.* (1971, 1986) have shown that part of our social identity comes from which groups we associate with. We show a strong bias in favour of 'in-group' members, even when groups are arbitrarily formed. Tajfel demonstrated this in an experiment where he assigned people randomly into groups (and everyone saw it was random), but soon people showed a preference for members of their group over other people, even giving rational arguments about how unpleasant and immoral the 'out-group' people were.

* *Key influencers:* Psychologists have identified that we are open to influence from people in authority or people we like. When we are influenced by authority (an expert, someone with legitimate power to direct our actions, someone who can either reward or punish us) the effects are less likely to be lasting than when we are influenced by information by someone we like (Halpern *et al.* 2004). However, care should be taken when using persuasion: knowing that someone is trying to persuade us generally makes us take the opposing view.

Economists Fehr and Fischbacher (2004) have looked recently at why social norms are important from an evolutionary point of view, and they have shown that groups are biologically fitter (have more offspring) when social norms are enforced. (See section on Principle 3: 'People are motivated to do the right thing'.)

Although they have no independent theories of human behaviour, the 'new' disciplines of system dynamics and agent-based modelling in economics can incorporate behavioural traits, and in particular dynamic 'feedback' from other people's behaviour into social norms. In systems with feedback – where the output (the typical way people behave in a particular instance) affects the input (how people choose to behave) – there is no single stable equilibrium (as in rational-man economics), but temporary equilibria occur which depend on the history of the system. For examples of such modelling see Paul Omerod's (1998) book *Butterfly Economics*.

### Examples

The enforcement of seatbelt wearing is now hardly necessary as it has become a social norm, and for most of us a habit. When the compulsory wearing of seatbelts in cars was introduced in the 1970s there was widespread public resistance. By 2002 when a survey was carried out to assess public support for state intervention about 94 per cent of the people asked supported compulsory wearing of seatbelts (Halpern *et al.* 2004).

The theory of reasoned action has been used to model the uptake of technologies by farmers, and it identifies which communication strategies could potentially speed up the adoption of these strategies (Garforth 2003). Vets were identified as key influencers in this study, and government officials as amongst the least influential.

A famous example of the influence of authority is an experiment done by Milgram (1974). A doctor told participants to increase the level of electric shocks apparently being applied to a patient – who screamed louder and louder and showed more and more signs of distress as the level of shock was increased. The participants, however, went on increasing the level as directed by the doctor.

### Relevance to policy

Policy makers focusing only on rational-man economical analysis may often devise a system that has an immediate effect; however, this may not last. For example knowing that there is a fine for speeding and a high likelihood of getting caught I will probably drive more slowly – but I will drive just as fast once I realise the chance of being caught is low. However, if policy makers can change the social norm – perhaps in this case by encouraging us to frown on others who drive dangerously fast with campaigns against dangerous driving – then less enforcement will be needed after the change. In other words policy makers might want to take preferences as fixed in the short term, but as part of a sustainable intervention they should consider shifting preferences in the medium term. An example where policy appears to have successfully changed people's preferences in the US is banning smoking in public places. This change appears to reduce the 'social proof' (which in some way reinforces smoking behaviour as pro-social), thereby reducing the amount people smoke in private (Trotter *et al.* 2002).

Once policy makers have identified the particular behaviour they are trying to change, they can evaluate the role that social norms play in influencing this behaviour. If other people's behaviour plays an important role perhaps this could be leveraged. Malcolm Gladwell (2000) describes how small numbers of key people can have a big impact in his book *The Tipping Point*. He divides such people into three groups: the Mavens, the Connectors, and the Salesmen. The Mavens are people who have such expert knowledge that you would take their advice if given it (and Mavens enjoy giving it for free). The Connectors have many connections, so information they have has the potential to be distributed to a large number of people. The Salesmen are people with the power to persuade us to change our behaviour. Policy makers may find it useful to focus their efforts to create behaviour change on these specific types of people who will help promote wider change.

## Principle 2: Habits are important

### *Introduction*

When we do something out of habit, we use little or no cognitive effort. Most of us do not spend a long time each morning deliberating on what to eat for breakfast or how to travel to work: such daily routines quickly become ingrained habits. Even when we consciously think about what we do, it can be difficult to change our behaviour. Perhaps I think it is a good idea for people to use public transport, but I don't know where the bus stop is or when the bus runs. I think I should find out, but I don't know how, so I continue using my car. The rewarding feeling – 'my journey by car was easy and hassle free' – reinforces my old bad habit.

### *Theory*

In rational-man economics the assumption is made that people act rationally to maximise their *utility*, given their particular preferences (utility broadly means happiness or satisfaction, but usually a financial measure is taken as a proxy for this). Doing something out of habit, for example choosing my normal coffee in the usual sized jar when shopping, is outside of rational-man theory, in which I would do a full analysis of the all the available coffee/jar-size/price options. Habits can, however, be viewed as rational when considering that we have limited cognitive ability – and as such it is a type of procedural rationality along with the influence that social norms have on us, as described in the section on Principle 1: Other people's behaviour matters.

As in the case of social norms, psychologists have long accepted that the frequency of our past behaviour influences our current behaviour (see, for example, Triandis 1977, Bagozzi and Warshaw 1990).

Just as rational-man theory does not really recognise the existence of habits, it does not acknowledge the effort we need to expend in overcoming them. Again, this is addressed by many psychological theories. Jager (2003) has found that the strength of a habit (i.e. how difficult it is to change) is generally determined by:

- How often the action is repeated (it is more difficult to change something I do daily than something I do annually).
- The strength and frequency of the reinforcing *reward*, and its proximity to the behaviour in question (the reward from smoking a cigarette is immediate and satisfying feeling, thus it is hard to break the habit by thinking of the long-term health incentive).

Several psychologists have similar theories on changing habits (Lewin 1951, Dahlstrand and Biel 1977). These generally involve first *unfreezing* the subconscious action and raising it to a conscious level where we can consider the merits of alternative behaviours. This is followed by adopting the new behaviour which, with time, becomes *frozen* as a new habit. We are more likely to think consciously about something (and thus be able to break our habit) when:

- What we are trying to do is complex.
- The consequences of our decisions/actions are important to us.
- We have enough time, cognitive capacity and knowledge to do so.

To change deeply ingrained habits, a Pavlov-type conditioning can be used to create associations between the desired behaviour and a reward. This is especially effective where the reward can be given immediately after the desired behaviour (Halpern *et al.* 2004).

### *Examples*

Actions such as recycling rather than just throwing everything in the rubbish can become habits. However, when we are used to just throwing things away, it takes a lot of mental effort to think about whether the empty jar in our hand is recyclable or not, and what to do with it if it is. In this case cues such as visible recycling facilities, or being provided with coloured bins, can help remind us to recycle, as well as making it easier to recycle (Jackson 2005).

The deregulation of the utilities companies and the increase in choice of supplier was meant to reduce prices through competition. This policy has not been as successful as expected as people have been reluctant to change supplier. It appears that habit is key to people's behaviour here, and the barriers to changing these habits were higher than expected: there is the hassle associated with changing (identifying which new supplier, filling out forms etc.) and there is a perceived risk – perhaps the new supplier will not be so reliable. Conversely, the financial gain (which was expected to dominate) is not immediate but comes as a small decrease in future bills. Some of this problem is captured in the conventional economics notion of 'transaction costs' but we would argue that these have generally not taken into account the role of habit.

### *Relevance to policy*

When aiming to change people's behaviour, the role habits play should be considered. Are there any habits that are likely to be barriers to behaviour change, and if so, how strong are they likely to be? How can any such habitual behaviours be raised to people's conscious awareness? What incentives (financial and non-financial) can people be given to help them change their behaviour, and what feedback can be given to help reinforce the new behaviour and cement it as a new habit? Can this feedback be tailored to occur close in time to the action to maximise this learning effect?

For example, a habit-changing policy with extremely successful results has been the introduction of a charge (15p) for plastic shopping bags in Ireland. Since the introduction almost everyone brings their own shopping bags when grocery shopping. Although most people could easily save a little money on their shopping basket by carefully choosing which brands and quantities to buy, most people don't bother (due to habit). However, when they must *explicitly* pay 15p extra for a plastic bag, this acts as a strong incentive (cue) to bring their own bags. This is not to say that user charging – a traditional 'rational-man' policy intervention – is always successful (see examples from Principle 3). In this case the charge is quite out of proportion to the regular cost of a plastic bag (perhaps in the region of 1500 per cent). The level of the price acts as a trigger to unfreeze the existing habit and create a new one. If the policy had internalised the cost of environmental externalities of the bag it is likely that the price of the bag would have been much lower, and that the policy would not have changed habits very much.

## Principle 3: People are motivated to 'do the right thing'

### *Introduction*

There are many cases where we do things for other people for which we would be insulted if they paid us, for example when we invite friends for a meal. In such cases it is clear that a financial reward would be thoroughly de-motivating to continuing the behaviour. Even in less extreme cases such as doing volunteer work, money can be de-motivating as it detracts from the warm feeling of having done something good.

In cases where we are naturally motivated to 'do the right thing' we feel bad and have a guilty conscience when we fail. This guilt can be offset if we receive a punishment (e.g. a fine) because after being punished we feel we have paid for our misdeed and we have a clean conscience. This can result in punishments having counter-productive effects: we continue with our bad behaviour together with accepting the punishment.

People also have an inbuilt sense of fairness. In situations where one person clearly has a stronger bargaining position, very often they will not use this and will split the gain from the transaction 50/50 rather than demanding more for themselves. Our sense of fairness also drives us to punish the wrongdoing of others, even at a personal cost to ourselves.

### *Theory*

A rational-man analysis would add up the financial costs and benefits, so financial rewards would always be expected to encourage and financial fines would always be expected to discourage. People would also be expected to take advantage of any bargaining position that they had; further, the fact that people are willing to punish the wrongdoing of others at considerable cost to themselves without any obvious benefit cannot be explained by rational-man theory.

Many economists have turned their attention to the related topic of altruism. Most argue that any altruism is in fact selfishly motivated, as people either expect something in return or some (weird) people have altruistic *preferences*, hence they are maximising their utility (in a broad sense rather than a financial sense) by behaving altruistically. Such people are generally taken as the exception rather than the rule. However, Herbert Simon (1993) showed that in societies where people have less than full knowledge and the cognitive ability to analyse it (i.e. when people must act with procedural rationality), people with some true altruistic tendencies will be evolutionarily fitter (have more offspring) than people without. This is because their tendency to follow social norms gives them a competitive advantage in a society of procedural rationality. Thus we are 'hardwired' with some altruistic tendencies and behaving properly or fairly *can* be expected to give us a good feeling (or utility). This is corroborated by research by Fehr and Fischbacher (2003) on the evolution of behavioural traits in simulated prisoner's dilemma games, and from direct measurements of activity in the reward centre in people's brains when they decide whether to punish the wrongdoing of others (Fehr 2004). (Here it should be noted that what counts as wrongdoing depends on the social norms in the society [Gintis 2003].)

Social scientists make the distinction between our intrinsic and extrinsic motivations. Deci *et al.* (1999) define intrinsic motivation as what we have when 'activities provide their own inherent reward, so motivation for these activities is not dependent on external rewards'. Hence intrinsic motivations are related to our internal value system, whereas extrinsic motivations are influenced from external incentives such as rewards, tax systems etc. Under this system it is possible for extrinsic motivations to 'crowd-out' intrinsic motivations and thus be counter-productive (Frey and Jegen 2001 and examples in Deci *et al.* 1999). For example financial rewards, the threat of punishment and deadlines can decrease intrinsic motivation (Carr 2004).

Experimental economists have found that fairness often counts for more than a rational-man analysis would indicate in non-repeated experimental games, and that repeated games with the same people builds trust and enhances *fair* behaviour (Kagel and Roth 1995). Perceived fairness is also found to be important, and it appears to be considered fair that higher status individuals receive higher-than-expected rewards. People's willingness to pay for a public good has also been shown to be moderated by fairness (Ajzen *et al.* 2000) – people believe that costs should be fairly distributed between the people responsible for the necessity of the public good, and the people who will benefit from it. With higher perceived fairness people are willing to contribute more.

### Examples

In his classic work *The Gift Relationship*, Titmuss (1970) argues that, contrary to expectations, not only did more people give voluntary blood donations compared to donations made with financial incentives, but also the voluntarily donated blood was of a higher quality.

When questioned about volunteering, 97 per cent of respondents believed they were fulfilling an important task for society and less than 25 per cent thought that the work should be rewarded financially. This is consistent with *intrinsic motivation* – people feel the task is worth doing for its own sake, rather than for reward, and as such this feeling can be offset by *extrinsic motivations* such as pay, which can reduce the overall incentive. This is corroborated by a study of Swiss volunteers (Frey and Goette 1999). The average volunteering time was fourteen hours per week but those who were paid did approximately four hours a week *less* volunteering work than unpaid volunteers.

In a nursery school the result of issuing small fines when parents arrived late to collect their children *increased* the frequency that they arrived late (Gneezy and Rustichini 2001). It appears that by making a payment the parents no longer felt guilty about arriving late, and treated the situation as if they were paying for a service.

Several examples are given in the paper *Introducing Procedural Utility: Not only What, but also How Matters* by Bruno Frey *et al.* (2004):

- The treatment of taxpayers: Taking into account of the probability of being caught evading taxes, and the size of the punishment if caught, a rational-man analysis indicates that taxpayers should evade taxes more than they actually do. It appears that people are motivated to 'do the right thing' and further, the more fairly and respectfully the tax authorities treat them, the more willing they are to pay their taxes.
- Public good allocation: To overcome the problem of NIMBY (not-in-my-back-yard) projects, rational-man economics has a solution: as the benefits to the wider community are greater than the costs, the prospective gainers should be taxed and this revenue redistributed to the prospective losers. It has turned out, however, that this approach meets with much resistance as people feel they are being bribed to accept the project, thus undermining their motivation to 'do the right thing'. A more successful approach is to directly address people's concerns. For example, if people object to a new airport being built nearby, then they could be helped to insulate their homes against the noise.
- Law: A study of the acceptance of awards from court-ordered arbitration found that the litigants who judge the arbitration process as fair are much more likely to accept the award from the arbitration process and not take the case to formal trial, irrespective of the outcome.

### *Relevance to policy*

Policy makers should consider how people perceive the behaviour they are trying to change. If it is normally considered shameful, it might be counter-productive to introduce fines, and if it is normally considered the right thing to do it may be counter-productive to bring in financial rewards. The size of any financial (dis)incentives should also carefully be considered – a big enough fine will be a disincentive, and paying a volunteer a high enough salary may be an incentive. Consideration should also be given to appealing to people's sense of fairness, and conversely care should be taken to not make people feel a policy is unfair, even if it is of overall benefit.

## Principle 4: People's self expectations influence how they behave

### *Introduction*

We have expectations about our own behaviour, and perceptions about the expectations other people have about our behaviour. We don't like to feel our actions are out of synch with these expectations or our values or attitudes – it makes us feel uncomfortable. If we find ourselves often doing something that sits uncomfortably with our attitudes, values or expectations of ourselves, then we may well change our *attitudes and values* to justify our actions. However, where we have expressed our beliefs openly, then we are more likely to change our *behaviour* to remain consistent with these expressed beliefs. In this way commitments can be very important: when someone has promised to do something, they are likely to stick to this even without rewards or punishments. Who and how the commitment is made can also have a strong influence: when a whole group with high social capital publicly makes a commitment this is likely to be more influential on the individuals than when an individual by himself/herself makes the commitment. The more public commitments are, the stronger they are, and written commitments are stronger than spoken ones. People who have made a small commitment (for example, signing a petition) appear to change their view of themselves, and if asked a few days later to make a much larger commitment (for example, donating money) are more likely to agree.

### *Theory*

A rational-man analysis would disregard self-expectations and commitments, as these would be expected to influence our preferences, but preferences are taken as 'given' in this analysis. Promises are irrelevant in rational-man theory unless they are backed by sanctions.

The psychologist Leon Festinger (1957) developed the *cognitive dissonance theory*, which proposes that people feel uncomfortable when they feel a clash or 'dissonance' between their actions and attitudes or values. Daryl Bem (1972) postulated that we infer our attitudes from observing our own behaviour, which means that when our behaviour is out of synch with our attitudes, we may well change our attitudes (rather than our behaviour). Higgins' *self-discrepancy theory* (1987) has built on cognitive dissonance theory. He maintains we have three views of ourselves: actual, ideal and ought-self (how we have a duty to be). We have corresponding perceptions of how we think other people assess these three views of ourselves, thus we have six distinct types of self-concept. Differences between these give rise to different (negative) emotions such as guilt, shame or disappointment. It would appear that making commitments, especially publicly, strengthens the feeling of how we should behave, and the shame if we fail to live up to the commitment. A useful guide to using commitments in changing behaviour is given by a psychologist, Doug McKenzie-Mohr (1999).

## *Examples*

A Canadian programme using a combination of public commitments and visible signals was used to establish a strong community composting norm. Several months later an exceptionally high proportion (80 per cent) of the people originally approached were found to be composting (Mckenzie-Mohr 2000).

In a staged crime, individuals who had agreed to watch over a bag were four times more likely to attempt to prevent a theft as individuals who were aware the bag was being stolen but who made no commitment to watch over it (Halpern *et al.* 2004, p. 19).

When voters in the US were asked one day before an election 'Do you expect you will vote or not?' they all agreed and this action appeared to increase the likelihood of them voting by 41 per cent (Greenwald *et al.* 1987).

## *Relevance to policy*

Policy makers should consider whether it could be practical to get people to make commitments, and if so, how to make the commitment as strong as possible. Some examples taken from Doug McKenzie-Mohr's book *Fostering Sustainable Behaviour* (1999) include:

- Emphasise written over verbal commitments.
- Ask for public commitments.
- Seek group commitments.
- Actively involve the person.
- Consider cost-effective ways to obtain commitments.
- Use existing points of contact to obtain commitments.
- Help people to view themselves as environmentally concerned.
- Don't use coercion (commitments must be freely volunteered).

For large businesses the threat of externally imposed regulation has, in some cases, precipitated self-imposed voluntary agreements (Khanna 2001). Policy makers could consider whether it would be beneficial to use such tactics more broadly to encourage small businesses (or better still groups of small businesses) to make commitments. Another alternative could be to get business owners to make a written commitment, then to use the threat of naming and shaming those that don't keep the commitment. In particular consideration should be given to 'stepping' commitments from the very easy to the more demanding, thus changing identity and self-expectations in the process. For example small business may be asked to register for free information on how to improve their environmental impacts. They might then be invited to a meeting, and then asked to commit to certain actions.

## Principle 5: People are loss averse

### *Introduction*

People naturally have inbuilt biases:

- People are loss-averse which means they will go out of their way to avoid losses, while at the same they would not bother to go out of their way to gain something. This can mean people may take large risks to avoid losses whilst at the same time avoiding even small risks to make gains.
- People try to keep something that they consider is 'theirs', even when it is quite arbitrarily given and where the beneficiary's pre-established preferences would indicate that they would prefer to swap it. It is as if as soon as I consider something 'mine', I confer some extra value onto it.

### *Theory*

In rational-man theory people are expected to have a preference on risk (i.e. be either risk-takers or risk-avoiders) but it is usually assumed that people are neutral to loss or gain, meaning that the amount of effort I should put into saving £100 of my money should be the same as the amount of effort I would put into gaining £100. Kahneman and Tversky's *Prospect Theory* (1979) shows that this is not the case, and people generally use a relative assessment of losses and gains (rather than considering their total wealth position) and they value losses more than gains.

It is also usually assumed in rational-man theory that someone's 'willingness-to-pay' is the same as their 'willingness-to-accept'. This means they would sell something they own for just about the same price as they would be willing to buy it if they didn't already own it. The *endowment effect* (Kahneman *et al.* 1991) shows that this is not the case and in practise environmental economist David Pearce (2002) has found it is usual for the selling price or willingness-to-accept to be up to 20 times the buying price or willingness-to-pay.

### *Examples*

An extreme case of loss-aversion is the case of Nick Leeson: after he incurred losses from (illegally) trading from a secret account, he tried to re-coup these losses by taking gambles – and as the losses grew he started taking increasingly large gambles, which ended with the collapse of Barings Bank in London.

An example of a thought experiment is taken from Richard Layard's (2005) book on happiness. How much would you need to be paid to mow your neighbour's lawn? How much would you pay your neighbour to mow your lawn?

Most people would need to be paid much more to mow someone else's lawn than they would be willing to pay to have their own lawn mowed.

An example of a study in which people were willing to pay only a little to have something (or in this case maintain it) compared to demanding a lot to give it up concerns duck-hunters in the US: it was found that they would pay $247 each to maintain a wetland suitable for ducks, but asked $1044 to give up the wetland (Kagel and Roth 1995, p. 665).

In one intriguing experiment students were (randomly) given either pens or money. From observing the subsequent trade, *indifference curves* were generated. Indifference curves plot how much of one good we are willing to give up to get another. An early lesson from standard economics is that they should never intersect. However, the results showed that the group of people who were endowed with pens wanted more dollars per pen than the group endowed with money – and the indifference curves from the two groups intersected (Kahneman *et al.* 1991).

### *Relevance to policy*

This is a case where the theory is directly applicable within economic cost–benefit-type analyses that include valuations of non-market goods (such as valuations of pollution damage). Policy makers have a choice as to whether to use willingness-to-pay or willingness-to-accept, and as these may vary by up to a factor of 20 the outcome of such an analysis may well depend on which value is chosen. David Pearce (2002) has written an extremely useful paper addressing this issue. He proposes that where people reasonably have a 'right' to something that might be taken away from them, the willingness-to-accept value should be used. On the other hand, when people only reasonably have a 'right' to the status quo and an improvement is proposed, then the willingness-to-pay is the correct value to use. Unfortunately it often proves difficult in practice to elicit an unbiased estimate of willingness-to-accept.

In general, policy makers should consider the relative incentives given by fines or punishments (including loss of reputation) compared to rewards. A further point is the risks that people are likely to take to avoid a loss can be large, so punishments designed to curb slightly bad behaviour could have the adverse effect of encouraging people to do something much worse to avoid being caught. For example, to avoid being caught with an old bottle of a polluting chemical that is now banned, people might well do something drastic (pour it down the drain) rather than admitting to having it.

A further implication of loss-aversion is in tax collection: taxes taken at source may give less resentment and therefore be easier to introduce than taxes which must be actively paid.

## Principle 6: People are bad at computation

### *Introduction*

We are naturally very bad at calculating things, especially probabilities, and our choices are strongly influenced by how a problem is presented to us. Our usual internal biases are:

- *Salience:* We overestimate the likelihood of something that we can easily imagine (especially if it would be particularly frightening like a plane crash), something that has given us a short-lived extreme experience or of something we have recently experienced. Likewise we underestimate the likelihood of things that happen relatively often.
- *Discounting and time preferences:* We often underestimate the importance or relevance of something that might happen in the distant future. Our preferences are inconsistent over time: if asked to do either 5 hours of an unpleasant task today compared with 5½ hours tomorrow we often put off the unpleasant task, however if asked whether we would choose 5 hours in a month's time, or 5½ hours in a month and a day's time we would choose the former. This often manifests itself in people choosing short-term gratification over longer-term rewards leading to policy issues such as obesity or lack of savings for old age (O'Donoghue and Rabin 2000).
- *Framing:* If we must make a decision between two actions, we are strongly influenced by how the two possible outcomes are presented to us. If one is dressed up as a loss, and the other as neutral or as a gain then we will avoid the apparent loss – even when the two outcomes are mathematically identical.
- *Defaults:* We are strongly influenced by 'defaults' set for us by authorities, for example when money is transferred into a voluntary pension scheme by default few people choose to opt out, and the pension contributions are much higher than when people have to opt in (Madrian and Shea 2001). Sunstein and Thaler (2003) argue strongly in favour of using this bias when designing policy, which they call 'Libertarian Paternalism'.
- *Intuition:* We jump quickly to intuitive answers, which can be wrong, even to very simple mathematical questions. Where an outcome is particularly important to us, we are more likely to engage our active conscious thinking to evaluate the situation.
- *Fundamental Attribution Error:* We like to think we have control over situations, so we often assume that when something happens to someone it must be their fault – rather than it being an unfortunate random event (Ross 1997).
- *Price can signal value:* When offered 'something for nothing' we tend to undervalue what we are offered. For example, when a course on social entrepreneurship was offered free to a number of government people, no one signed up. When it was re-advertised three months later for AUD2,500, however, more than 20 people enrolled.

*Theory*

Often the necessary calculations are complex and would require lots of time and cognitive effort, thus using heuristics (rules of thumb) to quickly come to an intuitive answer or choosing the default option is a type of procedural rationality. A good discussion of these (in particular salience, discounting, framing and intuition) is given in Kahneman's Nobel Prize lecture (Kahneman 2002). These are not included in rational-man theory, in which the assumption is made that people act rationally and logically, and that they are capable of making the 'best' choice, given their preferences.

A thorough review of our preferences regarding time discounting has been made by Frederick *et al.* (2002). They show that the discounted utility model used as standard in economics for making valuations at different points in time bears almost no relationship to how people make such valuations. Unfortunately (from the point of view of ease of analysing problems) people use different discount rates depending on their (often competing) psychological motives. In some cases the rational-man theory can be adapted to better describe how people actually behave, for instance by using a non-standard discounting function (typically hyperbolic) which gives more weight to events nearer in time (Liabson 1997).

Framing appears to be a particularly powerful psychological effect: we use different heuristics depending on how a problem is framed. A useful review of the use of framing messages to motivate healthy behaviour is given by Rothman and Salovey (1997).

*Examples*

An example of a simple mathematical problem where our intuition is often wrong is given in Kahneman's paper (2002): 'A bat and a ball cost $1.10 in total. The bat costs $1 more than the ball. How much does the ball cost?' Most people answer 10 cents, including 50 per cent of Princeton students. This answer is wrong!

An example of framing is given by Redelmeier *et al.* (1993). When a risky medical procedure is proposed, people (including doctors) are far more likely to agree to it when it is positively framed:

*of those who have this procedure, 90 per cent are alive after five years*

than when it is framed as a loss:

*of those who have this procedure, 10 per cent are dead after five years*

This shows that how a problem is framed makes a difference: the prospect of a 90 per cent chance of living is better than a 10 per cent chance of dying.

An example of how our time-discounting biases do not conform to theory is that when asked what people would accept to swap $15 now for a sum in the future, the (median) answers are $20 in one month, $50 in one year, or $100 in ten years (Frederick *et al.* 2002). The rational-man economic theory would predict that if you are happy with $100 after ten years, then you should be happy with $18 after one year or $15.24 after one month.

An interesting example from Rothman and Salovey's paper (1997) involves our attitudes to loss-aversion, time-scales and framing with regard to women's behaviour relating to breast self-examination. As detection behaviour can lead to the undesirable knowledge that they have a lump (which can be thought of as a type of loss), the short-term incentive is not to have a test. Of course, taking account of the longer-term outcome and choosing to do detection tests is by far the most rational approach for women who value longevity. Research on messages to promote detection behaviours found that framing the message to emphasise the possible long-term loss (of not doing detection tests) is particularly effective in this case.

### *Relevance to policy*

Policies that involve financial incentives or disincentives should take account of people's biases and intuition about probabilities, and positively make use of framing effects:

- If punishments are to be used for non-compliance, information published about them should be vividly described to trigger the imagination into thinking 'how horrible' it would be to be to be punished. Conversely, if rewards are to be used to enhance compliance these should also be very salient.

   The Royal Mail has successfully used salience to encourage employees not to take sick leave by entering all staff who had not taken sick leave for a six-month period into a lottery to win a car or a holiday (Kwan Yuk and Gilies 2005). This reduced absenteeism in the 170,000-strong workforce from 6.4 per cent to 5.7 per cent meaning approximately 1,000 more people were working every day. The cost of the prizes was about £500,000. A neo-classical analysis would wrongly predict that as the expected value of the lottery ticket is small (about £6) compared to the utility of an extra day's free time when 'taking a sickie' (presumably a day's pay) then not many people would be influenced by the incentive, unless people placed a huge value on the 'fun' of participating in the lottery. The behavioural economics approach is that we are influenced by salience: as with all lottery prizes our imagination is caught by the idea of winning the holiday or the car thus we overestimate the chances of winning.
- Immediate losses are stronger incentives than long-term rewards. Programmes should, if possible, be devised to avoid immediate losses.

   An example where this has been successfully used is in a water conservation scheme in Barry, Canada where the up-front costs of installing water-saving equipment have been avoided (Holdsworth and Steedman 2005). To encourage people to install ultra-low-flow toilets and showerheads, the city

offered purchasers an interest-free loan to be paid off as part of the water bill. As the water is metered, the water saving offset the cost of the repayments making the equipment appear effectively free. The added incentive was that water bills would be cheaper in the future.
- The use of 'libertarian paternalism' devices could be very influential. Default options for individuals could be set to promote the relevant policy, for example, smaller servings of food in restaurants to counteract obesity. Further, in order to help people counteract the natural tendency to overly discount the future, small barriers or what Avner Offer (2004) has called 'commitment technologies' can be created or should be preserved. (An example of this is that students find it easier to write an essay with an externally imposed deadline.) This might suggest, for example, that people should not be allowed to easily raid their pension funds for present-day expenditure.

## Principle 7: People need to feel involved and effective to make a change

### Introduction

People hate feeling helpless and out of control and when they have such feelings they feel incapable of doing anything to change the situation. Conversely, when they feel in control, they can be highly motivated to change things for the better. This has implications on information, choice and the importance of participation:

- Information overload: Too much information can lead to a feeling of helplessness and inaction. For example: I care about the planet and climate change, but it is all just so complicated to solve that I don't know where to start – so I will continue behaving as before.
- Too much choice can also have a counter effect. We feel overwhelmed and don't know what to choose, thereby often not making any choice at all. Even when we do choose something we are often dissatisfied, thinking we have probably made the wrong choice.
- A participatory approach to problem solving can be highly motivational and effective in encouraging behaviour change, as well as making people happier.

### Theory

In rational-man theory, people are expected to rationally make the 'best' choices given their preferences, independent of how these choices are presented. Therefore more information and choice are always considered good. Using this theory, policy makers should ensure that people always have as much information and as many things to choose between as possible, and the process of introducing policy is irrelevant. However, ideas from behavioural economics indicate this is not the right approach.

We know from experimental economics (see examples below) that more choice and more information can be overwhelming and lead to a feeling of helplessness or reduced self-efficacy. Bandura (1977b), a psychologist, published a theory on how self-efficacy or 'people's judgments of their capabilities to organize and execute courses of action required to attain designated types of performances' affects our behaviour. He argues it affects the choices we make, how much effort we put into what we do, how long we persist in a task before giving up and how we feel. Psychologists Ajzen and Madden (1986) have developed a model using this idea called the *Theory of Planned Behaviour*. This is basically similar to the *Theory of Reasoned Action* (Fishbein and Ajzen 1975) but it includes a parameter of 'perceived behavioural control' which is a measure of self-efficacy. This model has greater predictive capabilities than the *Theory of Reasoned Action*.

Kaplan (2000), a psychologist, has proposed a participatory approach to problem-solving. He suggests that telling people what to do is demotivating (reducing self-efficacy), is likely to encounter resistance and ignores the possibility that the local knowledge people have may yield better solutions to a problem. Instead, providing people with 'opportunities for understanding, exploration and participation' engages 'powerful motivations' for 'competence, being needed, making a difference, and forging a better life'. In summary, people's self-efficacy increases and they are motivated towards implementing the solutions – i.e. changing their behaviour in a desired way.

A final argument for a participatory approach is that it not only improves policy, but it also makes us happier. This is the finding of research comparing Swiss cantons (districts), which differ in the extent to which they use referenda for making major decisions (Frey and Stutzer 2002). Most interesting of all, around two thirds of the well-being effect can be attributed to actual participation itself, and only one third to the improvement in policy as a result of the participation. This was discovered through looking at the well-being of foreigners resident in Switzerland, who get the well-being benefit from the improved decision making, but not from the participation itself. This implies that an increased ability to participate – both in politics and in the way public services are delivered – may have positive well-being dividends.

### Examples

An experiment was carried out whereby a stall was set up in a supermarket for jam tasting. On one day the stall had 24 jams, and on a different day only six jams. Although the stall with more jams attracted more attention (60 per cent of the people passing by stopped, compared with only 40 per cent for the small-selection stall), of the people who stopped only 4 per cent at the stall with the extensive selection subsequently bought a pot, whereas 30 per cent of the people who stopped at the small selection stall went on to buy a pot (Iyengar and Lepper 2000).

Out of a group who expressed they are interested in environmental issues, the most important factor in whether they actually behaved in an environmentally friendly way was 'personal control' which was defined as 'the extent to which participants felt their actions could benefit the environment' (Kaplan 2000).

The freeing-up of the market for telephone directory enquiries is an example of counter-effective choice. Since the introduction of over 100 new directory enquiry numbers to try to promote competition the use of the service has fallen; this is thought to be due to increased confusion and perception of higher costs, although increased use of internet services is also thought to play a role. Also most residential customers are paying more than they did before (although a quarter of the new numbers offer cheaper services), with no increase in the quality of the service (National Audit Office 2005).

### *Relevance to policy*

Policy makers should note that, contrary to rational-man theory, too much information or choice can be counterproductive. They should make sure that the target individuals are not bombarded with information or long manuals of regulations. In particular, policy makers should beware that people do not necessarily want more choice (as exemplified by the multitude of directory enquiries numbers).

Emphasis should be placed on helping people to believe that they do have it within their power to change their behaviour in a desired way. A study published by the National Consumer Council (Holdsworth and Steedman 2005) on ways to promote sustainable behaviour analyses 19 case studies and finds that in every case 'once enlisted, people have been persuaded to make major changes in their lives' and that in the UK:

> Consumer-facing policies have largely been limited to traditional information provision and awareness-raising. These policies have not had a transforming effect on mainstream society. Only now is it being recognised that preaching to people is a poor substitute for enlisting them as active partners.

Where possible, government should identify problems and encourage groups of people affected by the issue to work together with experts to find solutions. In particular government should build on existing groups and initiatives, rather than creating new processes and structures without buy in.

## Discussion and future research

These seven principles have been distilled from the many observed human traits coming from the fields of psychology, behavioural and experimental economics.

In most cases these principles cannot be used directly as part of any mathematical economics analysis, but highlight situations where this rational-man analysis might not accurately describe human behaviour or might have unintended consequences if used to design policy.

The academic research is well developed to support the theory behind the seven principles. There are, however, research gaps around the reality of the application of the principles. These fit around three related areas:

- Consideration of the relevance and materiality of the principle: Relevance (*is one or more of the principles applicable?*) is usually possible to judge for any particular case. Materiality (*does the principle make a significant difference?*), however, requires judgement to be informed by more case studies and research.
- Work on the different policy interventions that flow from the principles, and their efficacy: The sections on policy implications in this chapter are indicative. The academic research has not focused particularly on the translation of the principles into practice. There is a need for far more systematic work to take place looking at how to best translate the principles into policy, and how to make them most effective. Our research review does suggest, however, that the policy implications could be quite powerful as the behavioural approach provides quite different lines of analysis to the rational-man economics model.
- Understanding of the interplay between the principles: There is little research on how the principles interact, where they might conflict and how they can be combined to maximum effect.

To bridge the gap identified as to when these principles are relevant and make a significant difference to the outcome of a rational-man economic analysis (and therefore the policy levers which should be used) we recommend that a systematic study be undertaken relating expected outcomes of different policy approaches to actual outcomes. Where differences arise (either better-than-expected or worse-than-expected), what are they attributed to? Could these have been foreseen taking account the principles from behavioural economics? In which situations does the rational-man analysis give realistic predictions, and in which situations do the principles outlined in this chapter need to be accounted for? An on-going database could become a powerful tool for the future.

## Further reading

Tim Jackson's (2005) report *Motivating Sustainable Consumption* has an extensive survey of models of consumer behaviour and behaviour change, most of which are applicable to a far wider field than sustainable consumption.

David Halpern's (2004) report *Personal Responsibility and Changing Behaviour: the state of knowledge and its implications for public policy* gives theories of behaviour change and examples of where these are being applied to public policy. He argues that: policy outcomes will be much enhanced with the participation of citizens; there are strong moral and political arguments for protecting and enhancing personal responsibility; and that behaviourally based interventions can be significantly more cost effective than traditional service delivery.

Doug McKenzie-Mohr (1999) has developed a tool *Community-Based Social Marketing* to change people's behaviour towards environmentally friendly behaviour. This is underpinned by psychological theories of human behaviour.

Useful texts on bounded rationality include Daniel Kahneman's (2002) Nobel Prize lecture *Maps of Bounded Rationality: A Perspective on Intuitive Judgement and Choice* and *Why Bounded Rationality?* from John Conlisk (1996).

Many relevant papers from behavioural economics can be found through Joe Pomykala's (2005) website *Behavioural Economics: a crash course.*

The paper *Libertarian Paternalism is Not an Oxymoron* by Cass Sunstein and Richard Thaler (2003) references many psychological and behavioural-economic texts to argue that choice should be allowed but the default option should be what the authority thinks is 'best'.

The paper, *A Better Choice of Choice*, by Levett *et al.* (2003) argues that the choices that consumers make lead to other choices no longer being available. For example, giving people the choice of shopping at an out-of-town superstore as well as having local shops can lead to the local shops shutting down, which then reduces the choice of shops available – an outcome no individual would have chosen (Sims *et al.* 2002). In this case allowing 'freedom of choice' can disadvantage the elderly and people without cars. This effect cannot be modelled with the static approach taken by neoclassical economics, but has significant implications for policy design.

## Note

1 Copyright of this chapter is retained by the New Economics Foundation.

## References

Ajzen, I. and Madden, T., 1986. Predictions of goal-directed behaviour: attitudes, intentions and perceived behavioural control. *Journal of Experimental Social Psychology* 22, 453–474.

Ajzen, I., Rosenthal, L.H. and Brown, T.C., 2000. Effects of perceived fairness on willingness to pay. *Journal of Applied Social Psychology* 30(12), 2439–2450.

Bagozzi, R. and Warshaw, P., 1990. Trying to consume. *Journal of Consumer Research* 17, 127–140.

Bandura, A., 1977a. *Social Learning Theory.* Englewood Cliffs, NJ: Prentice Hall.

Bandura, A., 1977b. Self-efficacy: Toward a unifying theory of behavioral change. *Psychological Review*, 84, 191–215. See www.emory.edu/EDUCATION/mfp/self-efficacy.html for further references.

Bem, D., 1972. Self-perception Theory. *In*: Berkowitz, L., ed. *Advances in Experimental Social Psychology 6.* London: Academic Press, 1–62.

Carr, A., 2004. *Positive Psychology.* Hove: Brunner Routledge.

Cialdini, R., 1993. *Influence: Science and practice.* 3rd edn. New York: HarperCollins.

Conlisk, J., 1996. Why Bounded Rationality? *Journal of Economic Literature* 34, 669–700.

Dahlstrand, U. and Biel, A., 1997. Pro-environmental habits: propensity levels in behavioural change. *Journal of Applied Social Psychology* 27, 588–601.

Darley, J., and Latane, B., 1968. Bystander intervention in emergencies: Diffusion of responsibility. *Journal of Personality and Social Psychology*, 8, 377–383.

de Botton, A., 2004. *Status Anxiety.* London: Hamish Hamilton.

Deci, E.L., Ryan, R.M. and Koestner, R., 1999. A meta-analytic review of experiments examining the effects of extrinsic rewards on intrinsic motivation. *Psychological Bulletin* 125, 627–668.

Frederick, S., Loewenstein, G. and O'Donoghue, T., 2002. Time discounting and time preference: a critical review. *Journal of Economic Literature*, 40(2), 351–401.

Fehr, E. and Fischbacher, U., 2003. The nature of human altruism. *Nature* 425, 23 Oct 2003, p. 785.

Fehr, E. and Fischbacher, U., 2004. Social norms and human cooperation. *Trends in Cognitive Sciences*, 8 (4), April 2004.

Fehr, E., 2004. Press release, University of Zurich, 26 August 2004. Available from: www.iew.unizh.ch/home/fehr/science/Press_Release_for_Neural_Basis_of_Alt_Pun. pdf.

Festinger, L., 1957. *A Theory of Cognitive Dissonance.* Stanford: University of California Press.

Frey, B.S. and Goette, L., 1999. *Does Pay Motivate Volunteers?* Working Paper No. 7. Institute for Empirical Research in Economics, Universität Zürich.

Frey, B.S. and Jegen, R., 2001. Motivation crowding theory: a survey of empirical evidence. *Journal of Economic Surveys*, 15 (5) 589–611.

Frey, B.S. and Stutzer, A., 2002. *Happiness and Economics.* Princeton University Press, Princeton.

Frey, B.S., Benz, M. and Stutzer, A., 2004. Introducing procedural utility: not only what, but also how matters. *Journal of Institutional and Theoretical Economics*, 160, 377–401.

Fishbein, M. and Ajzen, I., 1975. *Belief, Attitude, Intention and Behavior: an introduction to theory and research.* Reading, MA: Addison-Wesley.

Garforth, C., 2003. *Improving the Targeting of Knowledge and Technology Transfer in the Livestock Sector by Understanding Farmer Attitudes and Behaviour*, Final report from LINK sustainable Livestock Production Programme, Project LK0647. Reading University, available from c.j.garforth@reading.ac.uk.

Gintis, H., 2003. The hitchhiker's guide to altruism: gene-culture coevolution and the internalization of norms. *Journal of Theoretical Biology*, 220, 407–418.

Gladwell, M., 2000. *The Tipping Point.* Little Brown and Company.

Gneezy, U. and Rustichini, A., 2001. A fine is a price. *Journal of Legal Studies*, XXIX, 1, part 1, 1–18.

Greenwald, A., Carnot, C., Beach, R. and Young, B., 1987. Increasing voting behavior by asking people if they expect to vote. *Journal of Applied Psychology*, 72, 315–318.

Halpern, D., Bates, C., Beales, G. and Heathfield, A., 2004. *Personal Responsibility and Changing Behaviour: the state of knowledge and its implications for public policy* [online]. Cabinet Office publication available from: www.pm.gov.uk/files/pdf/pr.pdf.

Higgins, T., 1987. Self-discrepancy: a theory relating self to affect. *Psychological Review* 94, 319–340.

Holdsworth, M. and Steedman, P., 2005. 16 pain-free ways to help save the planet [online]. National Consumer Council report available from www.ncc.org.uk/responsibleconsumption/16ways.pdf.

Iyengar, S. and Lepper, M., 2000. When choice is demotivating: can one desire too much of a good thing? *Journal of Personality and Social Psychology*, 79, 995–1006.

Jackson, T., 2005. *Motivating Sustainable Consumption* [online]. Available from the Sustainable Development Research Network at www.sd-research.org.uk.

Jager, W., 2003. Breaking bad habits: a dynamical perspective on habit formation and change. *In:* L. Hendrick, Wander Jager, L. Steg, eds. *Human Decision-Making and Environmental Perception – Understanding and Assisting Human Decision-Making in Real Life Settings.* Libor Amicorum for Charles Vlek, Groningen: University of Groningen.

Kagel, H. and Roth, A.E. eds. 1995. *The Handbook of Experimental Economics.* Princeton University Press.

Kaplan, S., 2000. Human nature and environmentally responsible behaviour. *Journal of Social Sciences.* Fall 2000.

Kahneman, D. and Tversky, A., 1979. Prospect theory: an analysis of decisions under risk' *Econometrica*, 47, 313–327.

Kahneman, D., Knetsch, J.L. and Thaler R.H., 1991. Anomalies: the endowment effect, loss aversion, and status quo bias. *Journal of Economic Perspectives*, 5 (1) 193–206.

Kahneman, D., 2002. *Maps of Bounded Rationality: A Perspective on Intuitive Judgement and Choice*, Nobel Prize Lecture, 8 Dec 2002.

Kaplan S., 2000. Human nature and environmentally responsible behaviour. *Journal of Social Issues*, 56(3), 491–508.

Khanna M., 2001. Non-mandatory approaches to environmental protection. *Journal of Economic Surveys*, 15 (3).

Kwan Yuk, P. and Gilies, C., 2005. 'Royal Mail to continue rewarding healthy staff' 'Simply sums play part in lottery's success' in the Financial Times, Tuesday 26th April.

Layard, R., 2005. *Happiness: Lessons from a New Science.* Penguin Press HC.

Levett, R., Christie, I., Jacobs, M., and Therivel, R., 2003. *A Better Choice of Choice.* London: Fabian.

Lewin, K., 1951. *In:* D. Cartwright ed. *Field Theory in Social Science; Selected Theoretical Papers.* New York: Harper & Row.

Madrian, B. and Shea, D., 2001. The power of suggestion: inertia in 401(k) participation and savings behavior. *Quarterly Journal of Economics* 116, 1149–1525.

McKenzie-Mohr, D. and Smith, W., 1999. *Fostering Sustainable Behavior: An Introduction to Community-Based Social Marketing.* New Society Publishers. Also available from: www.csbm.com.

McKenzie-Mohr D., 2000. Promoting sustainable behaviour: an introduction to community-based social marketing. *Journal of Social Issues* 56(3) 543–554.

Milgram, S., 1974. *Obedience to Authority.* New York: Harper and Row.

National Audit Office, 2005. *Directory Enquiries – From 192 to 118.* Report 18 March, 2005 [online]. Available at www.nao.org.uk/pn/04–05/0405211.htm.

O'Donoghue, T. and Rabin, M., 2000. The economics of immediate gratification. *Journal of Behavioral Decision Making*, 13(2), 233–250.

Offer, A., 2004. Passions and interests: self-control and well-being' Chapter 3 from man uscript draft of *Challenge of Affluence.* Oxford: All Souls College.

Omerod, P., 1998. *Butterfly Economics.* London: Faber and Faber.

Pearce, D., 2002. *The Role of 'Property Rights. Determining Economic Values for Environmental Costs and Benefits* [online], Report to the Environment Agency. Available from: www.environment-agency.gov.uk/commondata/103599/wtawtp_paper_778397.doc.

Pomykala, J., 2005. *Behavioural Economics: a crash course.* Website: www.altruists.org/static/files/A%20Page%20on%20Behavioural%20Economics.htm [accessed 2005].

Redelmeier, D., Rozin, P. and Kahneman, D., 1993. Understanding patients' decisions: cognitive and emotional perspectives. *Journal of the American Medical Association* 72, 73.

Ross, L., 1997. The intuitive psychologist and his shortcomings: distortions in the attribution process. *In:* Berkowitz, L. ed. *Advances in experimental social psychology*, Vol. 10. New York: Academic Press.

Rothman, A.J. and Solovey, P., 1997. Shaping perceptions to motivate healthy behaviour: the role of message framing. *Psychological Bulletin* 121 (1) 3–19.

Simon, H., 1957. *Models of Man.* New York: John Wiley.

Simon, H., 1993. Altruism and economics. *The American Economic Review*, 83 (2), Papers and proceedings of the hundred and fifth annual meeting of the American economics association (May 1993), 156–161.

Sims, A., Oram, J., MacGillivray, A. and Drury, J., (2002). *Ghost Town Britain: The threat from economic globalisation to livelihoods, liberty and local economic freedom.* London: nef.

Sunstein, C.R., Thaler, R.H., 2003. *Libertarian Paternalism is not an Oxymoron*, Chicago Public Law and Legal Theory Working Paper No 43. Available from: www.law.uchicago.edu/academics/publiclaw/resources/43.crs.paternalism.pdf.

Tajfel, H., Billig, M., Bundy, R., and Flament, C., 1971. Social categorization and intergroup behaviour. *European Journal of Social Psychology*, 1, 149–77.

Tajfel, H., and Turner, J., 1986. The social identity theory of inter-group behaviour. *In:* S. Worchel and L. W. Austin, eds. *Psychology of Intergroup Relations*. Chicago: Nelson-Hall.

Titmuss, R.M., 1970. *The Gift Relationship.* London: Allen and Unwin.

Triandis, H., 1977. *Interpersonal Behaviour.* Monterey, CA: Brooks/Cole.

Trotter, L., Wakefield, M. and Borland, R., 2002. Socially cued smoking in bars, nightclubs, and gaming venues: a case for introducing smoke-free policies. *Tobacco Control*, 11(4), 300–304. Available from www.tobaccocontrol.com.

# 5   The 'whole systems' approach in ecological economics

*Terry Barker*

The systems approach to studying environmental and economic issues has grown significantly over recent years. Whereas between 1980 and 1990 only four articles in the *Science Citation Index* (SCI) and *Social Science Citation Index* (SSCI) contained reference to *environment, ecological* and *system* in their topic, during 2000–2009 the comparable figure had increased over a thousand fold to 1345 articles.[1] This rate of growth is much faster than the overall rate of growth of scholarly articles included in the SCI and SSCI and thus reflects the growing importance of the whole systems or earth systems approach within science and social science research. This chapter looks at the characteristics of this 'earth systems' or 'whole systems' approach to ecological economics.

The chapter is organised as follows. Section 1 defines the *whole systems* or *earth systems science* approach to environmental issues and considers its relationship with ecological economics. This discussion uses Hardin's (1968) conceptualisation of the tragedy of the commons to illustrate a number of earth systems science concepts, most notably the possibility of systems effects. Sections 2, 3 and 4 compare and contrast ecological economics with traditional environmental economics and discuss a number of characteristics of the whole systems approach and their policy implications, dealing with areas where the two approaches use different underlying methodologies, including models of rationality and the role of social values. Finally, Sections 5 and 6 focus on politics and social choice and the case of governance-based policy solutions to global warming.

## 1   Earth systems science and the whole systems approach in ecological economics

The essence of the systems approach is that the behaviour of the system cannot be understood by focusing on the behaviour of its individual components alone. Interaction between components leads to outcomes at the system level that differ, in some cases diametrically, from the behaviour of individual components. Classic examples of such systems effects include the 'tragedy of the commons' (Hardin, 1968, 1998), Keynesian unemployment (Keynes, 1936) and lock-in to inefficient technologies (David, 1985). The tragedy of the commons starts by assuming individual utility (or profit) maximisation but when all participants adopt this behaviour, joint utility (or joint profits) are not maximised:

> With Adam Smith's work as a model, I had assumed that the sum of separate ego-serving decisions would be the best possible one for the population as a whole. But presently I discovered that I agreed much more with William Forster Lloyd's conclusions, as given in his Oxford lectures of 1833. Citing what happened to pasturelands left open to many herds of cattle, Lloyd pointed out that, with a resource available to all, the greediest herdsmen would gain – for a while. But mutual ruin was just around the corner. As demand grew in step with population (while supply remained fixed), a time would come when the herdsmen, acting as Smithian individuals, would be trapped by their own competitive impulses. The unmanaged commons would be ruined by overgrazing; competitive individualism would be helpless to prevent the social disaster.
>
> (Hardin, 1998, p. 682)

Similarly, Keynes' analysis of unemployment highlights contradictions between the profit maximising behaviour of individual firms and the macroeconomic consequences of their actions. Faced with a fall in demand it makes sense for individual firms to cut back employment to reduce output. However, the macroeconomic effect of these individual actions is a further fall in demand, still higher unemployment and lower profits.[2] Interaction between individual components, dynamics and feedback effects are all part of the complexity of systems level analysis. David's (1985) study of the origin and persistence of the QWERTY keyboard analyses a similar contradiction between individual and system-wide effects in the case of lock-in to an inefficient technology.[3]

The systems wide perspective has come to be applied to earth sciences[4] where Pitman (2005 p. 139) has defined *earth system science* as:

> the study of the Earth as a single, integrated physical and social system ... Earth System Science is not 'Earth Sciences' – the addition of 'system' fundamentally changes the focus of this super-discipline. Earth Systems Science studies the functioning of, and *interactions between* Humans (including population change, economic growth, social change) and biophysical systems (including soils, hydrology, the atmosphere, ocean, cryosphere and ecology).

This has particular resonance when applied to the issue of climate change:

> The uncertainties surrounding global climate change provide ample evidence, if any were necessary, of the need for a whole-system view of the Earth ... It is important to understand the Earth system as a *system*, rather than as a set of disconnected components.
>
> (Kirchner, 2003, pp. 21–22)

The *earth systems science* approach is interdisciplinary, but its roots are to be found in science and many of its scholars would claim science as their primary discipline. Closely related and coming at the same issue from the perspective of social science is *ecological economics*, which studies how ecosystems (large and small) interrelate with economic systems. It is a new discipline that developed partly in response to the limitations of neo-classical economics in its treatment of the interaction of human society and the natural environment. The subject encompasses a more general view of values, including intrinsic rights of ecosystems to exist. It emphasises uncertainty in effects and the major intergeneration problems associated with irreversible damage to natural systems caused by human activity. In its application to partial systems (e.g. Florida wetlands) ecological economics is only one of a set of disciplines required to understand the problems. There is an emphasis on the interconnections within and between natural and social systems. Environmental problems are seen as highly specific in terms of physical effects, location and timing. Their solution in terms of portfolios of policies adopted by government is to be set in a social context, allowing for institutions and inertia.

The development of ecological research combining science and social science disciplines was marked by the establishment of the journal *Ecological Economics* in 1989. The opening article of the journal defines the area:

> *Ecological Economics* addresses the relationships between ecosystems and economic systems in the broadest sense. These relationships are the locus of many of our most pressing current problems (i.e. sustainability, acid rain, global warming, species extinction, wealth distribution) but they are not well covered by any existing discipline. Environmental and resource economics, as it is currently practiced, covers only the application of neoclassical economics to environmental and resource problems. Ecology, as it is currently practised, sometimes deals with human impacts on ecosystems, but the more common tendency is to stick to 'natural' systems. *Ecological Economics* aims to extend these modest areas of overlap.It will include neoclassical environmental economics and ecological impact studies as subsets, but will also encourage new ways of thinking about linkages between ecological and economic systems.
>
> (Costanza, 1989, p. 1)

As the above definition makes clear, ecological economics addresses the problems brought about by the damaging impact of modern economies on the environment, i.e. environmental pollution. There are many aspects to these problems as covered in this chapter, namely the relationship of economics to other disciplines; the traditional treatment of the problem; the concepts of externalities, rights, obligations and valuations; and finally social choice. The social and individual views of pollution are influenced by the societies that produce the pollution and those that suffer from it. The problems are evident at all spatial scales from the local to the global, and as such, the solution in terms of social policy becomes complex, involving all scales of government as well as individual personal behaviour.[5]

## The tragedy of the commons

Hardin's (1968) seminal article on the tragedy of the commons is central to understanding the arguments for a systems approach that integrates science and social science research. Hardin's paper showed that the destruction of grazing pastures, over-fishing and pollution were all examples of a class of problems with 'no technical solution', but rather can only be solved by society, requiring an interdisciplinary approach that combines science and social science.[6] Writing on the 30th anniversary of the publication of *The Tragedy of the Commons*, Hardin (1998) called for greater interdisciplinary research to solve the tragedy, noting that 'economics and ecology are now in the process of being combined into *ecological economics*' (p. 682). However, he remained cautious, recognising the difficulties of interdisciplinary research:

> The more specialities we try to stitch together, the greater are our opportunities for mistakes – and the more numerous are our willing critics. Science has been defined as a self-correcting system. In this struggle our primary adversary should be 'the nature of things'. As a matter of policy, we must not reply in kind to those critics who love to engage in name calling. (They are all too numerous in interdisciplinary undertakings.) But critics who, ignoring personalities, focus on the underlying nature of things are the true friends of science.
>
> (Hardin, 1998, p. 683)

The social problem of pollution arises from the use of inadequately regulated common resources, i.e. open resources such as the atmosphere, rivers, seas, or public land, or infrastructure, such as parks or roads. The 'tragedy of the commons' is the idea that since the social costs are not paid, the use of the open resource will continue increasing indefinitely, as long as the private or market benefits exceed the costs, since those polluting may not take into account the social costs of the activity. The common resource can be 'over consumed' to the point of destruction if the rate of depletion exceeds the rate of assimilation. It is not in the interest of any single party to undertake action to preserve the common resource unless others also act. If governments do take action and regulate or price the open resources, then all those using the resource will benefit. However, if each is self-interested they will prefer that others take costly action, so they can benefit without cost. This is the additional problem of 'free riding': some individuals may seek to avoid or evade the regulations or prices and use the common resource for their benefit at the expense of others. In the case of pollution, there is the added difficulty that often the accumulation of pollutants is very slow and we may be ignorant of their toxic effects. Moreover, these may arise far away from the region or country where they were produced.

Nevertheless, there are qualifications to the free-rider problem. First, social groups are also concerned with effects on others such as future generations – especially when the open resource is a basic need (clean air and water) – and institutions have been developed to protect common resources. As Spash (1999, p. 430) says, 'the historical tragedy has been the destruction by private profiteers of customs and cultures which managed resources in common and prevented overexploitation.' Second, if the 'free riding' group is less well-off, then costly action by the better-off group can improve equity. Third, there are also interactions between social problems and solutions, so that actions in one area by one group may be offset by actions elsewhere by another group. In other words there may be potential for alliances, so that institutions can be developed to ease or remove the 'free rider' problem (Coase, 1974, Ostrom 1990). The literature on how to resolve the tragedy has grown significantly since the 1990s and encompasses both traditional neoclassical treatments advocating market-based instruments (see for example, Arrow *et al.*, 1996) and newer institutional analyses of governance-based solutions (see for example, Dietz *et al.*, 2003).

Studying the ecological and economic systems in tandem highlights the fact that the problems associated with pollution may be made much worse by the pursuit of development and growth by governments. As Arrow *et al.* (1996, p. 13) point out 'National and international economic policy has usually ignored the environment'. The possibility of a major disaster means that great caution is required. Without special measures being taken, or special techniques being introduced, the higher the level of national output, the higher the level of pollution, but because increases in pollutants are gradual, the reduction in living standards due to the environmental degradation may go almost unnoticed, or, it is assumed that such costs are an inevitable concomitant of development if people are to be decently fed, housed and clothed.

Traditionally the various methods of controlling pollution have been divided into command and control-type instruments and market-based instruments. Each has a role to play, and include:

1   *Outright Ban*: Certain poisons are so potent and have such long-term effects that a complete ban on their production and use seems appropriate. However, this is an extreme measure: most pollutants are associated with activities which also produce desired outputs, which may more than compensate for the undesired pollution. Fierce penalties must be imposed on those who ignore the ban if it is to succeed.

2   *Prescribed Limits*: Very often a low pollution content (as in river water) is not harmful to life or noticeable to the nose or eye. Once the tolerable limit has been decided, then the would-be polluters can bid among themselves for the right to pollute up to the limit (i.e. permit trading or 'cap-and-trade'), with the state being able to benefit from the auction of such rights. Or, more simply, the state can allow unhindered pollution as long as it is beneath the limit, as for example it does at present with noise levels. Again there is a

need for penalties if the limits are exceeded and they must be graded to suit the social and personal costs imposed by the excess.

3    *Taxes*: This is a very flexible means of imposing the social costs of the pollution directly on the producer or consumer. This encourages them to absorb or restrict their waste wherever possible, or to use more expensive but less polluting techniques of production or consumption. It also makes high-polluting products more expensive, and therefore cuts back their demand.

4    *Property Rights*: Provided the costs of transactions and litigation were low and the individuals' property rights in the environment were clearly and precisely defined, a system of property rights could ensure that some forms of pollution were held down to socially acceptable levels. However, this outcome depends on the existing distribution of income and property also being acceptable. Unfortunately, so many forms of pollution affect so many people (e.g. jet exhaust in the upper atmosphere) that it would be very difficult to enforce the property rights even if they could be defined.

## 2  Ecological economics and traditional environmental economics

As ecological economics has developed it has stimulated interest in systems-based approaches to economics that fit more congenially with the evolutionary systems approach adopted in ecology and the natural sciences, than neoclassical economics based on instrumental rationality and equilibrium analysis. Beinhocker (2006) defines 'traditional' environmental economics as 'the set of concepts and theories articulated in … textbooks. It also includes concepts and theories that peer-reviewed surveys claim, or assume, that the field generally agrees on.' (p. 24). Traditional environmental economics can be contrasted with ecological economics, allowing for complexity, evolutionary and Post Keynesian theory, and emphasising institutions, non-linear dynamics, and deep uncertainty. While both traditional and ecological economists tend to share a common conceptual definition of sustainability, they differ in their modes and extent of analysis and, in particular, in their policy recommendations (see Illge and Schwarze, 2009).

Traditional neoclassical environmental economics emphasises instrumental rationality, via the use of utility maximization, and equilibrium, downplaying fundamental uncertainty (Dequech, 2008, p. 290). The traditional approach adopts a version of expected utility theory with human welfare usually translating into private market consumption per head in the applied models. The theory is applied to utility across countries with huge differences in consumption and many years into the future, when consumption can rise perhaps many times over. This method rests on the idea that individual preferences are fixed and utilities can be aggregated and converted into well-behaved mathematical equations in a 'social welfare function', and differentiated to give stable marginal properties, as the basis for policy. It also crucially assumes that all natural services can be converted to money and back again at any time, i.e. that there are no irreversible effects in this sense (Ackerman and Heinzerling, 2004).

When the usual assumptions of traditional environmental economics are compared with the realities of everyday life, a dissonance becomes apparent. All activities take place in specific locations at particular times. Externalities are actually pervasive, returns to scale (whether increasing or decreasing) are intrinsic in economic activity, and indivisibilities are a necessary feature of biology and technology. Economic organisations are evidently multi-tasking and have multiple objectives. A theory that assumes human beings are identical is offensive in the sense that each of us expresses our creativity and humanity in a different way, a point that is reflected in models of 'expressive rationality' (Hargreaves Heap, 1989, 2004). Moreover, the instrumental model of human motivation and behaviour that underlies neoclassical economics has been found wanting by the growing body of empirical evidence resulting from research on experimental economics, which finds that even in the case of simple socio-economic choices under full information and a single time frame, participants frequently adopt strategy choices that contradict the model of instrumental rationality (Andreoni, 1995, Hargreaves Heap and Varoufakis, 2002 and Ostrom, 2006, 2007). These realities mean that traditional approaches in which space and time are treated as if they are complications to basic theory rather than intrinsic to the problem are unsuited to environmental analysis where location and timing of pollution is critical.

Moral philosophers have long debated the relative weighting to be given in utility theory between social groups. Broome (2006) makes uncomfortable reading for traditional economists, partly because he insists, rightly, that economics is not ethics-free, that basing economics on the ethics of individuals assumed to be entirely self interested can go badly wrong, and that 'willingness to pay' is invalid as a means of valuation (Broome, 2005). This is in direct contradiction to the analyses of Pearce *et al.* (1995, pp. 196–197), when they contrast prescriptive with descriptive valuations of human life. In considering the ethics of climate change, Broome positions *justice* centre stage, arguing that those who cause the global pollution should cease to do so because it is unjust, and if they cannot cease, then they should compensate those who suffer.

Ecological economics seeks to conceptualise and abstract in directions that are more intuitive and more in accordance with natural behaviour and evolutionary theory. In particular, it asserts that all people and all groups are different, and that these differences should be one of the foundations of economic analysis.

## 3 Externalities

I define externalities at their most general as effects emanating from one locality at a particular time and affecting other localities at later times or periods. The effects occur later and are spread wider as time passes, depending on geography, climate, and the physical characteristics of the emissions, sources, transmission routes and destinations. Externalities are pervasive and their collective effects impact on people, animals, vegetation, buildings and other infrastructure, now and in the future. In order to define an externality the source must be defined in a locality with a boundary. The effects within the boundary can be termed 'internalities' as opposed to the externalities outside the boundary. The externalities considered in this chapter are mainly *economic* externalities, i.e. those externalities associated with economic activity or affecting economic activity.

The nature of externalities has significant implications for how they are managed. Some externalities are local, some are regional, and yet others are global, such as the emission of greenhouse gases produced by the burning of fossil fuels. Externalities can be classified as intended or unintended. They can also be classified as stock or flow externalities: the stock externalities are those that add to a stock of the pollutant dispersed over one or more regions, and the flow externalities are those which flow into other regions. The externalities can be positive or negative, a positive externality being one that is a benefit, and a negative externality being one that is a cost. The externalities can be large and obvious or small and barely noticeable; they can be concentrated or diffused over space, or time, or both. The huge number of possible types of externalities, and the fact that all externalities are context-specific, occurring at specific places and times, means that they are very difficult to conceptualise (Papandreou, 1994, especially pp. 195–196 and p. 281). Moreover their valuation is problematic and the cause of deep controversy.

Timing of the externality can be critical. Typically the environmental effects are within a non-linear complex system with chaotic behaviour (e.g. the atmosphere), where timing and duration of pollution and effects are intrinsic to understanding the problem. As a result, locating the social optimum, such that taxes compensate for social cost, is almost impossible.

Irreversibilities can arise through accumulation of stocks e.g. those of heavy metals or greenhouse gases. Problems are often systemic; e.g. the climate change problem involves long-term interactions between the economic and energy systems, the coupled ocean-atmospheric system and the biosphere. Technological change is often central to the solution of the problem, since technologies are often instrumental in producing the emissions and controlling them. And there are uncertainties in the costs of changing technologies and in the eventual damage and its location from emissions. The evolutionary option of exploiting and polluting natural resources until an area becomes uninhabitable, then moving on, is less and less viable as the whole planet has become affected via the ozone layer, chemical residues, or climate change.

Recently there has been a revival of interest in Hardin's 1968 article that focuses on how society or groups may govern the commons (see for example, Feeny *et al.* 1990, Ostrom 2000, Dietz *et al.*, 2003, Lloyd, 2007). Institutions may make use of, or manage, or capture, beneficial externalities if it is either possible or viable, in the sense that organisations can provide and market services based on the externalities (e.g. a hotel in a particularly attractive location, or a lighthouse [Coase, 1974]). In order to do this, they must make sufficient profit to stay in business, or if this is not possible (and it is deemed socially necessary to manage the externality) they may be provided with a public subsidy to do so. Firms capture some of the externalities associated with research and development (R&D), by patents, copyright and brand names; they also manage to a greater or lesser extent their 'internalities' such as noxious fumes from chemical processes.

Institutions also manage many other costly externalities, such as those associated with traffic congestion and water and air pollution; usually this is a function of government, e.g. laws governing traffic and pollution. Governments manage social order, in the sense that there are social and economic benefits from a framework of law and regulation, enforced in a socially agreed manner. Markets manage information and have rules to reduce the propagation of misinformation and abuse.

The complexity of each environmental problem suggests that a portfolio of instruments may be needed to solve them (regulations, taxes and government spending) depending on climate, geography, institutions and technologies. Since problems often interact, solving one may help or hinder solving others. In addition, instruments have different side-effects. These effects suggest that the portfolio should contain complementary policies to address the unwanted side-effects of some of the instruments, and to address interacting problems. The standard neoclassical approach tends to favour market based instruments, such as taxes and subsidies. There are well-known limitations to this approach – most notably the difficulty of valuing externalities – which makes it difficult for governments to act with any precision. This problem has arguably been side-stepped by tradable policy instruments, such as carbon trading schemes. However, as Lloyd (2007) points out, a review of emissions trading schemes by Choi (2005) finds no hard evidence to suggest that they work.

## 4 Obligations, rights and values

There are two mutually-exclusive positions that can be taken regarding values. One is the absolute assertion of obligations and rights, e.g. the obligation of mankind not to destroy the global ecosystem, or the right of a species not to be made extinct by our own species. The other is the implicit relative value system derived from traditional utilitarianism, which is the basis of much of modern welfare economics. In this system, value is derived from maximisation of individual utility. It has its most formal expression in the general equilibrium solution. In this, utility is maximised to the point that no one can be made better off without making someone else worse off (the Pareto Optimum), the allocation of production is at maximum efficiency, and all prices and wages are determined by the market. It is solved to give the best possible outcome for the most people possible. The flaws in this system are that: it has an inadequate treatment of spatial and temporal aspects of economic activity and its effects; damaging externalities are not included; there is no treatment of pervasive increasing returns and endogenous technical progress; and equity issues are set aside to be treated by the tax system.

How is the value of goods and services, and hence the appropriate level of social pricing, to be determined, when allowing for environmental externalities? The values are social concepts, and depend on social agreement and custom. This is made obvious by comparing valuations or prices in different cultures and economic systems. Values in a specific location at a specific time are influenced by values in adjacent locations and times (the recent past in the same location and in other regions in the same industry, and in other industries in the same region). The valuations are partly trial and error, since both producers and consumers, and both buyers and sellers, are uncertain as to what the 'correct' values are. The process has to be like this because producers do not know the extent of the economies of specialisation and scale they can achieve. They do not know the extent of the market at a particular price (this demand may be years in the future at the time the production facilities are being designed). Market clearing, if it takes place at all, is by adjustment over a range of variables, including prices.

## 5  Global warming as an externality

From a policy perspective, the problem of global warming possesses a number of characteristics that affect the means by which it can be regulated. On the one hand, while there is no economic technology to absorb the primary greenhouse gas, $CO_2$, any abatement policy must focus on source reductions and not clean-up technologies. Moreover, since each of the individual fuels possesses distinct, but unique, carbon contents, $CO_2$ emissions are strictly a function of the type of fuel used. And finally, since global warming is a global common property, the issue of the location of emission sources is irrelevant to the determination of environmental damage. For these reasons, differential taxation of fuel types will effectively tax carbon inputs, $CO_2$ emission outputs, and environmental damages. (This is in contrast with the abatement of acid rain. Since different grades of coal possess widely varying sulphur content, since 'end-of-pipe' abatement technology such as flue-gas desulphurisation exists, and since there is spatial differentiation in environmental effects, the relationship between fuel and environmental damage is not unique.)

Moreover, since the different primary energy carriers (coal, oil, and gas) have clearly defined markets and sources of supply, it is a relatively straightforward matter to apply such tax rates. And finally, given that the fuels are already taxed or subsidised extensively, the administrative and institutional costs of further taxation are relatively small (the administrative costs of excise duties in the UK for example are a fraction of those of the value-added tax, VAT). In addition emissions of most non-$CO_2$ greenhouse gases are closely associated with the burning of fossil fuels (the exceptions being CFCs and methane from gas leaks, animals and waste tips). For these reasons, most of the literature (e.g. Barker *et al.*, 1995) is concerned with $CO_2$ abatement in particular rather than with greenhouse gas abatement in general. An economic instrument for abatement is a carbon tax, which in turn is expected to change energy and fuel prices and, via price elasticities, energy demands and $CO_2$ emissions (see Ekins and Barker, 2001).

Carbon taxation and emission trading schemes are market-based instruments and depend fundamentally on the efficient working of the market system for their success. This efficiency has many requirements and implications. First the legal and institutional structure should ensure that contracts are (1) available, (2) freely entered into by both or more parties and (3) enforceable under clear and widely accepted laws and rules; thus countries beset by bribery and corruption may not be able to use taxation because the taxes will be evaded or become an excuse for further corruption. A second requirement is that prices should reflect costs to some degree, so that the policy will increase the price of carbon-intensive production; in some special circumstances, e.g. if the carbon-based energy is rationed, then the extra tax may have no effect on demand. Third, buyers and sellers should be well informed as to the costs and availability of alternatives and that future outcomes (even if not known) should at least be considered; in some cases, especially amongst some socially disadvantaged groups such as the elderly, there may be an unwillingness to consider alternatives, so extra taxation may have very inequitable effects.

A further important limitation in using the price mechanism is the fact that the outcome of the use of a tax or emission permit scheme may be more uncertain than that following direct regulation of the industries and others. Of course the outcome of a regulatory regime is also uncertain: the rules may not be clear; they may not be enforceable; and it may be impossible to monitor the effects of the regulation on the emissions. However, even assuming that the regulations are effective, the uncertainty of taxation is not much of a limitation for two reasons. First the dichotomy between taxes and regulations is a false one; an effective scheme may well combine both taxes and regulation, with each instrument supporting the other depending on the countries, sectors and institutions concerned. Second, since some pollution abatement does not require a precise abatement by a definite date, the aim of policy must be to achieve significant reductions over a number of years, with policies adjusting to outcomes repeatedly over the years. In fact the risk is that fixed targets for individual sectors achieved by regulation will be highly inefficient in that the same target might be reached by means of taxation at much lower costs.

A final limitation here is that in order to achieve the targets, the increase in prices from the policies may have to be very high, as suggested in some studies. It is argued that they may be unenforceable or they may distort the market. The first point to note is that proposed and implemented taxes should have started at very low levels with the intention of assessing the outcomes before tax rates are increased. The second is that the usual case will be that the tax signal is made clearer and indeed amplified by changes in regulations, advertising and energy-saving campaigns, so that the results from the studies are likely to be over-estimates of the required increases in taxes to achieve a target. The argument regarding distortion is completely misplaced. The whole point of the increase in price is to improve the market signals so as to include the social costs of pollution; this is not a distortion but a correction. It is the market prices for polluting activity without the taxes that are distorted; indeed, in terms of the traditional treatment, it is the whole allocation of resources that is distorted and inefficient if the damaging externality is excluded from prices at whatever taxation level which may be required.

## 6 Politics and social choice in economics

Beder (1996) has argued that firms tend to favour and negotiate price-based instruments over less attractive (from the firms' perspective) stricter controls. More fundamentally, Lloyd (2007) has argued that the structure of the modern corporation and its prioritisation of shareholder value places a *duty* on corporations not to be neutral in negotiations but to argue for policy measures that maximise private (but not social) returns. The systems-based approach recognises that all agents – government, firms, etc. – may influence the strategy choices of other agents, this is an intrinsic element of the systems approach. There is no impartial government, agent or auctioneer, overseeing the economic system; government, policy makers and firms are all part of the system.

A related difference between neoclassical economics and complex systems analysis is that the latter relaxes the assumption of instrumental rationality. This assumption implies that all agents are instrumentally rational and follow maximising rules at all times, ignoring social norms and conventions. In contrast ecological economics and complex systems theory allow for the possibility of agent-based modelling whereby different agents follow different rules. Rules and norms evolve over time. If this is the case, then it is easy to imagine that the whole feedback process could work just as well to initiate and confirm cooperative rather than competitive behaviour. This takes the form of social groups devising institutions that reward cooperation more than competition, a key skill in the evolution of human society (Ostrom, 1990).

Mancur Olson (1965, 1982) analyses the formation of social groups under the assumption that all the individuals forming the groups are rational and self interested. The basic point is

> the larger the number of individuals or firms that would benefit from a collective good, the smaller the share of the gains from action in the group interest that will accrue to the individual or firm that undertakes the action. Thus, in the absence of selective incentives, the incentive for group action diminishes as group size increases, so that large groups are less able to act in their common interest than small ones.
>
> (1982, Chapter 2)

He concludes that for groups beyond a small size, no rational individual would join voluntarily because the costs would exceed the benefits. 'Free riding' is the preferred option, always assuming that there is a vehicle with spare capacity going in the right direction at the right time. In the case of collective goods with open access by all, then the rational choice is to let others provide the goods, and then enjoy them without paying for them. The problem is that with these assumptions and without institutional structures to provide incentives, no collective goods will be supplied by society, even though every member will benefit from them. The role of government is to provide the coercive framework to provide collective goods, such as clean air or reduced risk of climate change, and pay for any costs by taxing social groups to provide government revenues.

The first and main problem with Olson's thesis is the assumption regarding personal motivation. He assumes that rational individuals are entirely self-interested and that implicitly the welfare of others does not affect the individual's decisions or actions. It is as if social groups were collections of self-interested individuals without a legal structure, history, and means of achieving consensus and sets of institutions of their own. A second problem with the theory is that both the assumptions about personal motivation and some of the results that have been tested are not consistent with empirical evidence on personal and group behaviour (Ostrom, 1990, 2006, 2007).

A more promising approach is to assess how different social groups have solved the problems posed by open access resources. Essentially, the problem is solved by the development of institutions to manage it. This is Ostrom's view:

> The central question in this study is how a group of principals who are in an interdependent situation can organize and govern themselves to obtain continuing joint benefits when all face temptations to free-ride, shirk, or otherwise act opportunistically.
>
> (1990)

Social choice involves social groups, 'stakeholders', such as government, industry, NGOs, and political parties, in a process of consensus. But it also involves information. A real choice requires the equal and simultaneous presentation of feasible alternatives. When a policy is the subject of political debate and possible implementation by government, policy advisors consider the benefit that such implementation would produce in each of various mutually exclusive 'states of nature' that might follow it, the good being considered for each group affected over space and time.

A key issue for mitigation policies, nevertheless, is how to get sovereign nations and different social groups to agree to cooperate on the management of open access resources. Ostrom studied a variety of social groups in different cultures and times to derive the following general conditions under which groups can manage open access resources successfully: the people involved recognise the mutual benefit in cooperation; the group has low discount rates, so takes account of future effects; there is substantial mutual trust in others following the agreed rules and behaviours; there is a capacity to communicate; there is a possibility of entering into legal agreements regarding the resource and any property rights are respected and secure; and arrangements are made for monitoring the use and condition of the resource and enforcing any agreements.

One of the great insights of Hardin's analysis of the tragedy of the commons is that he recognised that the problem of the over-use of common resources could not be solved by science alone: it was a problem for science and society.

Hardin's work both called for and inspired more interdisciplinary research and was instrumental in encouraging the development of ecological economics and the systems approach to environmental questions such as pollution. Forty years on there is still doubt about whether it is possible to govern the commons and much need for further research. However, there is greater understanding of the different types of instrument that may be used. Not all of these are market based or command based: many are governance and institution based. As Dietz *et al.* (2003) note, the effects of this greater understanding leaves the question of the *commons* open:

> Is it possible to govern such critical commons as the oceans and the climate? We remain guardedly optimistic.... Systematic multidisciplinary research has ... shown that a wide diversity of adaptive governance systems have been effective stewards of many resources. Sustained research coupled to an explicit view of national and international policies as experiments can yield the scientific knowledge necessary to design appropriate adaptive institutions.
>
> (Dietz *et al.*, 2003, p. 1910)

## Notes

1 Source: *Web of Science* database, accessed on 20 May 2010.
2 In this regard, Keynes' theory embodies the central characteristic of a complex system – a systems-wide effect that is counterintuitive and unwanted.
3 This is discussed in more detail in the chapter by Michie and Oughton in this volume.
4 See for example, Kirchner (2003), Lovelock (2003).
5 On this topic see the chapter in this volume by Whitmarsh.
6 See Chapter 3 of this volume by Michie and Oughton which discusses Axelrod's solution based on evolutionary game theory. This solution is perhaps the closest to a purely technical solution to the problem, however, it requires 'rational' agents to believe in the possibility (however small) of their own immortality, which is at odds with the assumption of instrumental rationality and does not, therefore, provide a technical solution to the game on the terms set out by Hardin (1968).

## Acknowledgements

The author wishes to thank the editors for helpful suggestions and The Three Guineas Trust, one of the Sainsbury Family Trusts, for financial support in writing this chapter.

## References

Ackerman, F., Heinzerling L. (2004) *Priceless: On Knowing the Price of Everything and the Value of Nothing.* New York, The New Press.
Andreoni, J. (1995) Warm-Glow versus Cold-Prickle: The Effects of Positive and Negative Framing on Cooperation in Experiments, *The Quarterly Journal of Economics*, 110:1:1–21.
Arrow, K., Bolin, B., Costanza, R., Dasgupta, P., Folke, C., Holling, C., Jansson, B.-O., Levin, S., Mäler, K.-G., Perrings, C. and Pimental, D. (1996) Economic Growth, Carrying Capacity and the Environment, *Ecological Applications*, 6:1:13–15.

Barker, T., Ekins, P. and Johnstone, N. (1995) (eds) *Global Warming and Energy Demand*, London, Routledge.

Beinhocker, E. (2006) *The Origin of Wealth: Evolution, Complexity and the Radical Remaking of Economics*, Random House Business Books.

Broome J. (1992) *Counting the Cost of Global Warming*, White House Press, Cambridge, UK.

Broome J. (2005) Why economics needs ethical theory, *Pelican Record*, 42:80–88; reprinted in Basu K., Kanbur, R. (eds) (forthcoming) *Welfare, Development, Philosophy and Social Science: Essays for Amartya Sen's 75th Birthday, 3*, Oxford University Press.

Broome J. (2006) Valuing policies in response to climate change: some ethical issues, contribution to the work of the *Economics of Climate Change: The Stern Review*, Stern, N. (2007).

Choi, I. (2005) Global climate change and the use of economic approaches: the ideal design features of domestic greenhouse gas emissions trading with an analysis of the European Union's CO2 Trading Directive and Climate Stewardship Act, *Natural Resources Journal*, 45:865–952.

Coase, R. (1974) The Lighthouse in Economics, *The Journal of Law and Economics*, 17:2:357–376.

Costanza, R. (1989) What is ecological economics? *Ecological Economics*, Vol. 1, pp. 1–7.

David, P. (1985) Clio and the Economics of QWERTY, *Economic History*, 75:1:332–337.

David, P. (2001) Path dependence, its critics, and the quest for 'historical economics' in Garrouste, P., Ioannides, S. (eds) *Evolution and Path Dependence in Economic Ideas: Past and Present*, Edward Elgar, London.

Dequech, D. (2008) Neoclassical, mainstream, orthodox, and heterodox economics, *Journal of Post Keynesian Economics*, 30:2:279–302.

Dietz, T., Ostrom, E., and Stern, P. (2003) The Struggle to Govern the Commons, *Science*, 302:1907–1912.

Ekins, P. and Barker, T. (2001) Carbon taxes and carbon emissions trading, *Journal of Economic Surveys*, 15: 3 (Special Issue on Issues in Environmental Economics, eds, Nick Hanley and Colin Roberts) pp. 325–376.

Feeny, D., Berkes, F., McCay, B. and Acheson, J. (1990) The Tragedy of the Commons: Twenty-Two Years Later, *Human Ecology*, 18:1:1–19.

Hardin, G. (1968) The Tragedy of the Commons, *Science*, 162:3859 (13 December, 1968), pp. 1243–1248.

Hardin, G. (1998) Extensions of 'The Tragedy of the Commons', *Science*, 280:5354:682–683.

Hargreaves Heap, S. (1989) *Rationality in Economics*, Basil Blackwell, Oxford.

Hargreaves Heap, S. (2004) A note on participatory decision making and rationality, *Cambridge Journal of Economics*, 28:3:457 467.

Hargreaves Heap, S. and Varoufakis, Y. (2002) Some experimental evidence on the evolution of discrimination and fairness, *Economic Journal*, 112, July, 679–703.

Hodgson, G.M. (2007) Evolutionary and institutional economics as the new mainstream? *Evolutionary and Institutional Economics Review*, 4:1:7–25.

Illge, L. and Schwarze, R. (2009) A matter of opinion – how ecological and neoclassical environmental economists think about sustainability and economics, *Ecological Economics*, 68:3:594–604.

Keynes, J.M. (1936) *The General Theory of Employment, Interest and Money*, London, Macmillan Press (1973).

Kirchner, J. (2003) The Gaia Hypothesis: conjectures and refutations, *Climatic Change*, 58:21–45.

Kirman, A.P. (1992) Whom or what does the representative individual represent? *Journal of Economic Perspectives*, 6:2:117–136.

Lloyd, B. (2007) The commons revisited: the tragedy continues, *Energy Policy*, 35:5806–5818.

Lovelock, J. (2003) GAIA and emergence: a response to Kirchner and Volk, *Climate Change*, 57:1–3.

Maréchal, K. (2007) The economics of climate change and the change of climate in economics, *Energy Policy*, 35: 5181–5519.

Olson, M. (1965) *The Logic of Collective Action*. Cambridge, Harvard University Press.

Olson, M. (1982) *The Rise and Decline of Nations*. New Haven, Yale University Press.

Ostrom, E. (1990) *Governing the Commons: The Evolution of Institutions for Collective Action*, Cambridge University Press.

Ostrom, E. (2000) Collective Action and the Evolution of Social Norms, *The Journal of Economic Perspectives*, 14:3:137–158.

Ostrom, E. (2006) The value-added of laboratory experiments for the study of institutions and common-pool resources, *Journal of Economic Behavior and Organization*, 62:149–163.

Ostrom, E. (2007) *The Challenge of Crafting Rules to Change Open Access Resources into Managed Resources*. Available at SSRN: http://ssrn.com/abstract=1304827.

Ostrom, E., Burger, J., Field, C., Noogaard, R. and Policansky, D. (1999) Revisiting the Commons: Local Lessons, Global Challenges, *Science*, 284:278–282.

Papandreou, A.A. (1994) *Externality and Institutions*, Clarendon Press, Oxford.

Pearce D.W., Cline, W.R., Achanta, A.N., Fankhauser, S., Pachauri, R.K., Tol, R.S.J., Vellinga, P. (1996) The social costs of climate change: greenhouse damages and the benefits of control, Bruce, J., Lee, H., Haites, E. (eds) *Climate Change 1995—economic and social dimensions of climate change*. Cambridge University Press, Cambridge, pp. 125–144.

Pitman, A. (2005) On the Role of Geography in Earth System Science, *Geoforum*, 36:137–148.

Spash, C. L. (1999) The development of environmental thinking in economics, *Environmental Values* 8:4: 413–435.

Stern, N. (2007) *The Economics of Climate Change: The Stern Review*. Cambridge, UK, Cambridge University Press.

# Part II
# Innovation

# 6 Systems of innovation

## National, regional and technological innovation systems

*Timothy J. Foxon*

## 1 Introduction

A number of the chapters in this volume have already referred to the value of systems approaches in addressing environmental economics and policy issues. This chapter discusses important developments over the last two decades in understanding innovation from a systems perspective, and examines the framework this provides for drawing policy implications in relation to promoting innovation for environmental and sustainability ends. More specific questions on the argument for environmental innovation policy and the types of policy instruments available are taken up in Chapter 7.

We begin, in Section 2, by briefly reviewing the main conceptual models used within economics to understand innovation: *induced innovation, evolutionary approaches* and *path-dependent* models. In Section 3, we introduce the development of thinking on systems of innovation, and examine *national, regional* and *technological innovation systems*. In Section 4, we look at recent work on *functions* of innovation systems and the implications for understanding the 'life cycle' of a new technology's development and deployment. In Section 5, we address the 'non-optimality' of innovation systems, and introduce the notion of 'systems failure' as a rationale for policy intervention. We conclude, in Section 6, by briefly discussing the policy implications of these ideas, which are further developed in Chapter 7.

## 2 Conceptual models of innovation

Though classical economists from Adam Smith to Karl Marx were very much concerned with issues relating to technological and institutional change, the first systematic attempt by an economist to understand the processes of innovation was the work of Joseph Schumpeter in the first half of the twentieth century. He identified three stages of the innovation process – *invention, innovation* and *diffusion* – a classification which is still widely used, though, as we shall see, is now being challenged as over-simplistic. He identified *invention* as the first practical demonstration of an idea; *innovation* as the first commercial application of an invention in the market; and *diffusion* as the spreading of the technology or process throughout the market. The classical representation of the diffusion process is by an S-shaped curve, in which the take-up of the new technology begins slowly, then 'takes off' and achieves a period of rapid diffusion, before gradually slowing down as saturation levels are reached. Schumpeter also undertook deep assessments of the drivers of the innovation process. In his early work, he stressed the role of 'heroic' entrepreneurs as the (usually) men who drove a new technology to the market (Schumpeter, 1911/1934). His later work, reflecting institutional changes in the 1920s and 1930s, stressed the role of large firms which have the resources to conduct extensive research and development (R&D) and support new technologies in the early stages of their development (Schumpeter, 1939). His metaphor of 'creative destruction' to describe the process of the replacement of old firms and old products by innovative new firms and products has also been widely influential, both in the popular conception of capitalism and in inspiring more recent understanding of the process of innovation.

This three-stage classification underlies what is often referred to as the 'linear model of innovation'. This describes innovation as a process of more-or-less continuous flow through the three stages, from basic research to applied research to technology development and diffusion. This leads to the identification of two main drivers of innovation. The first is the process of *technology-push*, i.e. new technologies arising through the processes of research and development without particular applications in mind. The second is that demand for new products and services is more important in stimulating inventive activity than advances in the state of knowledge, so-called *demand-pull*. As we shall see, more recent theoretical approaches accept the importance of both technology-push and demand-pull, but also stress the importance of feedbacks between the supply and demand sides. Crucially, *innovation* can be thought of as the process of matching technical possibilities to market opportunities, through activities including experimental development and design, trial production and marketing (Freeman and Soete, 1997). These interactions occur within an *innovation system*.

Before going into more detail on innovation systems approaches, it is helpful to review three broad approaches to understanding the economics of technological change and innovation which go beyond the linear model – *induced innovation, evolutionary approaches* and *path-dependent models* (Ruttan, 2001). Ruttan argues that these three approaches represent complementary elements of a yet to be developed more general theory. Other useful recent reviews of technological innovation in relation to environmental policy may be found in Kemp (1997), Grubler (1998), Jaffe *et al.* (2003), Foxon (2003) and Stern (2007, Chapter 16).

## 2.1  Induced innovation

Induced innovation approaches emphasise market drivers and analyse the impact of changes in the economic environment on the rate and direction of technical change. The importance of demand-pull mechanisms has already been mentioned. Another key insight dates back to classical economist John Hicks (1932)

– that a change in the relative prices of factors of production is itself a spur to innovation directed at economising the use of the factor that has become relatively expensive. This implies that if, for example, labour becomes relatively more expensive compared to capital, say because of labour shortages, innovation will be directed towards more labour-saving technologies. It has been argued that the combination of relatively high wages and cheap energy, in the form of easily-accessible coal, in Britain in the eighteenth century stimulated the innovation of labour-saving technologies, such as the steam engine and cotton spinning jenny at the start of the Industrial Revolution (Allen, 2009).

### 2.2 Evolutionary theory

The modern approach to an evolutionary theory of technical change was pioneered by Richard Nelson and Sidney Winter, culminating in their book *An Evolutionary Theory of Economic Change* (Nelson and Winter, 1982). This builds on two foundations – the Schumpeterian understanding of innovation, and the idea of 'bounded rationality', first put forward by Herbert Simon. Simon (1955, 1959) noted that decision makers, either individuals or firms, are limited in their ability to gather and process information and so, rather than being perfectly rational profit-maximisers, they make decisions that satisfy whatever are their most important criteria, i.e. they 'satisfice' rather than optimise.[1].Nelson and Winter thus jettison much of what they consider to be the 'excess baggage' of the neoclassical microeconomic model, including the global objective function, the well-defined choice set, and the profit-maximising assumption. Instead, they replace the production function of the firm by the concept of 'routine'. A routine could be any technical, procedural, organisational or strategic process or technique used by a firm as part of its normal business activities, for example, its R&D strategy. Routines change by a process of *searching* for better techniques. Successful routines, and firms that employ them, are then *selected* by the process of market competition. Because firms are assumed to have 'bounded rationality', search processes will usually look for incremental improvements in techniques or imitation of the practices of other firms, and will be terminated when firms satisfice by attaining a given aspiration level.

### 2.3 Path dependent models

'Path dependency' is the idea that the successful innovation and take up of a new technology depends on the path of its development, including the particular characteristics of initial markets, the institutional and regulatory factors governing its introduction and the expectations of consumers. This arises as a consequence of 'increasing returns' to adoption, i.e. positive feedbacks which mean that the more a technology is adopted, the more likely it is to be further adopted. Arthur (1994) identified four major classes of increasing returns: *scale economies, learning effects, adaptive expectations* and *network economies. Scale economies* reflect the fact that unit costs decline as fixed costs are spread over increasing production volumes, causing demand to increase. *Learning effects* reflect product improvements and cost declines as experience is gained in the production and application of a technology. *Adaptive expectations* arise as increasing adoption reduces uncertainty and both users and producers become increasingly confident about quality, performance and longevity of the current technology. *Network* or *coordination effects* occur for technologies for which the more users there are, the more useful the technology becomes, such as for mobile phones. Arthur (1989) showed that, in a simple model of two competing technologies, these effects can amplify small, essentially random, initial variations in market share, resulting in one technology achieving complete market dominance at the expense of the other, so-called technological 'lock-in'. He speculated that, once lock-in is achieved, this can prevent the take up of potentially superior alternatives. A series of historical studies showed the plausibility of arguments of path dependency and lock-in, including the QWERTY keyboard layout (David, 1985) and the light-water nuclear reactor design (Cowan, 1990).

### 2.4 Towards a more general theory

The evolutionary and path-dependency approaches emphasise the importance of past decisions, embodied in technologies and institutions, constraining present innovation, whilst the induced perspective stresses the long-run importance of changes in relative prices in driving the direction of technical change. We shall see how aspects of these three models – induced, evolutionary and path dependent, have appeared in more recent approaches which take a dynamic, systems perspective, looking in more detail at the actors involved, their behaviour and the feedbacks between elements of the system.

## 3  Systems of innovation

The systems approach was first applied to the idea of a national system of innovation by Chris Freeman, working at the University of Sussex, in a pioneering study of the then successful Japanese economy in the late 1980s. Freeman (1987, 1988) defined a national system of innovation as 'the network of institutions in the public and private sectors whose activities and interactions initiate, import, modify and diffuse new technologies.' Freeman stressed the positive role of government, working closely with industry and the science base, to create a *vision* and provide *long-term support* for the development and marketing of the most advanced technologies; the *integrated approach* to R&D, design, procurement, production and marketing within large firms; and the high level of general *education* and scientific culture, combined with thorough practical *training* and frequent up-dating in industry.

Two major studies in the early 1990s by Lundvall (1992) and Nelson (1993) analysed national innovation systems in more detail. Lundvall (1988, 1992) defined a national system of innovation as constituted by 'the elements and relationships which *interact* in the production, diffusion and use of new, and economically useful, knowledge ... either located within or rooted inside the borders of a nation state.' He stressed the role of interactions between *users* and *producers*, facilitating a flow of information and knowledge linking technological capabilities to user needs. Because of the fundamental *uncertainty* of innovation, these interactions go beyond pure market mechanisms, and rely on mutual trust and mutually respected codes of behaviour. Lundvall (1992) defines innovation as a process, which is *ubiquitous* and *cumulative*, involving new combinations of knowledge, produced through various forms of *learning*, including *learning-by-doing*, improvements in practices and processes increasing the efficiency of production operations (Arrow, 1962), *learning-by-using*, ways of improving the design and operation of new technologies that become apparent through feedbacks from the initial use of these technologies (Rosenberg, 1982), and *learning-by-interacting*, increasing efficiency of the system through user-producer interactions (Lundvall, 1988). Nelson and collaborators (1993) conducted a major empirical study and comparison of the national innovation systems of 15 countries. They concluded that 'to a considerable extent, differences in innovation systems reflect differences in economic and political circumstances and priorities between countries.' The differences identified in the institutional set-ups between different countries included systems of university research and training, and of industrial R&D; financial institutions; management skills; public infrastructure; and national monetary, fiscal and trade policies.

The concept of national innovation systems has been taken forward and used extensively by the OECD (1999, 2002, 2005), following these early studies. The innovation process is seen as characterised by the different roles of actors in creating or sharing knowledge (academics, technology developers, knowledge networks); disseminating and using knowledge (project developers, end-users); and setting rules and framework conditions (regulators, research funders, financers), and their interactions through flows of knowledge, funding and influence. These interactions take place within an institutional framework of formal rules (laws, regulations, contracts) and informal constraints (routines, conventions), which serve to create drivers for, or barriers to, innovation.

The concept of a system of innovation has also been applied at a regional level, to examine innovation clusters, such as Silicon Valley, and a sectoral level, to examine sectoral systems of innovation, such as pharmaceuticals, telecommunications or business services (Malerba, 2005), or technological innovation systems, such as renewable energy technologies (Carlsson and Stankiewicz, 1991, Jacobsson and Bergek, 2004).

Three key themes may be identified across these systems of innovation approaches.

## 3.1 Systemic interactions

The idea of a systems approach and systems thinking leads beyond the old linear model of innovation, whereby an increase in R&D going in will automatically lead to new products and services emerging at the end of the process. It also suggests that the rationale for government intervention to support innovation goes beyond a simple 'market failure' argument, whereby support reflects the difference between the private rate of return to R&D and the social rate of return. None of this argument serves to diminish the role or importance of R&D in generating innovation, but it provides a more complex picture of the drivers of the rate and direction of innovation, and the barriers that can prevent successful innovation.

The OECD (2002) study identified several broad trends that are combining to change the conditions for successful innovation:

- *Growing importance of linkages and interactions between the science base and the business sector*: the importance of feedbacks from the development, production and use phases to scientific research has been highlighted above;
- *More competitive markets and the accelerating pace of scientific and technological change are forcing firms to innovate more rapidly*: however, paradoxically, this innovation may be more likely to be directed along the prevailing technological trajectory (Dosi, 1982), as firms 'run fast just to stand still';
- *Increasing need for firms to engage in networking and collaboration*: this is particularly as a consequence of the growth and diversity of knowledge-intensive services to good business practice. This may take the form of *clusters* of innovative firms and other private and public knowledge-based organisations as key local or regional drivers of growth and employment;
- *Importance of technology-based start-ups, often small and medium sized enterprises (SMEs), in the development and diffusion of new technologies*: such firms help to instil a culture of innovation and encourage investment in skills;
- *Countries' innovation systems are becoming more interdependent as a result of globalisation*: this means that competitiveness of firms depends increasingly on their ability to link to international innovation networks.

### 3.2  Uncertainty and bounded rationality

The second common theme relates to the role of uncertainty and 'bounded rationality'. As emphasised within evolutionary approaches, 'bounded rationality' is the idea that firms or individuals are always limited in their ability to gather and process information relevant for their decision making. As a result, rather than making the optimum choice from a given range of options, they 'satisfice' by choosing an available option that meets their preferred criteria. Because firms are not assumed to have perfect knowledge, what they know and how they learn becomes central to understanding the innovation process. Much innovation consists of making new combinations of existing knowledge, as a result of the various forms of learning: *learning-by-doing*, *learning-by-using* and *learning-by-interacting*. Hence, it is important to work to better understand how these learning processes work for different technologies and industries. The ability to learn, and hence to innovate, also depends on the existing knowledge and skills of the firm's employees. Bounded rationality also implies that firms' expectations of the future are a crucial influence on their present decision making. Innovation is necessarily characterised by uncertainty about future markets, future technology potential and future policy and regulatory environments. Hence, firms' expectations of these factors will influence the directions of their innovative searches. As expectations are often implicitly or explicitly shared between different firms in the same industry, this helps to explain why the development of technologies follow particular path-dependent trajectories (Dosi, 1982). A shared expectation can even come close to being a self-fulfilling prophecy (MacKenzie, 1992).

### 3.3 Institutional set-up

The third common theme is the importance of the institutional set-up or framework in determining the rate and direction of technological innovation. Institutions can be thought of as providing the 'rules of the game', covering property rights, contractual relations and policy and regulatory frameworks (North, 1990). Institutional economics describes different levels of stability, ranging from market interactions that are continuously changing, through formal institutions with lifetimes of several years, to cultural values which only change over decades or centuries (Williamson, 1999; van der Steen, 2005). The prevailing set of technologies and institutions forms a technological *regime*, which helps to guide innovation. Recent thinking suggests that a transition to a new technological regime occurs through the development and cumulation of niches, in which learning can occur, at least partly insulated from the demands of the current regime (Kemp *et al.*, 1998; Geels, 2002).

## 4 Functions of (technological) innovation systems

Recent work applying these ideas to environmental challenges has largely applied a technological innovation systems approach to investigate innovation processes relating to renewable energy and other environmentally friendly technologies. A technological innovation system was defined by Carlsson and Stankiewicz (1991) as '...network(s) of agents interacting in a specific technology area under a particular institutional infrastructure to generate, diffuse, and utilize technology.' Hence, a technological innovation system is made up of thee main elements:

- *Actors*, including technology developers, users, policy makers and regulators. Again, these actors have limited ability to gather and process information for decision making – so-called 'bounded rationality' – but have particular capabilities or competences which they can employ.
- *Networks* through which actors share knowledge and exchange information. These include formal interactions, e.g. through exchange within markets, but also informal interactions, e.g. through trade associations.

- *Institutions* which stipulate the norms and rules for interactions between actors, and so influence the rate and direction of innovation.

The performance of an innovation system can be defined in terms of how well the system promotes the innovation and diffusion of its technology, i.e. the rate at which it gives rise to useful innovations that challenge incumbent technological systems. Synthesis of studies of past innovation systems has identified a number of key dynamic processes that need to occur for an innovation system to perform well (Jacobsson and Bergek, 2004; Hekkert *et al.*, 2007; Bergek *et al.*, 2008). These processes are referred to as 'functions of innovation systems', including:

- *Entrepreneurial activities*: both new entrants seeking business opportunities in new markets, and incumbent companies which diversify their business strategy to take advantage of new developments, in either case giving rise to experiments and learning;
- *Knowledge development*: R&D projects, patenting of new ideas and investments in R&D, also leading to learning within the system;
- *Knowledge diffusion through networks*: exchange of information between the different actors within the system and the networks through which they interact;
- *Guidance of search activities*: relating to selection between different technological options, including interactive and cumulative processes of exchanging ideas between users, producers and other actors, giving rise to changes in user preferences and the creation of positive expectations about the future potential of the technology;
- *Market formation*: activities that stimulate the creation of niche markets, either through entrepreneurial and learning activities, user demands, or specific policy incentives and measures;
- *Resources mobilization*: investment in both financial capital and human capital involving the accumulation of relevant skills and capacities;
- *Creation of legitimacy*: the action of advocacy coalitions to promote the adoption of new alternatives, and also responses to counter-actions by incumbent players seeking to maintain their current advantage.

In their study of the evolution of renewable energy technologies, Jacobsson and Bergek (2004) identified two broad phases in the evolution of a product or industry: a (1) 'formative period'; and a (2) 'market expansion' period. These differ in terms of the character of technical change in the period; patterns of firm entry/exit; and the rate of market growth.

The *formative period* of a technology's development is characterized by the existence of: a range of competing designs; many entrant firms, typically small; high uncertainties, in terms of technologies, markets and regulations; and niche markets. Niche markets provide 'incubation rooms', where learning can occur, the price/performance of technology may improve, and new customer preferences are formed (Kemp *et al.*, 1998). The formative phase is characterised by severe barriers to change, which may prevent the adoption of the new technology. These include: high uncertainty, with respect to the future of technologies, costs and market opportunities; lock-in of existing technologies and institutions; weak networks for change; and lack of long-term vision. As discussed briefly above and in the chapter by Hogg, lock-in arises because existing technologies have benefited from long periods of increasing returns to their adoption, as have the institutional structures that support those technologies. For example, actors with power in current techno-institutional systems act to reinforce their power by resisting changes to institutional structures that would weaken that power, for example by encouraging the development of competing technologies (North, 1990; Pierson, 2000; Foxon, 2007a). However, there are also, of course, drivers for change. These include: feedbacks from formation of markets, through learning effects and price/performance improvements; firm entry/new activity, which contributes to the creation of new knowledge and designs, and the supply of resources; and government policy, through support for R&D, investment subsidies, demonstration programmes and regulatory changes.

If the drivers for change prove to be stronger than the barriers in the specific technological and institutional setting, then increasing returns to the adoption of the new technology can kick in, leading to a *market expansion* phase. This is characterised by: emergence of a 'dominant design'; rapid market growth, as niche markets grow and coalesce; 'cumulative causation', in the form of adaptive expectations of further market growth; and eventual market saturation.

Recent work has examined in more detail the processes by which new technologies or organisational changes challenge the existing dominant regime. Again, positive feedbacks are important, as the functions may interact through 'virtuous cycles', i.e. successful activities relating to one function enable other functions to be successfully performed, leading to a process of cumulative causation (Hekkert *et al.*, 2007). For example, an increase in entrepreneurial activities may stimulate development of new knowledge and increases in lobbying and advocacy activities, creating higher expectations and guiding the search patterns of other actors. Similarly, in Spain, a supportive institutional framework for renewable energy, in the form of a 'feed-in' tariff system providing price support for renewable technologies, created pressure for investment in wind farms by incumbent firms. This led to development of relevant technological capabilities by these firms and lobbying by them for further enhancement of the feed-in system in a virtuous cycle leading to high levels of wind power adoption by the incumbents (Stenzel and Frenzel, 2007).

## 5 Non-optimality and systems failure

Systems of innovation approaches incorporate evolutionary economic ideas, referred to in Section 2. So, innovation systems help to guide firms in the process of *searching* for better routines, and influence the *selection* of successful routines, in terms of technical capability and market needs. Recent work has analysed the co-evolution of technologies, institutions and business strategies in creating wealth in Western countries (Nelson, 2005; Beinhocker, 2007) and in contributing to the innovation and deployment of renewable energy technologies and more sustainable business practices (Parrish and Foxon, 2009; Foxon *et al.*, 2010).

This has particular implications for the rationale for policy intervention. As firms have bounded rationality and operate under conditions of uncertainty, it implies that learning-by-doing, learning-by-using and learning-by-interacting, knowledge and skills, and positive expectations are important in promoting innovation. Together these imply that an innovation system never reaches a state of equilibrium: innovations are constantly occurring, through search and selection processes. Hence, it is not possible to specify an 'optimal' system of innovation (Foxon, 2007b).

The rationale for policy intervention, though, is usually framed in terms of 'correcting for market failure'. Following the principles of neo-classical welfare economics, well-functioning markets lead to 'Pareto optimal' states, in which no individual can be made better off without making another worse off. Whilst it is recognized that markets are never perfect in practice, these imperfections are referred to as 'externalities' and policy interventions are justified on the basis of correcting for these externalities to recover, as far as possible, the Pareto optimal solution. In considering environmental innovation, two main types of externality are recognized: the environmental externality, e.g. carbon emissions which have no value in market transactions, and the innovation externality. The latter arises from the fact that new knowledge, once created, is relatively easy to copy, so that the private returns to the innovator are less than the social returns of the benefit of the innovation to society, and hence there is a disincentive for private firms to undertake innovation.

The standard policy prescription is to argue for two different types of policy: generally, taxes or tradable permit systems to address environmental externalities, and support for R&D or other incentives to increase the rate of innovation. However, in practice, the two types of externality interact, further reducing the incentives to undertake environmental innovation (Jaffe *et al.*, 2005). Hence, policy measures which address these externalities separately may be too weak to promote socially-desirable levels of innovation. In the systems approach, because it is not possible to specify an optimal system of innovation, there is no clear notion of 'market failure' defined by comparing an existing innovation system to an optimal innovation system. For these two reasons, it is desirable to have a rationale for policy intervention which incorporates systems ideas.

Hence, the concept of 'systems failure' has been proposed as an alternative rationale for policy interventions (Edquist, 1994, 2001; Smith, 1992, 2000). This advocates undertaking concrete empirical and comparative analyses, using innovation systems concepts, to identify systems failures that can be rectified. These are defined in relation to objectives that have been socially-defined, through some public policy process. Two conditions must then be fulfilled for public intervention to be justified in a market economy (Edquist, 2001):

1    market mechanisms and firms fail to achieve the socially-defined objectives, i.e. a *problem* must exist;
2    public agencies must have the *ability* to solve or mitigate the problem, i.e. the issue of potential government and bureaucratic failure must be addressed.

In many cases, this concept of systems failure leads to similar or identical policy prescriptions to the concept of market failure, e.g. the use of market-based instruments to internalise negative environmental externalities. The crucial difference, however, is that it does not presume that public policy interventions can re-create ideal market solutions. This implies that an adaptive approach to policy-making is needed, emphasising the roles of policy learning and interactions with stakeholders (Foxon *et al.*, 2005; Foxon and Pearson, 2008).

Smith (2000) identifies four areas of systems or systemic failure, which could provide a rationale for specific policy interventions:

### 5.1  Failures in infrastructure provision and investment

Both physical infrastructures, such as for energy and communications, and science-technology infrastructures, such as universities, technical institutes and regulatory agencies, are important parts of innovation systems. However, because of their large scale, indivisibilities and very long time horizons of operation, private investors may fail to provide these sufficiently, and so there is a case for public support for infrastructure provision.

### 5.2  Transition failures

Because existing firms, especially small firms, are necessarily quite limited in their technological capabilities and horizons, they are likely to experience great difficulties in responding to technological changes due to developments outside their area of expertise, changes in technological opportunities or patterns of demand which push the market into new areas of technology, or major shifts in technological regimes or paradigms. Public policies may be used to help firms to cope with such changes.

### 5.3  Lock-in failures

Path dependence, due to system or network externalities combined with the fact that technologies are closely linked to their social and economic environment, can lead to 'lock-in' of existing technologies, creating barriers to the innovation and adoption of new technologies (Arthur, 1989; Unruh, 2000, 2002, 2006). New technologies must compete not only with an existing dominant technology, but also challenge the overall technological and institutional system in which it is embedded. This requires public policies to generate incentives for new technologies or technological systems, and to overcome barriers created by the prevalence of the incumbent technology or system.

### 5.4 Institutional failures

The set of public and private institutions, regulatory systems and the policy system creates a framework of opportunities and barriers to innovation by firms. Hence, the performance of these institutions and systems in regard to innovation should be monitored and assessed, and if they are judged to be creating unnecessary barriers, this would provide a rationale for policy changes or interventions.

## 6 Policy implications

The proposed policy response for identifying and addressing system failures is as follows (Foxon, 2007b). First, undertake empirical analyses of innovation systems, including comparative analyses between countries where appropriate. Second, identify system failures occurring within these systems, e.g. by identifying where the system is failing to fulfil any of the seven functions of innovation systems. Third, propose policy measures to address the systems failures. These should be appropriate to the stage of technological development and to the characteristics of the relevant national innovation system, such as current institutional frameworks and the level of skills developments. Finally, assess the likely effectiveness of policy measures, through the use of international comparisons and/or the development of socio-technical scenarios (Elzen *et al.*, 2004; Hofman *et al.*, 2004).

This concept of systems failure was applied in a study of UK renewable energy innovation systems. This identified systems failures relating to renewable energy technologies moving from the demonstration to pre-commercial (e.g. for wave and tidal power) and pre-commercial to supported commercial (e.g. offshore wind) stages of development (Foxon *et al.*, 2005b). The policy implications of the systems failure argument are discussed further in Chapter 7.

### Note

1  The counter-argument by Friedman (1953) that real firms behave 'as if' they are profit-maximisers, because only those firms will survive market competition, assumes the existence of perfect markets, which is highly unlikely in the face of rapid technological change and environmental and other externalities.

### References

Allen, R. (2009), *The British Industrial Revolution in Global Perspective*, Cambridge University Press.
Arrow, K. (1962), 'The economic implications of learning by doing', *Review of Economic Studies* 29, 155–173.

Arthur, W. B. (1989), 'Competing technologies, increasing returns, and lock-in by historical events', *The Economic Journal* 99, 116–131.

Arthur, W. B. (1994), *Increasing Returns and Path Dependence in the Economy*, University of Michigan Press.

Beinhocker, E. (2006), *The Origin of Wealth: Evolution, Complexity and the Radical Remaking of Economics*, Random House, London.

Bergek, A., Jacobsson, S., Carlsson, B., Lindmark, S. and Rickne, A. (2008), 'Analyzing the functional dynamics of technological innovation systems: A scheme of analysis', *Research Policy* 37, 407–429.

Carlsson, B. and Stankiewicz, R. (1991), 'On the nature, function and composition of technological systems', *Journal of Evolutionary Economics* 1, 93–118.

Cowan, R. (1990), 'Nuclear power reactors: A study in technological lock-in', *Journal of Economic History* 50, 801–814.

David, P. (1985), 'Clio and the economics of QWERTY', *American Economic Review* 75, 332–337.

Dosi, G. (1982), 'Technological paradigms and technological trajectories', *Research Policy* 11, 147–162.

Dosi, G., Freeman, C., Nelson, R., Silverberg, G., and Soete, L. (1988), *Technical Change and Economic Theory*, Pinter Publishers, London.

Edquist, C. (1994), 'Technology policy: The interaction between governments and markets', in *Technology Policy: Towards an Integration of Social and Ecological Concerns*, Aichholzer, G. and Schienstock, G. (eds), Walter de Gruyter, Berlin.

Edquist, C. (2001), 'Innovation policy – a systemic approach', in *The Globalizing Learning Economy*, Archibugi, D. and Lundvall, B.-A. (eds), Oxford University Press, Oxford.

Elzen, B., Geels, F., Hofman, P. S., and Green, K. (2004), 'Sociotechnical Scenarios as a Tool for Transition Policy: an Example from the Traffic and Transport Domain', in Elzen, B., Geels, F. W. and Green, K. (eds), *System Innovation and the Transition to Sustainability – Theory, Evidence and Policy*, Edward Elgar, Cheltenham.

Foxon, T. J. (2003), *Inducing Innovation for a Low-carbon Future: Drivers, barriers and policies*, Carbon Trust, London, also available at www.thecarbontrust.co.uk/Publications/publicationdetail.htm?productid=CT-2003-07.

Foxon, T. J. (2007a), 'Technological lock-in and the role of innovation', in Atkinson, G., Dietz, S. and Neumayer, E. (eds), *Handbook of Sustainable Development*, Edward Elgar, Cheltenham.

Foxon, T. J. (2007b), 'The rationale for policy interventions from an innovation systems perspective', in *Governing Technology for Sustainability*, Murphy, J. (ed.), Earthscan, London.

Foxon, T. J., Gross, R., Chase, A., Howes, J., Arnall, A. and Anderson, D. (2005), 'UK innovation systems for new and renewable energy technologies: drivers, barriers and systems failures', *Energy Policy* 33 (16), 2123–2137.

Foxon, T. J., and Pearson, P. (2007), 'Towards Improved Policy Processes for Promoting Innovation in Renewable Electricity Technologies in the UK, *Energy Policy* 35(3), 1539–1550.

Foxon, T. J., Pearson, P., Makuch, Z. and Mata, M. (2005), Transforming policy processes to promote sustainable innovation: some guiding principles, Report for policy makers, ESRC Sustainable Technologies Programme, ISBN 1 903144 02 7, March 2005 www.sustainabletechnologies.ac.uk/PDF/project%20reports/SI_policy_guidance_ final_version.pdf.

Foxon T. J., Stenzel, T. and Pearson, P. J. (2010), 'Industrial dynamics and firms' strategies for renewable energy innovation: a co-evolutionary approach', *Journal of Economic Behaviour and Organization* (submitted).

Freeman, C. (1987), *Technology and Economic Performance: Lessons from Japan*, Pinter Publishers, London.

Freeman, C. (1988), 'Japan: a new national system of innovation?', in Dosi *et al.* (1988).

Freeman, C. and Soete, L. (1997), *The Economics of Industrial Innovation* (3rd edn), Pinter, London.

Friedman, M. (1953), 'The methodology of positive economics', in *Essays in Positive Economics*, University of Chicago Press.

Grubler, A. (1998), *Technology and Global Change*, Cambridge University Press.

Hicks, J. (1932), *The Theory of Wages*, Macmillan, London.

Hofman, P., Elzen, B. and Geels, F. (2004), 'Sociotechnical scenarios as a new tool to explore system innovations: Co-evolution of technology and society in the Netherlands' energy system', *Innovation: Management, Policy and Practice* 6 (2), 344–360.

Jacobsson, S. and Bergek, A. (2004), 'Transforming the energy sector: the evolution of technology systems in renewable energy technology', *Industrial and Corporate Change* 13 (5), 815–849.

Jaffe, A., Newell, R. and Stavins, R. (2003), 'Technological change and the environment', in Mäler, K.-G. and Vincent, J. (eds), *Handbook of Environmental Economics*, Elsevier, North-Holland.

Jaffe, A., Newell, R., and Stavins, R. (2005), 'A tale of two market failures: Technology and environmental policy', *Ecological Economics*, 54, 164–174.

Kemp, R. (1997), *Environmental Policy and Technical Change*, Edward Elgar, Cheltenham.

Lundvall, B.-A. (1988), 'Innovation as an interactive process: from user-producer interaction to the national system of innovation', in Dosi *et al.* (1988).

Lundvall, B.-A. (ed.) (1992), *National Systems of Innovation: Towards a Theory of Innovation and Interactive Learning*, Pinter Publishers, London.

Malerba, F. (ed.) (2004), *Sectoral Systems of Innovation: Concepts, Issues and Analyses of six major sectors in Europe*, Cambridge University Press, Cambridge.

MacKenzie, D. (1992), 'Economic and sociological explanations of technological change', in *Technological Change and Company Strategies: Economic and Sociological Perspectives*, Coombs, R., Saviotti, P. and Walsh, V. (eds), Academic Press (reprinted in MacKenzie [1996]).

MacKenzie, D. (1996), *Knowing Machines: Essays on Technical Change*, MIT Press, Cambridge, MA.

Nelson, R. (1993), *National Innovation Systems: A Comparative Analysis*, Oxford University Press, New York.

Nelson, R. (2005), *Technology, Institutions and Economic Growth*, Harvard University Press.

Nelson, R. and Winter, S. (1982), *An Evolutionary Theory of Economic Change*, Harvard University Press, Cambridge, MA.

North, D. C. (1990), *Institutions, Institutional Change and Economic Performance*, Cambridge University Press, Cambridge.

Organisation for Economic Co-operation and Development (OECD) (1999), *Managing National Innovation Systems*, OECD, Paris.

OECD (2002), *Dynamising National Innovation Systems*, OECD, Paris.

OECD (2005), *Governance of Innovation Systems: Vol. 1: Synthesis Report* (Remoe, S.-O., ed.), OECD, Paris.

Parrish, B. D. and Foxon, T. J. (2009), 'Sustainability Entrepreneurship and Equitable Transitions to a Low-Carbon Economy', *Greener Management International*, Issue 55, 47–62.

Pierson, P. (2000), 'Increasing returns, path dependence, and the study of politics', *American Political Science Review*, 94 (2), 251–267.

Rosenberg, N. (1982), *Inside the Black Box: Technology and Economics*, Cambridge University Press.

Ruttan, V. W. (2001), *Technology, Growth and Development: An Induced Innovation Perspective*, Oxford University Press, New York.

Schumpeter, J. A. (1911/1934), *The Theory of Economic Development*, Harvard Univeristy Press, Cambridge, MA.

Schumpeter, J. A. (1939), *Business Cycles*, 2 Vols, McGraw-Hill, New York.

Simon, H. A. (1955), 'A behavioral model of rational choice', *Quarterly Journal of Economics* 69, 1–18.

Simon, H. A. (1959), 'Theories of decision making in economics', *American Economic Review* 49, 258–283.

Smith, K. (1992), 'Innovation policy in an evolutionary context', in Saviotti, P. and Metcalfe, J. S. (eds), *Evolutionary Theories of Economic and Technological Change: Present Status and Future Prospects*, Harwood Academic Publishers, Reading.

Smith, K. (2000), 'Innovation as a systemic phenomenon: Rethinking the role of policy', *Enterprise & Innovation Management Studies*, 1 (1), 73–102.

Stenzel, T. and Frenzel, A. (2007), 'Regulating technological change: The strategic reactions of utility companies towards subsidy policies in the German, Spanish and UK electricity markets', *Energy Policy*, 36 (7), 2645–2657.

Stern, N. (2007), *The Economics of Climate Change – The Stern Review*, Cambridge University Press, Cambridge.

Unruh, G. C. (2000), 'Understanding carbon lock in', *Energy Policy* 28, 817–830.

Unruh, G. C. (2002), 'Escaping carbon lock in', *Energy Policy* 30, 317–325.

Unruh, G. C. (2006), 'Globalizing carbon lock-in,' *Energy Policy* 34, 1185–97.

Van der Steen, M. (1999), *Evolutionary Systems of Innovations*, Van Gorcum Press, the Netherlands.

Williamson, O. E. (2000), 'The new institutional economics: Taking stock, looking ahead', *Journal of Economic Literature* 38 (September 2000), 595–613.

# 7 Policy support for environmental innovation

*Timothy J. Foxon*

## 1 Introduction

This chapter discusses policy support for environmental innovation, building on the systems perspective described in Chapter 6. It begins by reviewing the arguments around the so-called Porter hypothesis, that well-designed regulation can promote environmental innovation in a way that is also economically beneficial. The broader case for direct support for environmental innovation is then given, leading on to the types of policy instrument in relation to 'systems failure' arguments. Examples are then given of policy instruments to address systems failures in UK innovation systems for renewable energy technologies, and of a longer-term strategic policy framework to promote a transition to a low carbon economy.

## 2 Porter hypothesis and related arguments

There are two lines of argument put forward for the need for environmental innovation policy. The theoretical argument is that the neo-classical rationale for environmental innovation policy is limited, because the theory has an inadequate representation of innovation systems. The empirically-based argument is that regulation can be used to promote environmental innovation, generating 'win-win' solutions. We begin by addressing the latter, commonly referred to as the Porter hypothesis, after the arguments made by Michael Porter and colleagues (Porter, 1991; Porter and van der Linde, 1995a, 1995b), though essentially the same argument had previously been made by Nicholas Ashford (Ashford *et al.*, 1985; Ashford, 1993, 2000).

Porter's starting point, drawing on his research on strategic management (Porter, 1985), is that the competitive advantage of firms rests on their capacity for innovation. Neo-classical economists generally assume that, for firms operating in competitive markets, forcing those firms to meet regulatory standards will necessarily push up their costs. However, Porter argued that well-designed environmental regulation can trigger innovation giving rise to economic benefits that may offset the costs of compliance, so-called 'innovation offsets'. In this case, these offsets could lead to both reductions in environmental damage and competitive advantage for firms undertaking the innovation. For example, advantages could accrue to firms that are first movers in developing a new product or service that is then widely taken up. Porter argues, for example, that firms in countries that have strong environmental legislation promoting innovation are likely to have an advantage in that they will be a good position to export the results of that innovation when other countries introduce similar legislation. Thus, the Porter hypothesis argues that there are 'win-win' opportunities to be grasped that are both economically and environmentally beneficial, and that these can be promoted by the use of 'good quality' regulation.

This argument flies in the face of neo-classical economic thinking, and critics of Porter and van der Linde's paper called their argument 'somewhat astonishing' (Palmer *et al.*, 1995, p. 119). The criticism starts from the assumption that firms typically operate at or near the 'efficiency frontier', i.e. they minimse their private production costs. So, environmental regulations will necessarily raise costs, by forcing firms to take actions that they would not otherwise take. Furthermore, even if there were potential benefits to firms stimulated to make investments in reducing their environmental impacts, these investments should be judged against the 'opportunity cost' of other investments not made, because they have been 'crowded out'. Finally, the critique focuses on the question of why should regulators better understand the potential for efficiency improvements than firms themselves.

The response by Porter and others focuses on the dynamic incentives for innovation, potentially provided by flexible regulation. Porter (1985) argues that innovation is a key source of economic competitiveness, and so drivers for innovation do not just come from firms attempting to minimise their private costs. This fits well with innovation systems approaches, which emphasise the wider social and institutional drivers of innovation. More specifically, he argues that pollution is a form of economic waste, through inefficient use of natural resources. Innovation in production processes, which reduces or eliminates waste at source, is likely to be more economically beneficial to the firm than 'end-of-pipe' clean-up measures. This is similar to incentives to improve product quality, which are more likely to be successful when incorporated into the entire production process, rather than seen as an 'add-on' feature. Regulators do not need perfect information to stimulate change, because policy is based on social objectives. Furthermore, empirical evidence from a large number of case studies suggests that firms forced to search for efficiency improvements often find huge opportunities. Similar arguments for the potential for 'Factor Four' improvements in the efficiency with which firms use resources have been put forward by Amory Lovins and colleagues (von Weizsacker *et al.*, 1997; Hawken *et al.*, 1999).

However, it is clear that regulation needs to be 'well-designed' in order to promote economically beneficial outcomes (Ashford, 1993; Porter and van der Linde, 1995; Foxon and Kemp, 2006). Key criteria for well-designed regulation are:

- Set strict standards to promote innovation, but with flexibility as to the means;
- Focus on desired environmental outcomes, not particular technologies;
- Use market incentives to promote continuous environmental improvements;

- Make regulatory processes more stable and predictable, in order for firms to be able to undertake long-term planning;
- Employ phase-in periods, to enable firms to make innovations in line with normal capital turnover;
- Promote reduction at source, through input substitution, product reformulation or process re-design.

It is also important that regulatory and policy processes are improved, in order to promote better regulatory outcomes (Wallace, 1995; Kemp, 1997; Foxon *et al.*, 2005a). Greater coordination is needed of energy, environmental and innovation policies, in order to harmonise or converge policies, so that they promote consistent behaviour. This is likely to require an open, informed dialogue with stakeholders (industry, consumers, NGOs) from the beginning of regulatory process, and improvement in the competence and knowledge of regulators.

As we discussed in Chapter 6, these empirically based arguments are supported by theoretical arguments, underpinned by innovation systems theory. As discussed there, innovation is seen as a dynamic, non-linear process, and there is potential for 'systems failure' in achieving socially defined objectives. For example, technological lock-in can arise through increasing returns to adoption of technologies and associated institutions (see also Chapter 3), which prevents the innovation and adoption of potentially superior technological alternatives. This rationale for policy interventions, based on 'systems failures', goes beyond the neo-classical view of correcting for market failures. It argues that there is an interaction between innovation market failures, relating to the disincentive for private firms to innovate, as they cannot appropriate full benefits of their investment (so that social returns are greater than private returns), and environmental market failures, relating to unpriced environmental impacts (or externalities). Therefore, there are likely to be synergies arising from regulations that promote environmentally beneficial innovation. Thus, there are good theoretical, as well as empirical, arguments for policy support for environmental innovation. However, the systems theory of innovation is still incomplete and the empirical evidence is largely case-study based, and so is open to the existence of countervailing cases. Hence, further theoretical and empirical research, and closer relations between the two, are needed to strengthen the arguments for desirable innovation being driven by well-designed environmental regulation.

## 3 Types of policy instruments to promote environmental innovation

The case for direct support for environmental innovation is based on three related theoretical arguments (Anderson *et al.*, 2001; Gross and Foxon, 2003). First, the existence of positive externalities, i.e. opportunities and sources of productivity gain for future generations, relating to increases in environmental benefits. Second, it serves to create options for achieving environmental goals and reduce uncertainties, and so helps to define a dynamic path forward. Third, it creates opportunities for reducing costs, e.g. through 'learning-by-doing', so that technologies become competitive in self-sustaining markets.

As has been argued by the Stern Review on the economics of climate change (Stern, 2007), three types of policy instrument are needed to promote innovation to address climate change and other environmental problems:

- Measures to put a price on carbon emissions and other environmental externalities, such as a carbon tax or emissions trading scheme;
- Measures to promote technological innovation and deployment directly, as discussed below;
- Measures to alleviate institutional and other non-markets barriers that prevent the take-up of energy efficiency and low carbon alternatives, such as shared benefit schemes to overcome split incentives between landlords and tenants.

Measures to promote environmental innovation and deployment directly again cover three main types:

1 Basic R&D;
2 Market development policies;
3 Financial incentives.

Again, it is likely that a mix of all these types of instrument will be needed. The exact mix of instruments, and how they complement measures to price externalities and alleviate non-market barriers, will depend on the particular environmental problem and the political and institutional circumstances relating to their implementation (Alic *et al.*, 2003; Rennings *et al.*, 2003).

## 1 Basic R&D

As noted above, there is a well-known and widely accepted argument for government support for basic research and development (R&D). This is that the social returns to innovation exceed the private returns, since it is relatively easy for other firms to copy the knowledge needed once it has been developed, and so the level of innovation by private firms will be less than the socially desirable level. Hence, there is a strong case for public support for the earliest stages of innovation. Applying an evolutionary metaphor, R&D helps to create the variation, from which successful technologies can be selected.

## 2 Market development policies

Market development policies include long range targets and obligations; strategic niche management; and back-loading support.

*Long-range targets and obligations* should be defined in terms of environmental outcomes, rather than particular technologies, to maximise flexibility and encourage competition between different means of achieving the desired end. An example is provided by the California Zero-emission Vehicle (ZEV) Mandate

(Kemp, 2005). This was enacted by the California Air Resources Board in 1990, with the requirement that 10 per cent of the new cars offered for sale in California from 2003 would have to be zero emissions vehicles (ZEVs). This gave a relatively long time-scale for manufacturers to develop the technologies, and was based on a clear environmental outcome, i.e. zero local emissions. The flexibility of this mandate meant that, though it was originally designed with battery electric vehicles in mind, it helped to stimulate the development of hydrogen fuel cell powered vehicles and hybrid vehicles. Indeed, the ability to point to the intended market created by the ZEV Mandate was crucial in enabling the pioneering Canadian fuel cell developer Ballard to obtain private and public investment. However, the Mandate was fiercely opposed by the large auto manufacturers, and continued lobbying led to the postponement of the date of implementation and increased complexity of the regulations, for example, to allow for partial ZEV credits for hybrid vehicles. Thus, though the ZEV Mandate was relatively successful, it was not a simple story and illustrates the difficulties of overcoming incumbent vested interests to promote innovation.

Similarly, the Renewables Obligation, enacted by the UK government in 2002, placed an obligation on electricity suppliers to source an annually increasing proportion of their generation from renewable sources. Again, this was a long-term obligation, with the required proportion initially increasing from 3 per cent in 2003 to 10 per cent in 2010, and designed to remain in place at least at that level until 2026. The level of the Obligation has since been increased in further annual steps to 15 per cent in 2015, and subsequently to allow for further increases on a 'headroom' basis, to ensure a continuing long-term stretching target. The Obligation has been successful in creating a market for near-commercial renewable technologies, particularly onshore and offshore wind. However, it has not been so successful at stimulating other early-stage renewables that are currently further from commercialisation, leading to innovation 'systems failures' for these technologies (Foxon *et al.*, 2005b). It has been argued that mechanisms employed in some other European countries, such as 'feed-in tariffs' that provide a guaranteed price for renewable electricity generated, which differs for different technologies, have been more successful in stimulating a higher and more diverse level of renewables deployment (Mitchell *et al.*, 2006).

*Strategic niche management* relates to measures to create niche markets for new innovations, so that they can benefit from 'learning-by-doing', leading to cost reductions and performance improvements (Kemp *et al.*, 1998; Hoogma *et al.*, 2003). Strategic market niches can either be in the form of pilot projects in specific, local areas, or in particular sub-markets, for example through the use of public procurement programmes. Public procurement may also be used to support a number of small-scale demonstration projects, for example in schools or public bodies.

Public procurement may also be used as a form of *back-loading* support for innovation. This could involve offering prizes for innovative technologies that secure particular environmental objectives. The prize could be financial, or the reward could be in the form of a guaranteed niche market for the technology. Such a policy would provide a high profile launch pad for innovation. This type of prize has a long history – the most famous example being the prize offered by the British Admiralty in the eighteenth century for a precise way of measuring longitude at sea, which stimulated the development of the world's then most accurate clock (Sobel, 1998).

## *3 Financial incentives*

There is also a range of types of financial incentive for promoting innovation:

### *Capital subsidies*

Capital grants are usually aimed at supporting technologies in the early demonstration phase, when firms find difficulty in raising private investment for new technologies that are still seen as high risk. Capital grants of this type were provided in the UK for biomass energy crops and offshore wind development.

### *Tax credits*

Tax credits provide an alternative means for supporting investment in cost-effective technology improvements, by offsetting a proportion of the tax that would otherwise be payable by firms. In the UK, this has taken the form of Enhanced Capital Allowances for firms investing in specified energy efficiency improvements.

### *Hypothecation of revenues*

Hypothecation refers to the direct allocation of some or all of the revenues raised from other fiscal instruments to support innovation. For example, some of the revenue raised from the UK Climate Change Levy on the use of energy by businesses was allocated to setting up the Carbon Trust, which supports the innovation and deployment of low carbon technologies. It is argued that hypothecation is justified as an effective use of revenues, which also helps to create public acceptability for the original revenue-raising instrument. However, it tends to be unpopular with government treasuries, as it enforces limits on the flexibility of government spending.

### *New financing institution*

The creation of a new financing institution could help to lever private funding. An example is provided by the UN's Global Environmental Facility, which supports the deployment of environmental technologies in developing countries.

## 4 Informing the policy process to promote sustainable innovation

The range of types of policy instrument for promoting environmentally sustainable innovation leads to the question of how policy makers should determine an appropriate mix of instruments. Whilst the exact mix of instruments will depend on the particular environmental issue and the political and institutional circumstances, it is possible to examine how policy processes could effectively address this issue.

In work done by the author and colleagues at Imperial College London, we investigated policy processes to promote sustainable innovation (SI), through literature review, case studies and interactions with stakeholders from the policy-making, business and academic communities. This led to a set of guidelines for SI policy processes (Foxon *et al.*, 2005a; Foxon and Pearson, 2008):

1   Stimulate the development of an SI policy regime, bringing together *innovation, energy* and *environmental policy regimes*:
    These policies are currently largely addressed in separate regimes, with their own aims and criteria. Organisational changes are needed to bring these regimes together and to make sustainable innovation an explicit goal of policy making. The creation of the Department for Energy and Climate Change in November 2008 could be an important step towards this in the UK. An SI policy regime would also involve facilitating *systemic changes* to current technological and institutional systems; creating a *long-term, stable and consistent strategic framework* to promote a transition to more sustainable systems; and formulating clear, *long-term sustainability goals*. The Dutch transition management approach, discussed below, could provide an exemplar for promoting such long-term systemic change.

2   Apply *systems thinking and practice*:
    This would involve engaging with the complexity and systemic interactions of innovation systems and policy-making processes, to promote a transition to sustainability. For example, this could involve developing and applying the concept of *systems failures* as a rationale for public policy intervention; taking advantage of the appearance of 'techno-economic' and 'policy' *windows' of opportunity*; and promoting a *diversity of technology and institutional options* to overcome 'lock-in' of unsustainable technologies and supporting institutions.

3   Advance the *procedural and institutional basis* for delivery of SI policy aims:
    Delivering SI policy would require more effective interactions between policy makers and wider stakeholders. This could involve developing *public/private institutional structures* to enhance regulator/regulated relationships and stakeholder activities. It would also be important to ensure broad *stakeholder participation*, particularly from the *innovation constituency*, i.e. those innovative small firms and entrepreneurs who may need financial or other incentives to enable their involvement in policy-making processes.

4   Develop a more *coherent and integrated mix* of policy instruments to promote sustainable innovation:
    In order to ascertain whether certain types of instrument are likely to give rise to synergies when employed together, policy makers could apply *sustainability indicators* and *sustainable innovation criteria*; assess *benefits and costs* of likely economic, environmental and social impacts; utilise a

*dedicated SI risk assessment tool* in developing policy support instruments; and assess instruments in terms of appropriateness to *stages of the innovation process.*

5    Incorporate *policy learning* and *review* as an integral part of SI policy process:
To ensure that measures are successfully promoting sustainable innovation in practice, an iterative process of policy learning and review is likely to be necessary. This could involve learning at three levels: direct *monitoring and evaluation* of policy implementation; review of policy *impacts on sustainable innovation systems*; and learning to *enrich the policy process* itself.

## 5  Example – UK innovation systems for renewables

An example of a systems approach to the analysis of support for environmentally sustainable innovation is provided by the analysis of UK innovation systems for renewable energy technologies by the author and colleagues (Anderson *et al.*, 2003; Foxon *et al.*, 2003; Foxon *et al.*, 2005b). This work was undertaken as part of the former UK Department of Trade and Industry's Renewables Innovation Review. This involved the analysis of the UK innovation systems for six low-carbon technology areas: *wind, marine, solar PV, biomass, hydrogen from renewables* and *district and micro-CHP*. For each area, the key technologies and actors, flows of knowledge, influence and funding, and framework conditions were identified, following a methodology derived from the OECD (2002) national innovation systems approach (see Chapter 6). This included interviewing key stakeholders from industry and policy-making for each of these areas. A 'map' of the innovation system was produced for each technology area. An important finding was that different technologies were at different stages of development along the 'innovation chain' towards commercialisation.

This led to the identification of 'systems failures' in progressing certain renewables technologies along the innovation chain. For example, for early stage technologies, such as wav e and tidal power, there was a failure identified in going from first demonstration to pre-commercial stage, since it is difficult to get investment for scaling up, and the market pull from the Renewables Obligation (RO) is still too weak. This could be an example of where niche support would be helpful. For technologies that are more developed, such as offshore wind, a failure was identified in going from the pre-commercial stage to (supported) commercial, under the RO. These technologies still face multiple risks in relation to developing the technology, creating a market, responding to regulatory changes, and how the technology fits with existing systems and networks. This suggests a need to improve the risk/reward ratio for investment at this stage (Gross *et al.*, 2007).

In general, to address these systems failures and promote the successful innovation and deployment of renewable technologies, there is a need for a shared vision of technology development, and a need for perseverance of policy frameworks. Since that study was undertaken, the UK government has made

moves to strengthen the renewables policy framework, and to address some of
the failures. It has introduced banding of the Renewables Obligation, so that
early stage technologies qualify for multiple certificates, providing greater incentive for investment. In 2008, it undertook a Renewables Consultation on further
measures to meet the UK's target of 15 per cent of final energy (electricity,
heating and transport) from renewables by 2020, under the EU energy and
climate policy, agreed in December 2008. As was confirmed in the 2009 Renewable Energy Strategy, this implies meeting at least 30 per cent of UK electricity
from renewables by 2020, which would represent a step-change in levels of
activity (DECC, 2009; Committee on Climate Change, 2009).

## 6 Long-term frameworks – example of transition management

As noted, a major challenge for promoting environmentally sustainable innovation is to overcome the technological and institutional lock-in of existing
systems, which have benefited from long periods of increasing returns to adoption. This is likely to require not only incremental innovation, but also radical
systems-level change. In order to achieve such a systems change in a way that
ensures that services continue to be provided during the change, e.g. ensuring
sufficient power to keep the lights on, a stable, long-term policy framework is
required. A long-term framework for promoting systems change to address per-
sistent environmental problems has been developed in the Netherlands, referred
to as *transition management*.

Transition management was adopted as a policy-making process as part of the
4th Netherlands Environmental Policy Plan (NMP4), published in 2000 (see
Rotmans *et al.*, 2001; Kemp and Rotmans, 2005). It is now being implemented with
the 'energy transition' being led by the Dutch Ministry of Economic Affairs (2006).
This has so far involved the formulation of 26 transition paths, from four transition
platforms (with the themes of 'sustainable mobility', 'new gas and clean fossil
fuels', 'green raw materials' and 'chain efficiency'). For each platform, the aim is to
agree with stakeholders a strategic vision for the industry sector to 2050. In return,
the government agrees to provide political commitment and seeks to integrate the
relevant policy areas. The stakeholders, working together in a 'transition arena',
then agree long-term goals and transition paths for the period up to 2020. They then
undertake transition experiments along these paths, e.g. providing support for
niches, for a range of technology options. These experiments typically involve collaboration between technology developers, industrial partners, local authorities and
community groups, and are designed to test the social and technological feasibility
as well as the acceptability of the transition paths (Dietz, 2008). Thus, the transition
approach seeks to apply both technology and policy learning at all stages.

Of course, no single approach provides a panacea, and a framework
developed in one country needs to be adapted to the political and institutional
circumstances in other countries. There are also concerns that the transitions
approach risks capture by the incumbent energy regime, thereby undermining

the ambition for radical innovation of the energy system. This is exemplified by the fact that the Dutch energy transition taskforce, set up in 2005 to oversee the transition process and identify strategic directions, is chaired by the CEO of Shell Netherlands (Kern and Smith, 2007). However, the Dutch transitions approach provides useful ideas and lessons for developing long-term frameworks for promoting sustainable innovation for systems change.

The UK has begun to move towards a long-term framework by setting the legally binding target of an 80 per cent reduction in greenhouse gas emissions by 2050 under the Climate Change Act (2008). This involves setting five-yearly carbon budgets for emissions reductions towards that target, based on the recommendations of an independent Committee on Climate Change (2008, 2009). In July 2009, the UK government published its Low Carbon Transition Plan for meeting the first three carbon budgets, leading to a 34 per cent reduction in emissions on 1990 levels by 2020 (HM Government, 2009). The main measures to achieve this focus on reducing the carbon-intensity of electricity generation, through 30 per cent generation from renewables, four demonstration plants for capturing and storing carbon emissions from coal power stations, and facilitating the building of new nuclear power station by streamlining planning and licensing processes. Other measures aim to improve energy efficiency of homes, through incentives for insulation and smart meters, and to impose a long-range obligation on auto manufacturers to reduce emissions from new cars across the EU to $95gCO_2$/km by 2020. Despite rhetorical claims that the Plan will help by make the UK a centre of green industry, the additional levels of investment proposed are relatively small. There is also some scepticism about whether the other targets will be reached, particularly the 30 per cent renewable generation target. This shows that, as in the Dutch approach, long-term frameworks need to be complemented by shorter-term actions to demonstrate the feasibility and viability of proposed solutions.

## 7 Summary

This chapter has argued that there is a strong case for using well-designed environmental regulation, alongside other policy instruments, to promote environmental innovation, as suggested by the Porter hypothesis. Overcoming lock-in and promoting a transition to more sustainable systems may also require a long-term, strategic framework. The ideas presented here could provide a useful start, but more theoretical analysis and empirical evidence is needed to find appropriate mixes of policy instruments to promote sustainable innovation. In this regard, policy learning of what does and does not work may be as important as technology learning.

## References

Alic, J.A., Mowery, D.C. and Rubin, E.S. (2003), *US Technology and Innovation Policies: Lessons for Climate Change*, Pew Centre on Global Climate Change.
Anderson, D., Clark, C., Foxon, T.J., Gross, R. and Jacobs, M. (2001), Innovation and the Environment: Challenges and Policy Options for the UK, London: Imperial College

Centre for Energy Policy and Technology & the Fabian Society. http://www3.imperial.ac.uk/pls/portallive/docs/1/7294721.PDF.

Anderson, D., Arnall, A., Foxon, T.J., Gross, R., Chase, A. and Howes, J. (2003), *UK innovation systems for new and renewable energy technologies*, Report for DTI, London, June 2003, www.berr.gov.uk/files/file22069.pdf.

Ashford, N.A., Ayers, C. and Stone, R.F. (1985), 'Using Regulation to Change the Market for Innovation', *Harvard Environmental Law Review* 9, 419–466.

Ashford, N.A. (1993), 'Understanding Technological Responses of Industrial Firms to Environmental Problems: Implications for Government Policy', in Fischer, K. and Schot, J. (eds), *Environmental Strategies for Industry: International Perspectives on Research Needs and Policy Implications*, Washington, DC, Island Press.

Ashford, N.A. (2000), 'An Innovation-based Strategy for a Sustainable Environment', in Hemmelskamp, J., Rennings, K. and Leone, F. (eds), *Innovation-Oriented Environmental Regulation: Theoretical Approach and Empirical Analysis*, ZEW Economic Studies, Heidelberg, New York: Springer Verlag, 67–107.

Committee on Climate Change (2008), *Building a Low Carbon Economy – the UK's contribution to tackling climate change*, First Report.

Committee on Climate Change (2009), *Meeting Carbon Budgets – the need for a step-change*, First Annual Report to Parliament.

Department for Energy and Climate Change (DECC) (2009), *The UK Renewable Energy Strategy*, The Stationery Office, London.

Dietz, F., Brouwer, H. and Weterings, R. (2008), 'Energy transition experiments in the Netherlands', in van den Bergh, J. and Bruinsma, F. (eds), *Managing the Transition to Renewable Energy: Theory and Practice from Local, Regional and Macro Perspectives*, Edward Elgar, Cheltenham.

Foxon, T.J. (2003), Inducing Innovation for a Low-Carbon Future: Drivers, Barriers and Policies, London: The Carbon Trust, also available at www.thecarbontrust.co.uk/Publications/publicationdetail.htm?productid=CT-2003–07.

Foxon, T.J., Gross, R. and Anderson, D. (2003), *Innovation in long-term renewables options in the UK: Overcoming barriers and system failures*, Report for DTI, London, November 2003, www.berr.gov.uk/files/file22072.pdf.

Foxon, T.J., Pearson, P., Makuch, Z. and Mata, M. (2005a), *Transforming policy processes to promote sustainable innovation: some guiding principles*, Report for policy makers, ESRC Sustainable Technologies Programme, ISBN 1 903144 02 7, March 2005 www.sustainabletechnologies.ac.uk/PDF/project%20reports/SI_policy_guidance_final_version.pdf.

Foxon, T.J., Gross, R., Chase, A., Howes, J., Arnall, A. and Anderson, D. (2005b), 'UK innovation systems for new and renewable energy technologies: drivers, barriers and systems failures', *Energy Policy* 33 (16), 2123–2137.

Foxon, T.J. and Kemp, R. (2007), 'Innovation impacts of environmental policies', in Marinova, D., Annandale D. and Phillimore, J. (eds), *International Handbook on Environment and Technology Management*, Edward Elgar, Cheltenham.

Foxon, T.J. and Pearson, P. (2008), 'Overcoming barriers to innovation and diffusion of cleaner technologies: some features of a sustainable innovation policy regime', *Journal of Cleaner Production*, 16 (1), Supplement 1, S148–S161.

Gross, R. and Foxon, T.J. (2003), 'Policy Support for Innovation to Secure Improvements in Resource Productivity', *International Journal of Environmental Technology and Management*, 3 (2), 118–130.

Gross, R., Heptonstall, P. and Blyth, W. (2007), *Investment in Electricity Generation: the role of costs, risks and incentives*, Report by ICEPT for the UK Energy Research Centre.

Hawken, P., Lovins, A.B. and Lovins, L.H. (1999), *Natural Capitalism: Creating the Next Industrial Revolution*, Earthscan, London.

HM Government (2009), *The UK Low Carbon Transition Plan*, The Stationery Office, London.

Hoogma, R., Kemp, R., Schot, J. and Truffler, B. (2002), *Experimenting for Sustainable Transport: The Approach of Strategic Niche Management*, London, SPON Press.

Kemp, R. (1997), *Environmental Policy and Technical Change*, Edward Elgar, Cheltenham.

Kemp, R. (2005), 'Zero emission vehicle mandate in California: misguided policy or example of enlightened leadership?', in Sartorius, C. and Zundel, S. (eds), *Time Strategies, Innovation and Environmental Policy*, Edward Elgar, Cheltenham, pp. 169–191.

Kemp, R. and Rotmans, J. (2005), 'The Management of the Co-Evoultion of Technical, Environmental and Social Systems', in Weber, M. and Hemmelskamp, J. (eds), *Towards Environmental Innovation Systems*, Springer Verlag, Berlin.

Kemp, R., Schot, J. and Hoogma, R. (1998), 'Regime Shifts to Sustainability through Processes of Niche Formation. The Approach of Strategic Niche Management', *Technology Analysis and Strategic Management*, 10 (2), 175–195.

Kern, F. and Smith, A. (2008), 'Restructuring energy systems for sustainability? Energy transition policy in the Netherlands', *Energy Policy* 36 (11), 4093–4103.

Mitchell, C., Bauknecht, D. and Connor, P. (2006), 'Effectiveness through risk reduction: A comparison of the Renewable Obligation in England and Wales and the Feed-In system in Germany', *Energy Policy* 34 (3), 297–305.

Ministry of Economic Affairs (The Netherlands) 2006. *More with Energy: Opportunities for the Netherlands*, Energy Transition Action Plan. Online: www.senternovem.nl/energytransition/downloads/index.asp.

OECD (2002), *Dynamising National Innovation Systems*, OECD, Paris.

Palmer, K., Oates, W.E. and Portney, P.R. (1995), 'Tightening Environmental Standards: The Benefit-Cost or the No-cost Paradigm?', *Journal of Economic Perspectives* 9 (4), 119–132.

Porter, M. (1985), *Competitive Advantage: Creating and Sustaining Superior Performance*, New York, Free Press.

Porter, M. (1991), 'America's Green Strategy', *Scientific American* 264, 168.

Porter, M. and van der Linde, C. (1995a), 'Green and Competitive: Ending the Stalement', *Harvard Business Review*, 73 (5), 120–134.

Porter, M. and van der Linde, C. (1995b), 'Towards a New Conceptualization of the Environment-Competitiveness Relationship', *Journal of Economic Perspectives* 9 (4), 97–118.

Rennings, K., Kemp, R., Bartolomeo, M., Hemmelskamp, J. and Hitchens, D. (2003), Blueprints for an Integration of Science, Technology and Environmental Policy (BLUEPRINT), available at www.insme.info/documenti/blueprint.pdf.

Rotmans, J., Kemp, R. and van Asselt, M. (2001), 'More evolution than revolution: transition management in public policy', *Foresight* 3, 15–31.

Sobel, D. (1998), *Longitude*, Fourth Estate, London.

Stern, N. (2007), *The Economics of Climate Change: The Stern Review*, Cambridge University Press.

Von Weizsacker, E., Lovins, A.B. and Lovins, L.H. (1997), *Factor Four: Doubling Wealth, Having Resource Use*, London: Earthscan.

Wallace, D. (1995), Environmental Policy and Industrial Innovation: Strategies in Europe, the US and Japan, London: Royal Institute of International Affairs.

# 8 A paradigm shift in economics

## Endogenous technological change in economic models of climate change policy

*Jonathan Köhler*

## 1 Introduction

The balance of evidence suggests that anthropogenic emissions of greenhouse gases (GHG) (of which $CO_2$ is the most important) are having a discernible impact on the global climate and that this impact is expected to grow stronger over the next 100 years. The Intergovernmental Panel on Climate Change (IPCC 2007) has projected increases ranging up to 6.4°C in the global average temperature by 2100, with important regional variations. Consequently, there have been international efforts to develop policies that will control or reduce GHG emissions, culminating in the proposed setting of legally binding reductions targets at the 1997 Kyoto conference. These targets have been subsequently agreed by a large number of states and, with the exception of the USA (and a few other OECD states), now ratified as the Kyoto Protocol. The initial Kyoto agreements run until 2012 and negotiations are now under way for the 'post-2012' international climate change policy, which are planned to be agreed in a conference in Copenhagen in December 2009. This policy debate has been informed by economic and engineering assessments of methods of GHG mitigation and their economic consequences.

However, these analyses have resulted in considerable controversy, in particular as to their assessments of economic costs in terms of welfare and GDP losses. The USA based its decision to withdraw from the Kyoto process in part on the perceived high cost of mitigation for the US economy. While the estimation of the economic impact of global warming is subject to a great deal of uncertainty, economic analyses have also produced widely differing estimates of the economic implications of policies (e.g. carbon taxes) for emissions reduction. Barker and Rosendahl (2000), in an analysis of carbon taxation in Europe, estimate that the Kyoto target of an 8 per cent reduction in GHG emissions from 1990 levels by 2008–2012 can be achieved with an *increase* of 0.8 per cent in EU GDP over the baseline. In contrast, Cooper *et al.* (1999), in a paper estimating the costs of the US reaching its Kyoto target without international permit trading and holding emissions at their 1990 levels after 2010, estimate that US GDP is reduced by 4 per cent below the baseline by 2020.

### The controversy about economics

In the heated policy debate around the Kyoto Protocol, the differences in cost estimates from models have been used to support the different policy positions. Barker *et al.* (2002) show that the differences are due to different theories and structures used by the different modelling teams. As will be briefly surveyed below, there is a wide range of opinions about how economies and energy systems should be modelled. The debate in macroeconomics has been particularly bitter, with a 'mainstream' community wedded to Computable General Equilibrium models (CGEs), while Barker and his collaborators (including the author) argue for a disequilibrium approach, starting from 'Keynesian macroeconometric' models.

However, this debate is being transformed. All parties to the debate, both political and academic, agree that the widespread implementation of new, low carbon technologies will be crucial to climate change mitigation. This fits in well with US policy statements and the Joint Implementation (JI) and Clean Development Mechanism (CDM) introduced in the Kyoto protocol. Furthermore, there has been a major advance in the academic literature on energy analysis with the introduction of new models of endogenous technical change. These models were initially applied to economic models of energy markets and technologies. However, these models have fundamental implications for macroeconomic cost estimates of climate change mitigation policy, such that it is now accepted that it is necessary to incorporate these ideas in macroeconomic models of climate policy.

This is a big challenge for macroeconomic modelling. This chapter will argue that it exposes the limitations of the inherently static CGE approach. Nonetheless, there is now a new consensus in the economic modelling community. This may well eventually transform 'mainstream' economic modelling, away from static equilibrium methods to dynamic processes of technological development and diffusion.

This chapter will survey the debate and discuss the dynamic economic methods that are being employed to bring a new sophistication to climate change policy analysis. Section 2 will summarise the evidence for the range of estimates of mitigation costs of models and briefly describe the concepts used to build the models. Section 3 will discuss the role of technological change in the economics of mitigation policy and argue that a new approach is needed: disequilibrium analysis of economics *and* endogenous and induced technical change. Section 4 will explain the implications of endogenous technical change for economic models and describe two of the approaches being used to model technology dynamics. Section 5 draws some policy conclusions.

## 2 Economic models of climate change mitigation

Three different types of models have been used for most mitigation cost assessments:

### 1 Models of energy technologies and their costs

These are known as bottom-up models, because they calculate costs by adding up costs of individual technologies. As will be described later, these models have led the way in incorporating endogenous technical change in the model structure. They have also generated the lowest estimates of costs of climate change mitigation. It is argued that this is because they assume that the potential of new (low Carbon) technologies can be fully exploited, whereas macroeconomists argue that the limitations imposed by the rest of the economy must be considered as well.

Two types of macroeconomic models have been used:

## 2 CGE models

These models are based on the idea of equilibrium in perfect and well behaved markets. In economics, this means that the world is represented as a series of markets for the different goods, with a demand for the good and a supply of the good. The models are solved by assuming that the economy moves (instantaneously) to a state – equilibrium – in which demand equals supply. The models work through a price of the good, with firms supplying such that their costs are at least covered by the price and purchasers demanding as much of the good as they wish at the given price. The models vary the price in order to equate demand and supply. Walras' Law shows that, under conditions of perfect competition, an equilibrium is general – all the different markets are simultaneously in equilibrium. The main characteristic of CGE models is that they have an explicit specification of the behaviour of all relevant economic agents in the economy based on neo-classical economic theory. In the mitigation applications they have usually adopted assumptions of optimising rationality, free market pricing, constant returns to scale, many firms and suppliers of factors, and perfect competition in order to provide a market-clearing equilibrium in all markets. Any deviation from the assumed optimal equilibrium to accommodate environmental policies will by definition lead to costs in these models, unless the environmental benefits of abatement are incorporated into the optimal solution.

## 3 Macroeconometric models

These models are based on the 'Keynesian' macroeconomy identity

$$Y = AY_{IO} + C + I + G + X - M$$

Demand (i.e. output) = intermediate demand + consumption + investment + government spending + exports-imports

Intermediate demand is a representation of all the intermediate steps that go into the final consumer product (e.g. for a motor car, steel, tyres, paint etc.). These intermediate relationships are summarised in 'Input-Output' tables, measurements of the inputs into any one industry and the outputs from a single industry to all the other industries in the economy.

The equations in these models are statistically estimated as time-dependent relationships from economic data using time series econometrics. This is in contrast to most CGEs, which are calibrated to fit the data of a single year. We argue that, in order to look at the long timescales of climate change policy, 10–100 years ahead, starting off in the right direction is better than just starting off at the correct level in a single year.

### *Does it matter?*

While it is interesting that these different approaches exist, if the models agree about the costs of climate change mitigation, then it is just an academic debate. Barker *et al.* (2002) consider this question. They performed a meta-analysis, collecting data on cost estimates of mitigation from articles in the literature and also from the set of models used for the IPCC SRES analysis (Nakićenović *et al.*, 2000). The spread of results is shown in Figs 8.1 (models reported in the academic literature) and 8.2 (SRES).

These figures show change in GDP from a baseline against $CO_2$ reduction. For a range of regions (mostly world or the US) they display a wide range of results, to the extent that even the sign of the change of GDP is uncertain in Figure 8.1. The SRES results have a narrower range, showing the advantage of common assumptions. A regression analysis showed that *all* the various model characteristics are significant (in one form or another) at the 1 per cent level – i.e. different models do give consistently different results, even given the same

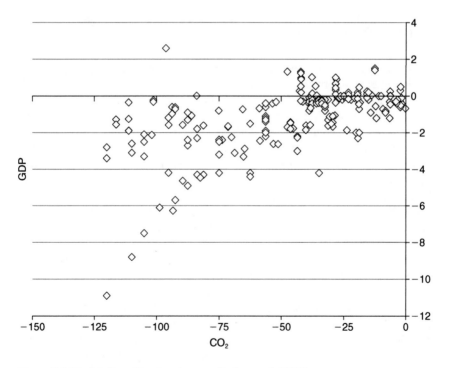

*Figure 8.1* Models from literature (source: Barker *et al.*, 2002).

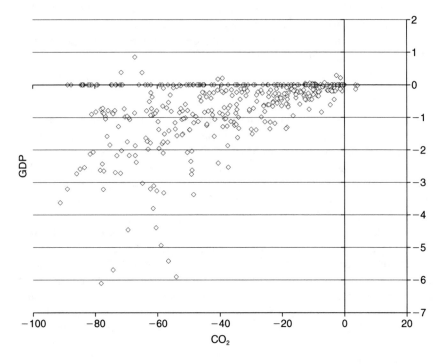

*Figure 8.2* IPCC IAM models (source: Barker *et al.*, 2002).

policy scenario. So the theoretical argument does matter, especially as these models directly inform policy making.

The importance of model structure was confirmed by the meta-analysis undertaken in the Innovation Modelling Comparison Project (IMCP). This project defined common climate change scenarios and ran a variety of climate-economy and energy-economy models, which incorporated the latest implementations of endogenous technical change (discussed in detail below). The theories applied in the models are discussed in Köhler *et al.* (2006) and results discussed in detail in Edenhofer *et al.* (2006). For a scenario of stabilisation of the atmospheric concentration of $CO_2$ at 450ppm, the change in Gross World Product in 2100 compared to the baseline ranged from more than +3.5 per cent to −10 per cent or more.

In addition to this, much of the variation results from choice of assumption, so these choices should be made explicit in reporting results. One major problem is that most models use discount rates for future costs and revenues of between 1 per cent and 5 per cent per year. These models are typically run for 100 years into the future, but even a 1 per cent rate effectively ignores the contributions to costs and benefits from around 2050 onwards. This is a very important assumption, for which there is no consensus. Worse than that, the discount rate is often not even reported!

The theoretical arguments about how to model economies remain unresolved. However, it has always been accepted that the introduction of new technologies will be fundamental to large scale greenhouse gas mitigation. There is a new consensus that the processes of technological change should be represented in the models. The next section explains the role and methods of technology modelling in economics and in climate policy models in particular, and suggests that most current models, the CGE models, face severe problems in incorporating new understandings of technological change.

## 3 Incorporating technology in economic models of climate change mitigation

Why is technology important for climate change analysis? There are two reasons:

1 technology has caused anthropogenic climate change,
2 a change to a low carbon society will require widespread development and mass deployment of new, low carbon technologies.

Both coal and oil were part of processes of transformations of economies and societies. The industrial revolution of the first part of the nineteenth century was founded on burning coal at rates never before attempted. It was used for home heating, steam engines in factories and on railways and later for electric power generation. In the twentieth century, technologies based on burning oil: cars, industrial chemicals and later air transport caused another major increase in GHG emissions. Motor vehicles and aviation are still diffusing through the world, providing the most serious challenge for policy to reduce the rate of climate change.

In order to avoid rates of climate change that will cause major changes to the climate and ecosystems, reductions in emissions of 60 per cent + from the industrialised world will be necessary. Even more important, countries that are becoming major world economies – China, India and Brazil are well known examples – will have to follow a different technological path, if GHG emissions are not to increase, let alone decrease. Therefore, addressing climate change requires a change in the structure of economic activity and in technologies used by society. Technology policy also has the potential to overcome some of the objections to climate change mitigation. US Policy statements have often argued that mitigation policy such as carbon or energy taxes are too expensive and that the problem can be solved by technological development. Hence, modelling technologies is particularly important for economic analysis of climate change mitigation.

### *Mainstream theories of technological change in modern economics*

Solow (1957) was for a long time the basis of thinking about the economics of technological change in macroeconomics. He studied US data on economic growth and his econometric analysis showed that there was an increase in productivity that was unexplained by the main economic variables. He then argued that the unexplained element of growth was due to technological progress. This became known as the 'Solow residual' – the residual part of the regression was taken to be technological change. The problem with this is that it is not actually a theory of technological progress, but just an argument to explain the inadequacy of the regression analysis. The next main contribution came from Romer (1986, 1990). He built a dynamic macroeconomic optimisation model with a variable – knowledge – that he assumed caused increases in productivity. Romer (1990) introduced a technological progress variable explicitly into an economic growth model. Thus these models incorporated endogenous technical change, as opposed to the models of growth with exogenous technical change i.e. where technological change was incorporated by assumption, but not included in the economic structure of the models.

In microeconomics, the literature asked the question: why develop new products? Dasgupta (1988) is a typical example of this literature. This assumes that firms engage in 'patent races', in which firms spend money on R&D to obtain patents. The patent gives a temporary monopoly on a new technology, which enables the firm to make monopoly profits by selling products incorporating the new technology for the period of the patent, or by licensing the technology to other producers.

### Other approaches

There are other theories of the dynamics of economies. Joseph Schumpeter considered processes of technological change and developed the idea of 'creative destruction' – the idea that new technologies 'destroy' the old. Also, there is a small tradition in Kondratiev waves or 'long waves' of economic growth of which the work of Nikolai Kondratiev is the most well known. Ernst Mandel, writing in the Marxist tradition, also made a major contribution to the study of Kondratiev waves (Mandel, 1975, 1995). These two traditions have found recent expression in the work of the 'neo-Schumpeterians'. Freeman and Louçã (2001) have developed a qualitative theory of Kondratiev waves. Perez (2002) has extended these ideas to include finance, showing how financial bubbles may occur which are part of the process by which a new technology takes off. Köhler (2002, 2003) has begun to apply these ideas to economic models of climate policy and this is described below. Evolutionary economics (Nelson and Winter, 1982) follows the Darwinian analogy of dynamic competition leading to selection (in economics, usually by price competition). Other economists such as Giovanni Dosi have studied dynamic processes in economies and there are also the Neo-Keynesians and Institutional economics. Technology is particularly interesting for alternative economic methods that concentrate on the dynamics of economies. This is because technological development is by its very nature a dynamic process. Outside mainstream economics, but very much part of the management/business literature, there is a large body of work on firms' R&D

decision making. Freeman and Soete (1997) is the standard reference work in this area.

## Technology in climate change economics

Economic modelling of climate change policy started out by using macroeconomic models in the mainstream tradition. Grubb *et al.* (2002) review the history of technology modelling in this area. In these models, relatively little attention was paid to how technical change occurs and in many economic models, technical change in energy demand is incorporated as an exogenous variable: the AEEI (Autonomous Energy Efficiency Improvement). Technological change is reflected through specific assumptions entered as data about improved efficiency and declining costs of certain kinds of technologies through time. This implies a modelling assumption that technical change is mainly an autonomous process: that it just happens in ways that do not depend upon other policy or economic variables. In other words, technology is 'manna from heaven'. In the wider literature on technical change, it is acknowledged that it is not an autonomous process, but that it occurs as a result of identifiable processes, such as government research and development, corporate technology

*Table 8.1* Distinction between autonomous and induced technical change

| | Technical change process | |
|---|---|---|
| | *Autonomous* | *Induced* |
| Defining characteristic | Independent of energy market conditions or expectations | Responsive to energy market conditions or expectations |
| Relationship to technology supply vs demand | Predominantly 'supply push' | Predominantly 'demand pull' |
| Dominant at which stage of technology development | Initial invention, declining importance in applied technologies | Innovation and development of applied technologies |
| Main potential sources of technical change | Inventors, university research, government research and development | Corporate research and development, learning by doing, scale economies |
| Corresponding representation in energy-economy modelling | Exogenous energy efficiency and technology cost assumptions | Endogenous influence on rates of efficiency, which change technology characteristics |

Source: Grubb *et al.* (2002).

Note
Explicit knowledge investment functions in models may span both government research and development and corporate research and development, and generally these models do not distinguish between the two. To the extent that such investment is made a function of market conditions, it represents a form of induced technical change.

investment, and economy-of-scale effects. A great deal of technical change is led by the private sector, being induced in response to government policies, market conditions, investment, and expectations. R&D is acknowledged to be exceptionally risky, often being characterised as 'the triumph of action over analysis'. In modelling terms, therefore, technical change really should be endogenous, i.e., dependent upon other parameters reflected within the model. Table 8.1 summarises the differences. If the technical change is autonomous, it can be treated as exogenous to the model. If technical change is endogenous to the model, i.e. dependent upon processes represented by variables/relationships in the model, technical change is induced as a response to economic conditions, including economic policy.

As has been argued above, modelling the processes of technical change is recognised to be very important, which in turn has very important implications for the processes that have to be represented in economic models of climate change mitigation. These are summarised in Table 8.2. The table shows that both the models and the results they generate change dramatically with a switch from autonomous, exogenous technology to endogenous technology in which technological change is induced by the economic environment.

The different approaches to economic modelling of technological change can be summarised as follows:

- AEEI – Autonomous Energy Efficiency Improvement;
- Experience curves or learning by doing;
    - From investment in new production capacity;
- Change in technology from price changes;
    - Induced technical change from policy;
- Changes in production function or structure;
    - Endogenous technical change (R&D), including Knowledge and Human Capital.

Typical applications of the AEEI are for example:

- the DICE Integrated Assessment Model (Nordhaus, 1994);
    - AEEI 1.41 per cent* $(1-e^{0.11t})$ per 10 years;
- the GEM-E3 (Capros *et al.*, 1996) and G-Cubed (McKibbin and Wilcoxen, 1993) CGE macroeconomic models;
    - AEEI 0.5–2.5 per cent per year;
- the OECD GREEN CGE macroeconomic model (Burniaux *et al.*, 1992);
    - AEEI 1 per cent per year.

The idea of a learning curve originated in the management literature. The basic idea is that R&D expenditures and also investment in new capital stock lead to new inventions, which reduce production costs. These relationships were found in empirical work, initially in the aviation industry. Work by IIASA pioneered the application of these ideas to energy technologies, gathering data on the costs

*Table 8.2* Implications of autonomous vs induced technical change

| | Autonomous technical change | Induced technical change 1 |
|---|---|---|
| Process: | Technical change independent of energy market conditions or expectations | Technical change responsive to energy market conditions or expectations |
| Modelling implications: Modelling term | Exogenous | Endogenous |
| Typical main parameter | AEEI and projected costs | Learning rate, knowledge investment function, price response |
| Mathematical implications | Usually linear | Nonlinear, complex |
| Optimisation implications | Single optimum with standard techniques | Potential for multiple equilibria, perhaps very diverse, complex techniques |
| Economic and policy implications: | | |
| Implications for long-run economics of climate change | Atmospheric stabilization below c.550ppm likely to be very costly | Atmospheric stabilization in range around 500ppm may not be very costly |
| Policy instruments and cost distribution | Efficient instrument is uniform Pigouvian tax + government research and development | Efficient response may involve wide mix of instruments, targeted to reoriented industrial research and development and spur market-based innovation in relevant sectors. Potentially with diverse marginal costs |
| Timing implications | Defer abatement to await cost reductions | Accelerate abatement to induce cost reductions |
| 'First mover' economics | Costs with little benefits | Costs with potential benefits of technological leadership |
| Spillover and leakage[2] implications | Spillovers generally negative (positive leakage) | Positive spillovers may dominate (leakage likely to be negative over time) |

Source: Grubb *et al.* (2002).

Notes
1 The differences are generally greatest for models with learning by doing based upon empirical experience curves, but other models with induced technical change show at least some of the characteristics indicated.
2 Leakage is the change in emissions in uncontrolled regions due to restrictions in controlled regions. Positive leakage implies that when one region controls emissions, emissions rise elsewhere.

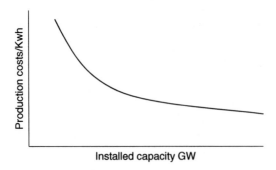

*Figure 8.3* A learning curve.

of energy technologies over time. These developments are surveyed in Grübler *et al.* (1999a). The application of a learning curve is illustrated in Figure 8.3, which shows a typical relationship between production costs of energy and the installed capacity or physical capital.

This has usually been applied as an exponential decay:

$$C(x)/C(0) = x/x(0))-b$$

C cost/kW
C(0) = cost of calibration unit
x = cumulative installed capacity or production
x(0) = installations at C(0)
b = learning parameter

The POLES energy market model (Bourgeois *et al.*, 1999) also incorporates learning curves for renewables. Typically the learning rate in energy technologies has been found to be around a 20 per cent decrease in cost per capacity doubling.

Learning curves fundamentally change the nature of economic analysis of climate change mitigation in two ways:

1   they are an example of increasing returns to scale: the product gets cheaper as more is produced.
2   they put the emphasis on investment in new technologies. This changes the nature of the economic debate. The main question used to be: what is the (optimal) tax or carbon permit trading system and what costs does this impose on an economy? Learning curves place the emphasis on investment: how should investment in new (low carbon) technologies be encouraged, so that even though they are currently more expensive than fossil fuel energy technologies, the learning effect will eventually make the new technologies competitive in energy markets?

As is shown in Table 8.2, this has considerable implications, both for the necessary theory of the economics of climate change mitigation and for the policy conclusions that can be drawn. The first consideration (i) above poses a particular problem for CGE models. CGE models have a series of perfectly competitive markets, in which the solution is the price at which demand equals supply. This is the market equilibrium, a situation where economic welfare in the economy is maximised, in the terms of these models – an optimum. Figure 8.4 represents this situation graphically; it can be found in all basic economics textbooks. Where the two curves cross is the equilibrium, the optimal solution. However, this assumes, the curves must actually cross. In most circumstances in energy markets, the demand for energy will decrease as the price increases i.e. the demand curve is downward sloping to the right. In order to ensure that the curves cross, CGE models assume that the supply curve slopes upwards to the right or at least that the supply curve is horizontal. The former implies that as more (energy) is produced, the cost of production and therefore the costs at which producers are willing to supply (energy) goes up. This is called decreasing returns to scale. A horizontal curve means costs are the same for all levels of output, which is called constant returns to scale.

We have seen that the empirical evidence shows that for energy technologies, the learning curve means that costs decrease as production increases, i.e. there are increasing returns to scale. The situation in a market then becomes much more complex, as is shown in Figure 8.5. If there is a part of the supply curve with increasing returns to scale, the supply curve moves parallel to the demand curve. This is illustrated in the central part of the supply curve in Figure 8.5. It is then an empirical question as to where the supply and demand curves are in relation to each other. If the demand curve is the thick dashed line, there will be a single equilibrium at high levels of production. If production is in the region of increasing returns, (small) changes in production lead to the supply and demand curves staying apart, there is no equilibrium point in this market. If the demand

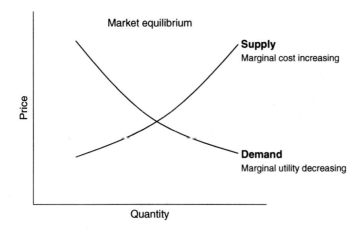

*Figure 8.4* Market equilibrium.

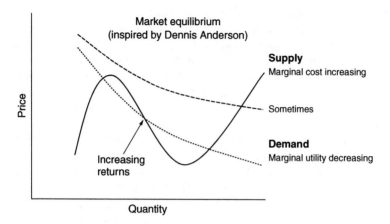

*Figure 8.5* A market with increasing returns to scale.

curve is the dotted line, the demand and supply curves cross in three places: there are three equilibria of which the central one is probably unstable. In either case, a CGE model which depends upon finding a single equilibrium to produce results will fail. This has been recognised by some economists.

Ackerman (2002) describes the problems with CGE models and DeCanio (2003) contains an extensive critique of CGE models in climate change. He builds a CGE and shows that it is unstable under many conditions. It is possible for a CGE to get around the problems illustrated in Figure 8.5, by making the learning curve have a small effect on the economy, or by only examining the points where the situation in Figure 8.4 applies, where the supply curve is upward sloping. The problem is that this contradicts the empirical evidence of increasing returns to scale through learning curves.

What is to be done? We argue that CGE models should be abandoned for models which allow explicitly for disequilibrium. This requires models of dynamic change, calibrated to match empirical data. In the next section, two examples of this are briefly described.

## 4  Some new methods

This section gives two examples of new thinking in climate change economics, both centered on modelling technological change. First, the IIASA work incorporating learning curves with uncertainty to look at energy costs is considered. Finally, new work on applying the ideas of Kondratiev waves to changes in economic structures is discussed.

### *Grübler* et al. *(1999b) – learning curves with uncertainty*

This paper reports the results of a bottom-up energy technology model. The simulations ran with a single trajectory of energy requirements out to 2030. The model included many different energy technologies with experience curves for cost reductions for the different technologies. Both fossil fuel and renewable technologies were considered. Uncertainty was incorporated as distributions of future costs of the energy technologies. Energy economics models of this type usually minimise the cost, summed over time, of meeting the assumed energy demand. This is not analytically possible for a stochastic model with significant increasing returns to scale. Instead, they defined 520 'technology dynamics' – different combinations of technologies through time that meet the demand – and ran 130,000 scenarios in a form of Monte Carlo analysis. This was an unusually computationally intensive task for an economic model, requiring a supercomputer and completed using parallel processing.

Fifty-three low-cost technology dynamics were identified representing 13,000 'best' scenarios with simultaneous cost and risk minimisation. This produced the frequency distribution shown in Figure 8.6.

Figure 8.6 plots the relative percentage frequency (i.e. out of 100 per cent) of the carbon emissions for the 13,000 scenarios (53 technology dynamics) that were low cost. All 53 technology dynamics have similar costs of meeting the assumed time path of energy demand to 2030. The surprising feature of the plot is that it does not have a smooth pattern across the range of emissions. Instead, it is double humped. There are a set of technology dynamics that have low carbon emissions and a set that have high carbon emissions. They represent very different energy futures. There are low carbon futures, where heavy investment in renewables rapidly brings down the currently relatively high costs of renewables. These technologies are new, they have had little development and investment. They are at the left-hand side of Figure 8.3 where the curve shows rapid decreases in costs with further investment. The high emissions technology dynamics are fossil fuel futures, where continued investment in coal, oil and gas technologies improves the performance of conventional technologies. Because the fossil fuel technologies are already mature, having

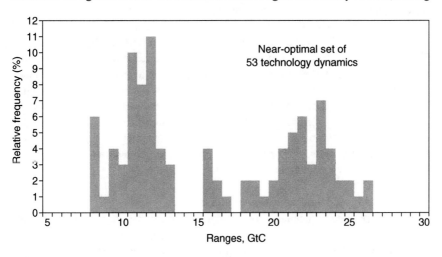

*Figure 8.6* Frequency distribution of carbon emissions (source: Grübler *et al.*, 1999b).

been the basis of the energy system for many years, they start on the right hand side of Figure 8.3 – their costs are already low, but only decrease slowly with further investment. This explains why the renewables have the same costs as fossil fuels over the period of analysis to 2030, even though they are more expansive now (in 2005). The policy implication of this is that if investment is concentrated on renewables, a low carbon energy system can be achieved at no greater cost than staying with the current fossil fuel system. A further result is that low carbon fossil fuel technologies, using carbon capture and sequestration, do not feature in the low cost technology dynamics. The cost of the carbon capture and sequestration equipment makes these technologies more expensive than renewables in the long run. Furthermore, recent high oil prices up to 2008 and the general acceptance that conventional oil reserves are limited suggest that in the medium to long run, oil prices will be much higher than in the 1990–2005 period, with forecasts of sustained prices in the $100/barrel range being common. This will make energy from oil-based technologies more expensive than assumed in Grübler *et al.* (1999b).

### *Models of industrial revolutions – Kondratiev waves*

The economic processes of long term growth and structural economic change have been called 'Kondratiev waves'. As outlined in Section 3 above, the literature on long term economic dynamics has tried to explain these waves, most successfully in qualitative terms. Each wave is associated with a new 'techno-economic paradigm'. An example of this is motorisation, in which the economies of first the US and then Europe and then Japan, Korea etc. were dominated by the automobile, with the oil industry providing the core resource together with the 'Fordist' industrial culture. Not only do these Kondratiev waves characterise long term economic development, but they embody changes in economic structures that have major impacts on the forms of energy use and hence climate change. The internal combustion engine and the diffusion of motor cars is an obvious example.

Work at the Tyndall Centre has developed a quantitative disequilibrium model of Kondratiev waves, with initial ideas reported in Köhler (2002, 2003). The objective was to build models that describe long term changes in industrial structure, when can then be used as components of a macroeconomic model. This work is in the Neo-Schumpeterian tradition, but for the first time is producing a dynamic simulation economic model that reproduces the features of Kondratiev waves, as classified by Freeman and Louçã (2001). They argue that technology systems operate in five interacting areas: science, engineering, economics, politics, culture. They identify five waves of technology and socio-economic activity since the industrial revolution in the UK:

1   Water powered mechanisation of industry;
2   Steam powered mechanisation of industry and transport, based on iron and coal;
3   Electrification of industry, transport and the home, with steel as a core input;

4    Motorisation of transport, civil and war economies, with industrial chemi-
     cals and oil as core inputs;
5    Computerisation of the economy.

The features of these waves are summarised in Table 8.3, taken from Freeman
and Louçã (2001, p. 141). Following Perez (1983), they characterise Kondratiev
waves as a succession of new technology systems (Freeman and Louçã, 2001,
pp. 147–148).

1    For each long wave, there are one or more scientific and technical discover-
     ies that make a 'core input' e.g. iron for the railway wave, very cheap and
     universally available. The process by which these discoveries are made is
     partly dependent on firms' R&D expenditure, but also on cultural and even
     personality factors (Freeman and Soete, 1997). This opens up new possibil-
     ities of production factor combinations. The sector producing these inputs is
     the 'motive branch';
2    New products based on the new factor combinations give rise to new indus-
     tries whose growth drives the whole economy e.g. railways; associated pro-
     duction of rails, locomotives, railway equipment;
3    There are new forms of organisation of production brought about by the
     new industries and products, a new 'techno-economic paradigm';
4    Such a fundamental change will lead to a period of turbulent adjustment
     from the old paradigm to the new.

Freeman and Louçã identify the following six phases in the life cycle of a technology system or Kondratiev wave:

1    Laboratory/invention;
2    Decisive demonstration(s) of technical and commercial feasibility. Continu-
     ing with the railways example, the opening of the Liverpool and Manchester
     railway in the UK in 1830 is an outstanding example;
3    Explosive, turbulent growth, characterised by heavy investment and many busi-
     ness startups and failures. There is a period of structural crisis in the economy
     as society changes to the new organisational methods, employment and skills
     and regime of regulation, brought about in response to the new technology;
4    Continued high growth, as the new technology system becomes the defining
     characteristic of the economy;
5    Slowdown, as the technology is challenged by new technologies, leading to
     the next crisis of structural adjustment (with unemployment and social
     unrest);
6    Maturity, leading to a (smaller) continuing role of the technology in the
     economy or slow disappearance.

As can be seen from Table 8.3, phases 2–5 have been found to take roughly
50 years. In phase 1, which is of indeterminate length, there is a negligible

Table 8.3 Condensed summary of Kondratiev Waves

| Wave | Decisive innovations | Carrier branches | Core input(s) | Infrastructure | Management; organisation | Upswing (boom), downswing (crisis of adjustment) |
|---|---|---|---|---|---|---|
| 1 Water powered mechanisation of industry | Arkwright's mill 1771 | Cotton spinning, Iron | Iron, Cotton, Coal | Canals | Factory systems | 1780s–1815 |
|  |  |  |  | Turnpike roads |  |  |
| Sailing ships Partnerships | Entrepreneurs 1815–1848 |  |  |  |  |  |
| 2 Steam powered mechanisation of industry and transport | Liverpool and Manchester railway 1830 | Railways, Steam engines, Machine tools, Alkali industry | Iron, Coal | Railways | Joint stock companies | 1848–1873 |
|  |  |  |  | Telegraph |  |  |
| Steamships | Sub-contracting to craft workers | 1873–1895 |  |  |  |  |
| 3 Electrification of industry, transport and the home | Bessemer steel process 1875 | Electrical equipment | Steel, Copper, Metal alloys | Steel railways | Specialised, professional management systems | 1895–1918 |
|  | Edison's electric power plant 1882 | Heavy engineering |  |  |  |  |
| Chemicals Steel products Telephone | 'Taylorism' giant firms | Steel ships 1918–1940 |  |  |  |  |

| | | | | | |
|---|---|---|---|---|---|
| 4 Motorisation | Ford's assembly line 1914<br>Burton process for cracking oil 1913 | Cars<br>Aircraft | Oil, Gas | Radio | Mass production and consumption | 1941–1973 |
| Internal combustion engines<br>Oil refining<br>Airports<br>Airlines<br>Hierarchies | Synthetic materials | Motorways | | | | |
| 5 Computerisation of the economy<br>Intel processor 1972<br>Software | 'Fordism' 1973–?<br>IBM computers 1960s<br>Computers | | | | | |
| Telecommunications equipment | Silicon 'Chips' (integrated circuits) | Internet | Networks: internal, local, global | approx. 1980–? | | |

Source: Freeman and Louçã (2001: 141).

macroeconomic effect. The timing of the invention leading to a breakthrough in the technology and the application in a 'decisive demonstration' is more or less random, viewed from a economic perspective. It is phases 2–5 that lead to the Kondratiev waves.

The model of Köhler (2002, 2003) describes the growth of a new industry, e.g. the railway industry in the UK in the nineteenth century or the automobile industry in the motorisation wave. It assumes a technological and/or an organisational breakthrough, which suddenly dramatically reduces production costs. The new technology is taken up by a 'Carrier branch' of industry (e.g. railway companies, or automobile manufacture), to use Perez' terminology (Perez, 1983). The new technology is embodied in a 'Core input' (trains or automobiles) whose price suddenly drops dramatically. This leads to 'super normal' profits in the carrier branch, which then leads to an expectation of high profits, resulting in many startups of firms with high R&D expenditure and investment. This leads to an investment boom (and initial bubble) which further decreases costs and develops whole new markets, leading to long term large-scale growth in the industry. The model has supply decisions for the future dependent on current profits, while price and demand are determined simultaneously given the previous period's supply decision. Production costs follow a learning curve, allowing prices to continuously fall. Investment is a non-linear function of the difference between desired supply and the current productive capacity i.e. capital stock. Supply also leads to a shift outwards of the otherwise linear demand function, thus allowing for endogenous expansion of the industry. Following the literature on the diffusion of new products, a logistic demand expansion is assumed. Including lags in supply decisions and in the expansion of the demand function, the power law for investment allows for overshoot of investment behaviour in response to the initial impulse, while allowing later long term growth. The overshoot (i.e. investment bubbles) is a typical historical feature of the early part of a Kondratiev wave e.g. the recent dot com bubble.

A typical indicative result is shown below in Figure 8.7. The model has been calibrated to railways in the UK in the nineteenth century, the 2nd Kondratiev wave. The curves show demand, supply, and investment in two inputs to the railway industries: infrastructure INVI and rolling stock i.e. trains INVV plotted against time. The economic variables are in £m in constant 1913 prices with time in years. The early investment bubble can be seen, declining to a growth path determined by expansion of the demand. After the bubble, as the industry establishes a new economic structure to take full advantage of the new techno-economic paradigm, the logistic change in the demand function leads to a period of expansion followed by a slow down, as the industry matures. Figure 8.7 demonstrates that the model is capable of generating investment bubbles and an initial boom – or rapid expansion of capacity. It also shows a fluctuating expansion of activity in the long term. In this parameterisation, long term growth is determined by the positive feedback of increases in supply increasing GDP, which shifts the demand function upwards. The expansion eventually settles down to match GDP growth, as the industry determines the course of industrial

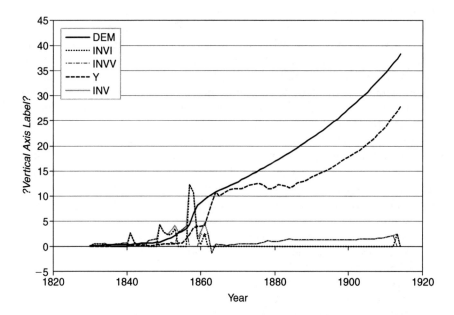

*Figure 8.7* Simulation of the second Kondratiev wave: UK railways 1829–1913.

expansion from 1850–1880 and then matures. The main features of a Kondratiev wave are therefore shown. The model has shown itself to be capable of generating unstable behaviour and the chaotic properties associated with non-linear dynamic systems.

Although this model does not consider energy technologies explicitly, this model is of fundamental importance for climate change economics. It has the potential to provide a theory of how economic structure changes in the 50–100 year timescales of climate change economics and thus provide a basis for considering how economic activity and hence energy demand may change. It may also provide insights into how to induce a Kondratiev wave of low carbon industries and technologies. This is critical to climate change mitigation, because the deep cuts in GHG emissions that are necessary to limit the rate of climate change will require widespread structural change in societies and economies.

## 5 Conclusions and policy implications

This chapter has described the controversy about the application of economic theory to climate change policy analysis. The early economic models that were developed to study the costs of climate change mitigation generated a wide range of results. They were extensively used to justify opposing policy positions in the climate change policy negotiations around the Kyoto Protocol. A meta-analysis showed that the differences in results were partly due to the different input assumptions about growth, policy and also discount rates. However, the different theoretical structures of the models also generate different results.

Recently, the ideas about what is necessary for an adequate model of climate change mitigation policy have changed. Led by the work of IIASA on learning curves for energy technologies, there is now a consensus that it is necessary to incorporate endogenous technological change in these models. This is a challenge for CGE models, which often assume constant or decreasing returns to scale to solve for a single (optimal) equilibrium. We argue that rather than trying to fit increasing returns to scale into CGE models, a more fruitful approach is to develop dynamic disequilibrium models, in order to directly represent the paths of technologies and economies through time. Two examples of such methods were described, a bottom-up energy technology model with learning curves and stochastic costs, and a model of Kondratiev waves of long run changes in economic structure.

The incorporation of increasing returns to scale dramatically changes the policy conclusions of economic analysis (Grubb *et al.*, 2002):

- **Low long-run costs**. The costs of moving to a low carbon energy system may be similar to a least-cost fossil fuel energy system.
- **Policy instruments for investment**. Far more attention should be given to technical change, but induced technical change greatly broadens the scope of technology-related policies. The main policy question is not: How much extra cost will climate mitigation policies impose on economies? Instead, policy should concentrate on enabling investment in new technologies that will move society towards a low carbon energy system and economy. The conventional instruments: carbon/energy taxes, GHG emissions permit trading schemes, regulation and standards need to be complemented by a wider range of policies to induce technological change.
- **Timing.** Induced technical change usually increases the benefits of early action, which accelerates development of cheaper technologies. This is the opposite of the result from models with autonomous technical change, which imply waiting for better technologies to arrive. Numerical studies of $CO_2$ abatement imply that for action taken at present, the benefits associated with induced technical change may be substantially larger than the direct Pigouvian benefits of internalising the present external costs of environmental damage (Grubb *et al.*, 1995; Grübler *et al.*, 1999b).
- **Spillover and leakage**. If climate change mitigation induces improved technologies in the industrialised nations, it is likely that these technologies will diffuse globally. This will result in a positive spillover that will offset the negative spillover usually hypothesised to result from the migration of polluting industries. This effect may dominate over time, which will result overall in negative leakage (i.e., reductions in industrialised countries may also result in reduced emissions in the rest of the world) because of the enormous leverage potentially exerted by global technology diffusion over decades.

This is an exciting time in climate change economics. These new ideas may cause a major change in economic ideas for climate change mitigation. The methods are still new: the details of what causes the increasing returns to scale of learning curves are poorly understood and the application of ideas of dynamic, disequilibrium economics to macroeconomic models is only just beginning.

## References

Ackerman, F. (2002) Still dead after all these years: interpreting the failure of General Equilibrium Theory, *Journal of Economic Methodology* 9(2), pp. 119–139.
Barker, Terry, Köhler, Jonathan and Villena, Marcelo (2002), The costs of greenhouse gas abatement: a meta-analysis of post-SRES mitigation scenarios, *Environmental Economics and Policy Studies*, 5(2), pp. 135–166.
Barker, T., Rosendahl, K.E. (2000) Ancillary benefits of GHG mitigation in Europe: SO2, NOx and PM10 reductions from policies to meet Kyoto targets using the E3ME model and EXTERNE valuations, Ancillary Benefits and Costs of Greenhouse Gas Mitigation, Proceedings of an IPCC Co-Sponsored Workshop, March, 2000, OECD, Paris.
Bourgeois, B., Criqui, P., Mima, S. 1999. *Technical change and sustainable development in the energy sector: first lessons from technology studies in quantitative assessment from the POLES model.* Institute for Economics Politics and Energy (IEPE) Working Paper. Grenoble, IEPE.
Burniaux, J.M., Martin, J.P., Nicoletti, G., Oliveira, J. 1992. *GREEN – A multi-region dynamic general equilibrium model for quantifying the costs of curbing CO2 emissions: a technical manual.* Work. Pap. 116. Econ. Stat. Dep., Paris, OECD.
Capros, A., Georgakopoulos, P., Zografakis, S., Proost, S., van Regemorter, D., *et al.* 1996. Double dividend analysis: first results of a general equilibrium model (GEM-E3) linking the EU-12 countries. In *Environmental Fiscal Reform and Unemployment*, ed. C. Carraro and D. Siniscalo. Dordrecht, Kluwer.
Cooper, A., Livermore, S., Rossi, V., Walker, J. and Wilson, A. (1999), 'Economic impacts of reducing carbon emissions: the Oxford model', *The Energy Journal*, Special Issue, pp. 335–65.
Dasgupta, Partha, 1988. 'Patents, priority and imitation or, the economics of races and waiting games,' *Economic Journal*, 98 (389), pp. 66–80.
DeCanio, Stephen J. (2003) *Economic models of Climate Change: a critique*, Palgrave Macmillan, New York and Basingstoke.
Edenhofer, O., Lessmann, K., Kemfert, C., Grubb, M. and Köhler, J. (2006). 'Induced technological change: exploring its implications for the economics of atmospheric stabilization synthesis report from the innovation modeling comparison project models.' *The Energy Journal Special Issue, Endogenous Technological Change and the Economics of Atmospheric Stabilization*, pp. 57–107.
Freeman, C. and Soete, L. (1997), *The economics of industrial innovation*, 3rd edn, London, Pinter.
Freeman, C. and Louçã, F. (2001) *As time goes by*. OUP, Oxford.
Grubb, M., Chapuis, T. and HaDuong, M. (1995). The economics of changing course: implications of adaptability and inertia for optimal climate policy. *Energy Policy* 23 (4/5), April/May, 417–431.
Grubb, M., Köhler, J., Anderson, D. (2002) Induced technical change in Energy and

environmental modeling: analytic approaches and policy implications, *Annual Review of Energy and the Environment*, 27, pp. 271–308.

Grübler, A. and Messner, S. (1998), Technological change and the timing of mitigation measures, *Energy Economics*, 20(5–6), pp. 495–512.

Grübler, A., Nakićenović, N., Victor, D.G. (1999a). Modeling technological change: implications for the global environment. *Annual Review of Energy and the Environment*, 24, pp. 545–569.

Grübler, A., Nakićenović, N., and Victor, D.G. (1999b) Dynamics of Energy Technologies and global change. *Energy Policy*, 27, pp. 247–280.

IPCC (2007) 4th Assessment Report, IPCC, Geneva www.ipcc.ch.

Köhler, Jonathan (2002), Long run technical change in an energy-environment-economy (E3) model for an IA system, *iEMSS proceedings: Integrated Assessment and Decision Support*, Lugano, 3, pp. 139–144.

Köhler, Jonathan (2003), Long run technical change in an energy-environment-economy (E3) model for an IA system: a model of Kondratiev waves, *Integrated Assessment*, 4(2), pp. 126–133.

Köhler, J., Grubb, M., Popp, D. and Edenhofer, O. (2006). The transition to endogenous technical change in climate-economy models: a technical overview to the Innovation Modeling Comparison Project.' *The Energy Journal Special Issue, Endogenous Technological Change and the Economics of Atmosperic Stabilization*, pp. 17–55.

Mandel, Ernest (1975), *Der Spätkapitalismus* (*Late Capitalism*, translated by Joris De Bres), London, NLB.

Mandel, Ernest (1995), *Long waves of capitalist development: a Marxist interpretation* (2nd edn) London, Verso.

McKibbin, W.J. and Wilcoxen, P.J. 1993. The global consequences of regional environmental policies: an integrated macroeconomic, multi-sectoral approach. In *Costs, Impacts, and Benefits of CO2 Mitigation*, ed. Y. Kaya, N. Nakićenović, W.D. Nordhaus and F.L. Toth. Laxenburg, Austria, IIASA.

Nakićenović, N., Alcamo, J., Davis, G., de Vries, B., Fenhann, G., Gaffin, S., Gregory, K., Grübler, A., Jung, T.Y., Kram, T., La Rovere, L., Michaelis, L., Mori, S., Morita, T., Pepper, W., Pitcher, H., Price, L., Riahi, K., Roehrl, A., Rogner, H.H., Sankovski, A., Schlesinger, M., Shukla, P., Smith, S., Swart, R., van Rooijen, S., Victor, N. and Dadi, Z. (2000) IPCC (Intergovernmental Panel on Climate Change) *Special report on emissions scenarios*, A Special Report of Working Group III of the Intergovernmental Panel on Climate Change, Cambridge University Press, Cambridge, UK.

Nelson, Richard R. and Winter, Sidney G. (1982) *An evolutionary theory of economic change*. Harvard University Press, Cambridge, MA, and London.

Nordhaus, W. (1994) *Managing the global commons: The economics of climate change*, MIT Press, Cambridge, MA.

Perez, C. (1983) Structural change and the assimilation of new technologies in the economic and social system, *Futures* 15, pp. 357–375.

Perez, C. (2002) *Technological revolutions and financial capital*, Edward Elgar, Cheltenham.

Romer, P. (1986) Increasing returns and long-run growth, *Journal of Political Economy* 94(5), pp. 1002–1037.

Romer, P. (1990) Endogenous technological change. *Journal of Political Economy* 98(5), S71–102.

Solow, Robert M. (1957) Technical change and the aggregate production function, *Review of Economics and Statistics* 39(3), pp. 312–320.

# 9  Modeling biased technical change

## Implications for climate policy

*Carlo Carraro, Enrica De Cian, and Lea Nicita*

## 1  Technical change: an ongoing debate

Climate-economy models aiming at quantifying the costs and effects of climate change impacts and policies have become important tools for climate policy decision making. These models reproduce energy and emission scenarios over time and can inform us about the costs of achieving a given stabilization target or the optimal policy path. Modeling results are quite heterogeneous and subject to a significant degree of uncertainty. Although there are several important dimensions along which models differ, this chapter focuses on a key component of climate change economics and policy, namely technical change.

Understanding and accurately characterizing the process of technical change is itself a challenging task. The ways in which economic incentives (endogenous technical change) or policy (induced technical change) can modify the pace and the direction of technical change are questions that do not have univocal answers.

The specification of the dynamics of technical change in climate-economy models has received increasing attention from modelers, but, as recently emphasized by Pielke *et al.* (2008), despite significant improvements, the appropriate way to model technical change is still a matter of debate.

A first tradition of models included the time evolution of technical change, but its determinants were left as exogenous, reflecting the pattern of historical data. Technical change, which is inherently unobservable and has conventionally been represented by proxy variables, was often approximated by a deterministic time trend (Nordhaus and Yang, 1996). Recent modeling efforts have focused on a more comprehensive description of technical change and specific models devoted to investigating induced technical change (ITC) have emerged. Overall, these models show that ITC substantially affects the long run costs of policy and the timing of actions, while broadening the scope of technology-related policies (Grubb *et al.*, 2002).

Nevertheless, most climate-economy models have limited their efforts to endogenize technical change in the energy sector, assuming autonomous trends of other forms of technical change or omitting them. These models implicitly assume that mitigation policies only affect investments in pollution-saving technology, and that other forms of technical change play no substantial role. The natural question to pose is why this should be the case. Whether technical change is energy-saving or energy-using[1] is an empirical question and the evidence supports the existence of both energy-saving and energy-using technical change (van der Werf, 2008; De Cian, 2009). Rising energy prices and more stringent environmental policies are likely to spur innovation especially in the energy field (Jaffe and Palmer, 1997; Popp, 2002), but still other types of innovations (e.g. labour or capital saving) will continue to occur. Moreover, the theoretical literature has shown how technical change is not necessarily pollution-saving, but it can also be pollution-using.

Whether technical change is good or bad for the environment depends on the direction it takes. In order to have sustainable growth, pollution-saving technical change must dominate other types of technical change, such as neutral technical change or labour-augmenting technical change, which tends to increase pollution (Bovenberg *et al.*, 1995; Brock and Taylor, 2004; Lopez, 1994).

In addition, the effects of technical change on production – and thus on the environment – depend on the substitutability among inputs. If technical change increases the productivity of inputs that are a gross complement to emissions, the overall effect of technical change may be to increase pollution (Lopez, 1994). For example, if energy is a gross complement to labour and capital, technical change directed towards those inputs may increase emissions. This indicates the key role played by the elasticity of substitution and the deep interconnections between substitution and technical change (Sue Wing, 2006).

This chapter tackles the issues of whether technical change is biased towards the energy sectors, the importance of the elasticity of substitution between factors in determining this bias and how a mitigation policy is likely to affect it. The analysis is performed using the World Induced Technical Change model, WITCH. The model has been modified to allow for factor-augmenting knowledge and to embody different assumptions about endogenous technical change. Three different versions of the model are proposed. The starting set-up includes endogenous technical change only in the energy sector. A second version introduces endogenous technical change in both the energy and non-energy sectors. A third version of the model embodies different sources of technical change, namely R&D and human capital. The analysis shows that there are substantial economic and policy implications of different assumptions about endogenous technical change.

## 2 Technological change and input substitution: contributions from the empirical literature

From an economic point of view, technological change can be defined as a change in the techniques of production.[2] Quoting Clarke and Weyant (2002) 'for technology to change, the production function must change...'. Indeed, the production function can be seen as a mathematical relationship between factors of production and output. There are two key parameters characterizing input-output combinations: (1) the elasticity of substitution and (2) input efficiency or productivity. Technology parameters may change over time exogenously (exogenous technical change) or with the change of other economic variables such as R&D, international trade and prices.

Climate-economy models represent the production side of the economy through production functions that can be parameterized in different ways, reflecting different assumptions about technology. The production structure, determining the way inputs are nested together, the elasticity of substitution, describing the ease with which inputs can be compensated with each other, and the technology coefficients, characterizing the efficiency of inputs, are the key factors that specify a production function. By shaping the production process, the way technical change is represented in climate-economy models influences the timing, costs and availability of policy options. For example, if energy can be easily substituted with capital or labour, an increase in energy prices induced by climate policies will not have high costs since the expensive input (energy) can be easily replaced with other factors of production.

The production structure adopted by climate-economy models varies from a Cobb–Douglas structure, which is used in many intertemporal growth models, to more flexible structures such as the Constant Elasticity of Substitution production function (CES), originally introduced in Computable General Equilibrium (CGE) models. Nevertheless, large differences exist with respect to the nesting structure used, the size of the elasticities and the way technological change is represented in the production function. While CES production functions allow for different elasticities of substitution among different pairs of inputs, the Cobb–Douglas production function has a major limitation in that it restricts the elasticity of substitution to one.

Equation 1 and Equation 2 provide a simple example of a nested production function. Final output, $Y$, is produced by a CES combination of capital-labour aggregate, $KL$, and energy input, $E$, and capital-labour aggregate is a Cobb–Douglas combination of capital input, $K$, and labor input, $L$.

$$Y = \left[ KL^{\rho} + E^{\rho} \right]^{1/\rho} \tag{1}$$

where

$$KL = K^{\alpha} L^{1-\alpha} \tag{2}$$

The elasticity of substitution, $\sigma$, between $KL$ and $E$, is related to the parameter $\rho$ according to the standard definition $\sigma = \dfrac{1}{1-\rho}$.

Figure 9.1 shows the production nest of the same function where $\sigma$ is set equal to 0.5.

The empirical literature on the elasticity of substitution is characterized by heterogeneous results, as recently reviewed in Carraro *et al.* (2009). Several

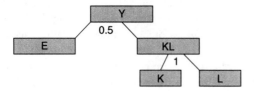

*Figure 9.1* Production nest.

studies focus on the estimation of the elasticities of substitution between energy, capital and labour in industry (Prywes, 1986; Manne and Richels, 1992; Chang, 1994; Kemfert, 1998; Kemfert and Welsch, 2000, Okagawa and Ban 2008), whereas others look at both industry and different countries (van der Werf, 2008). Overall, most of the estimates reveal that all three inputs – capital, labour and energy – are gross complements, and that the elasticity of substitution between capital and labour is higher than the elasticity of substitution between those inputs and energy (see Table 9.1).

This empirical literature, even if still in its infancy, provides important insights about the choice of the appropriate nesting structure. Kemfert and Welsch (2000), van der Werf (2007) and Markandya and Pedroso-Galinato (2007) all estimate alternative nesting structures of a two-level CES function in order to select those supported by the empirical evidence. Both van der Werf (2007) and Markandya and Pedroso-Galinato (2007) find that the structure in which capital and labour are nested together and then combined with energy, fits the data better than when capital and energy are nested together and then combined with labour. Nevertheless, van der Werf (2007) could not reject a non-nested structure in which capital, labour and energy can be substituted with the same elasticity. Kemfert and Welsch (2000) find that at a national level the KE-L structure fits the data best, while for industry, most often the KL-E structure performs better.

The empirical evidence on the direction of technical change is scarcer, as most literature has focused on measures of neutral technical change. Two recent contributions have undertaken a more systematic assessment of the direction and the sources of biased[3] technical change (van der Werf, 2007; De Cian, 2009). Both papers show that the rate of factor-augmenting technological change differs significantly across factors, empirically validating the theory of directed technical change.

## 3  Technical change in the WITCH model: a trilogy

The World Induced Technical Change Hybrid (WITCH) model (Bosetti *et al.*, 2006; Bosetti *et al.*, 2007) is an Integrated Assessment Model (IAM) designed to deal with the main features of climate change. The model has been developed along three different directions, each featuring different structures of production and sources of technical change. The Appendix shows the production nests and the elasticities of substitution of all three different versions.

*Table 9.1* Elasticities of substitution in empirical literature

**K/L**

| | |
|---|---|
| 0.88[A] | Prwes (1986) |
| 0.82[M] | Kemfert (1998) |
| 0.793[A] | Kemfert and Welsch (2000) |
| 0.224 to 0.616[A] | van der Werf (2007) |
| 0.07 to 0.33 | Okagawa and Ban (2008) |

**L/E**

| | |
|---|---|
| 0.88[A] | Prwes (1986) |
| 0.35[A] | Chang (1994) |
| 0.42[M] | Kemfert (1998) |
| 0.167[M] | Kemfert and Welsch (2000) |
| 0.517 to 0.863[A] | van der Werf (2007) |

**K/E**

| | |
|---|---|
| 0.87[M] | Chang (1994) |
| 0.65[M] | Kemfert (1998) |
| 0.871[M] | Kemfert and Welsch (2000) |
| 0.804 to 1.000[A] | van der Werf (2007) |
| 0.04 to 0.45 | Okagawa and Ban (2008) |

**KL/E**

| | |
|---|---|
| 0.4 | Manne and Richels (1992) |
| 0.42[A] | Chang (1994) |
| 0.5 | Kemfert (1998) |
| 0.698 | Kemfert and Welsch (2000) |
| 0.00 to 0.64 | van der Werf (2007) |

**KE/L**

| | |
|---|---|
| 0.681 to 1.159[A] | van der Werf (2007) |
| 0.00 to 0.94 | Okagawa and Ban (2008) |

Source Carraro et al., (2009).

Notes
A and M superscripts denote Allen and Morishima elasticities of substitutions, respectively.

In its basic set up, endogenous technical change enters only in the energy sector. The other two versions of the model add some complexity to the analysis, by modeling the productivity of non-energy inputs in an endogenous way. Overall the three variants of the model allow not only a deeper understanding of induced technical change, but they represent valuable means to compare the economic and policy implications of alternative assumptions about technical change, leading to important insights.

## *3.1  WITCH model: the basic set up*

### *3.1.1  Model structure and main features*

WITCH is an optimal growth model of the world economy that integrates sources and consequences of climate change in a unified framework. A reduced form climate module (MAGICC) allows for climate factors to feedback to the economic system.

It belongs to the class of hybrid model, embodying features of both top-down (TD) and bottom-up (BU) models. The TD component consists of an intertemporal optimal growth framework, the BU component allows for a representation of the energy sector of average complexity.[4]

The world economy is disaggregated into twelve macro regions[5] that interact strategically in a game theoretical setting. Channels of interactions are the presence of exhaustible resources, knowledge and experience spillovers, and the environment. International knowledge spillovers mimic the flow of ideas and knowledge across countries. Experience in the development of niche technologies such as renewable energy (wind and solar) and breakthrough technologies can also spill over internationally, over a reasonable window of time. In the presence of a climate policy, international emission trading can be simulated, adding an additional source of interaction.

The model can thus produce two different solutions: a cooperative solution, which is globally optimal because the social planner maximizes global welfare, and a non-cooperative solution (Nash equilibrium) which instead is strategically optimal for each single region. The latter solution better reflects the non-cooperative nature of international relations. As a consequence, it does not represent a first best outcome but rather it accounts for economic and environmental inefficiencies arising from the presence of global externalities (emissions, exhaustible resources, knowledge).

Regions face a problem that is economic and environmental. On the one hand, economic agents aim at maximizing welfare, thus consumption and production. On the other hand, production brings about an increase in GHG emissions that ultimately reduce consumption possibilities. In the optimisation process, each region chooses the dynamic mix of investments in capital stocks, innovation and energy technologies so as to optimally balance these two opposing forces.

Following the framework of neoclassical growth models, a unique final good is produced and employed for alternative uses (consumption, investments, reducing climate change damage). Production is characterized as a nested CES. At the top-nest level, the substitution possibilities between capital and labour are described by a Cobb–Douglas production function. The capital-labour nest can then be substituted with energy services. The lower flexibility in substitution between the capital-labour nest and energy is reflected in a low elasticity of substitution (0.5).

The only source of endogenous technical change appears in the energy sector, whereas increases in total factor productivity remains exogenous. Energy services are the result of a combination between raw energy and a stock of energy efficiency knowledge. This form of endogenous technical change captures improvements in overall energy efficiency in the economy and energy knowledge can substitute the use of the physical input. The flow of new ideas results from the combination of investment in R&D and the stock of cumulated knowledge, and contributes to increase the current stock of knowledge.

A wide set of different technologies, ranging from traditional coal/oil/gas power plants to carbon free options such as nuclear, renewables and biofuels, can be used in the generation of energy. The model also features new generation technologies – referred to as breakthrough technologies – which can become competitive in a few decades, provided sufficient investments in dedicated R&D are undertaken. Endogenous technical change in the energy sector can be driven by both Learning by Doing (LbD) and Learning by Researching (LbR). Both experience (LbD) and innovation (LbR) can bring down investment costs in specific technologies.

### 3.1.2 Climate policy: implications for the optimal investment mix

Contrary to most top-down macroeconomic models, WITCH features a portfolio of mitigation options that can be used to achieve low carbon scenarios. Key mitigation options include nuclear power, Carbon Capture and Sequestration (CCS), renewables and biofuels. Moreover, energy efficiency can improve endogenously with energy innovation and the deployment of breakthrough technologies can become competitive with a sufficient amount of targeted R&D.

In this setting, the carbon price is an important signal that provides the right stimulus for investment in R&D targeted to enhance energy efficiency and to increase the competitiveness of innovative low carbon technologies.

When a stringent climate policy is implemented, the world carbon price[6] increases rapidly in the first half of the century when a stronger signal is needed to stimulate an optimal reallocation of resources towards low carbon technologies (Table 9.2). This carbon pricing induces a four-fold expansion of energy R&D investments, raising the fraction of gross world product invested in energy innovation from 0.02 per cent up to 0.08 per cent, the peak level reached in 1980 after the oil price shock. A carbon price signal consistent with a 450 ppm $CO_2$ concentration stabilization target also induces large investments in low carbon technologies such as renewables, nuclear and CCS.

Additional investments in innovation and low carbon technologies come at the cost of overall economic growth, especially in the first half of the century

*Table 9.2* Climate policy effects: carbon price and macroeconomic costs

|  | 2025 | 2045 | 2065 | 2085 | 2105 |
|---|---|---|---|---|---|
| GWP (percentage change with respect to the baseline scenario) | −1.09% | −2.00% | −3.37% | −2.21% | −0.16% |
| Carbon price (USD/tCO$_2$) | 35 | 283 | 810 | 1083 | 1179 |

when more effort is needed to bring in breakthrough technologies. The economic losses computed in terms of Gross World Product (GWP) and its variation over time are displayed in Table 9.2.

### 3.2 Introducing directed technical change

The WITCH model as formulated in Bosetti *et al.* (2006) is an important contribution to the climate-economy literature as it presents a detailed treatment of the process of energy innovation and diffusion of both knowledge and experience. However, the modeling approach to technical change can be considered 'partial' in that it abstracts from other forms of innovation that may occur outside the energy sector and affect the overall macroeconomic structure.

More precisely, non-energy R&D expenditure is not explicitly modelled, instead it is included in the economy-wide investment variable, and an exogenous crowding out of investments by energy R&D expenditures is assumed to take into account the alternative and competitive uses of R&D funds.

However, as emphasized by Goulder (2004) it is not possible to rule out that forces other than the 'crowding out' effect may lower investments in other sectors and turn a de-carbonized economy into a less technologically advanced economy. For example, Goulder and Schneider (1999), Sue Wing (2003) and Gerlagh (2008), all find that climate policy induces substantial changes in total R&D investments and not only in the energy sector. Which forces mould such changes and how those changes affect the cost of policy are still open questions.

Also, as emphasized by Acemoglu (2002), technical change is not neutral. Since it is not possible to exclude the possibility that technical change in non-energy sectors affects energy demand, the direction of technical change and whether or not it is biased towards energy may have important implications for climate policy.[7]

### 3.2.1 Model structure and main features

With the goal of addressing questions about the impact of a long-term GHG stabilization policy on the direction and bias of technical change, and inspired by the contribution of Acemoglu (2002), the WITCH model has been modified to introduce factor-specific technical change.

A non-energy R&D sector, which enhances the productivity of the capital-labour aggregate, has been added to the energy R&D sector. By explicitly modeling directed technical change we can investigate whether technical change is biased and if a climate policy is likely to reverse that bias. Also, by relaxing any assumptions of exogenous crowding out between R&D sectors, we totally endogenize the impact of a strong mitigation policy on the rate of technical change both at sectoral and aggregate levels, and we are then in a position to disentangle those effects – other than crowding out – which affect the reallocation of investments in knowledge.

As specified above, gross output is obtained from a combination of energy services produced by the energy sector and capital-labour services produced in the non-energy sector, but with a different nesting structure of production. Two main modifications have been made. First, the Cobb–Douglas combination of capital and labour inputs is replaced with a CES nest. The elasticity of substitution between labour and capital, $\sigma_{KL}$, is now set lower than 1 and equal to 0.8, as suggested by the empirical evidence described in Table 9.1. Second, a new stock of knowledge that can enhance the productivity of capital-labour services is introduced. The resulting production structure therefore includes two input-specific knowledge stocks that characterize the productivity of energy and the capital-labour nest in an endogenous way. The production of new ideas and the evolution of the knowledge stock in the non-energy sector are characterized by intertemporal spillovers and decreasing returns, like the energy sector as described in Bosetti *et al.* (2006).

From the baseline scenario – which corresponds to the non-cooperative Nash equilibrium of the WITCH model under the assumption of no mitigation policy – we obtain the equilibrium investment trajectories, together with the equilibrium R&D investments, GWP and consumption path. The optimal equilibrium paths of R&D investments make it possible to analyse the predictions of the model about the direction of technical change.

Table 9.3 shows that R&D investments as a percentage of Gross World Product (GWP) slightly increase across the century. This is mainly due to a gently increasing investment path in non-energy R&D while energy R&D investment is slightly decreasing.

This result is in line with historical trends displayed in Figure 9.1. Historical data for OECD countries shows a trend over the past 13 years of slightly increasing total R&D investment over GDP, starting from 2.15 per cent in 1992 and reaching

*Table 9.3* Baseline trends in R&D investments

|  | *2005* | *2025* | *2045* | *2065* | *2085* | *2105* |
|---|---|---|---|---|---|---|
| Total R&D (% GWP) | 1.93% | 2.04% | 2.06% | 2.05% | 2.00% | 1.84% |
| Non-energy R&D (% GWP) | 1.92% | 2.03% | 2.04% | 2.03% | 1.98% | 1.83% |
| Energy R&D (% GWP) | 0.018% | 0.017% | 0.016% | 0.016% | 0.015% | 0.014% |
| Energy R&D (% total investment in R&D) | 0.0% | 0.82% | 0.79% | 0.77% | 0.76% | 0.75% |

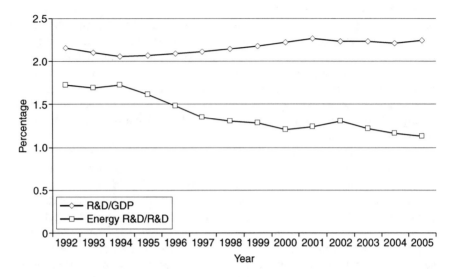

*Figure 9.2* R&D as a percentage of GDP and energy R&D as percentage of total R&D (OECD countries).

2.25 per cent in 2005, and a decreasing path of energy R&D over total R&D investment, starting from 1.7 per cent in 1992 and dropping to 1.1 per cent in 2005.

According to the outcomes of the model, technical change is mainly capital-labour augmenting and – most importantly – energy-biased because, as found by empirical studies and assumed in the model, the capital-labour aggregate and energy are complements. This means that R&D investments are mainly directed towards the capital-labour aggregate, but they also increase the productivity of the energy input relative to the productivity of the capital-labour aggregate. As a consequence, any increase in the stock of non-energy knowledge triggers an increase in energy demand.

### 3.2.2 Climate policy: impacts on the direction and magnitude of technical change, and on policy costs

In most climate-energy models which include endogenous technical change, the implementation of climate policy induces technical change in carbon saving technologies, but as emphasized above, the impact on other R&D sectors and on the overall rate of technical change is often omitted. By including directed technical change we are in the position to analyse the effect of the stabilization policy on the overall rate of technical change and to compare this result with the standard version of the model to see how different assumptions about technical change affect the cost of the policy.

When the stabilization target is implemented investments are made in the energy sector to accelerate the deployment of carbon-free technology and to increase energy efficiency by augmenting energy R&D capital stock. As shown in Table 9.4, we find that climate policy strongly re-directs investment to energy R&D. The opposite is true for the non-energy sector where the share of non-energy R&D investment declines more and more. Overall, since induced technical change in the energy sector is not enough to compensate the contraction of investment in capital-labour knowledge, the rate of technical change of the economy slows down. The stabilization policy has thus strongly affected the rate of knowledge accumulation and the economy becomes less and less knowledge intensive.

As shown in detail by Carraro *et al.* (2009) the reduction of the rate of investments in non-energy R&D does not result from a crowding out effect due to increased investment in energy R&D – as is often proposed in the literature – instead, it depends on the structure of the economy, as portrayed in the model. Since capital-labour augmenting technical change is energy-biased, when an ambitious climate policy is implemented, one channel to reduce energy demand, and therefore emissions, is by slowing down the pace of accumulation pollution-augmenting knowledge stock.

This result has important implications for the cost of policy. While omitting ITC in the Energy sector usually overestimates the cost of policy in terms of Gross World Product losses, omitting endogenous technical change in the non-energy sector actually underestimates it, because the negative impact of the climate policy on the rate of technical change of the entire economy is ignored.

### 3.3 Introducing human capital

In the WITCH model with endogenous energy technical change (Bosetti *et al.*, 2006) and in the version with directed technical change (Carraro *et al.*, 2009) the engine of endogenous technological change is the same: innovation, fuelled by expenditure in R&D. Another important source of endogenous growth is human capital (Lucas, 1988). Despite the existence of theoretical contributions about the relationship between human capital and growth on the one hand (Blankenau and Simpson, 2004) and human capital, innovation and the environment on the other (Gradus and Smulders, 1993; Hettich, 1998; Pautrel, 2008; Grimaud and Tournemaine, 2007; Ikazaki, 2006), the applied climate-economy literature has overlooked other forms of knowledge such as human capital.

*Table 9.4* Stabilization trends of R&D investments – percentage changes w.r.t. the baseline scenario

|  | 2025 | 2045 | 2065 | 2085 | 2105 |
|---|---|---|---|---|---|
| Total R&D (% GWP) | −3.78& | −6.90% | −8.14% | −7.87% | −7.03% |
| Non-energy R&D (% GWP) | −4.36% | −7.87% | −9.14% | −8.75% | −7.79% |
| Energy R&D (% GWP) | 66.71% | 116.25% | 121.04% | 107.76% | 93.79% |
| Energy R&D (% total investment in R&D) | 1.42% | 1.83% | 1.86% | 1.71% | 1.56% |

These theoretical contributions highlight how the relationship between environmental policy, human capital formation and economic growth hinges on the way human capital and education come into the model (in the utility function or as a production input) and on what is the source of pollution (output or inputs such as physical capital). When pollution depends on output, an environmental tax tends to reduce wages and thus education spending, with negative implications for human capital formation (Hettich, 1998; Gradus and Smulder, 1993). Instead, when pollution depends on capital, an environmental tax would increase wages relative to the rate of capital return, which boosts education investments.

Education spending can increase growth, but general equilibrium effects may crowd out other sources of growth, such as investments in physical capital and private human capital. The dimension of this crowding out effect depends on, among other things, how education expenditure is financed (Blankenau and Simpson, 2004). When education is financed with consumption taxes, the effects on growth are always positive.

Introducing human capital into the WITCH model as an additional source of endogenous growth makes it possible to assess the interplay between innovation, human capital and climate change policies.

### 3.3.1 Model structure and main features

The WITCH model version with human capital (Carraro *et al.*, 2008) builds upon recent empirical results (De Cian, 2009) which support the hypothesis that the sources of directed technical change are input-specific. Whereas human capital is an important driver of labour productivity, innovation, measured as the aggregate stock of knowledge, tends to enhance more capital and energy productivity, with a larger impact on the latter.

These findings have been fed back into the WITCH model by amending the top-level nest of the production function. Following the structural model estimated in De Cian (2009),[8] the three inputs are assumed to be substitutable with the same elasticity (non-nested production function). The productivity of each factor is described by a multiplicative input-specific coefficient. In other words, total factor productivity, which is exogenous in Bosetti *et al.* (2006), is now decomposed into endogenous factor productivities. Factor productivity – or factor-augmenting technical change – consists of two elements. An exogenous component, which captures the spontaneous time evolution of technical change, and an endogenous term, which links factor productivity to the economic variables indentified in the empirical work.

Capital and energy productivity are a function of knowledge, represented by the stock of aggregate R&D. Labour productivity, on the other hand, is related to human capital, which is approximated by the stock of total expenditure (both private and public) on education.

The production of both human capital and knowledge is characterized by intertemporal spillovers, which is similar to the specification used in Bosetti *et al.* (2006) and Carraro *et al.* (2009). The explicit representation of human capital makes it possible to account for the cross effects between innovation and human capital and therefore human capital contributes also to the formation of knowledge.

The resulting framework therefore includes not only energy-saving technical change, as in Bosetti *et al.* (2006) but also energy-using technical change, as in Carraro *et al.* (2009). The crucial element driving the implications of technical change for energy, and thus emissions, is the complementarity between inputs. Education investments, directed to improve the productivity of labour, have an effect that is pollution-using because more productive labour is complemented by more energy input. This feature is the main driver behind the implications of climate policies.

### 3.3.2 Climate policy: implications for knowledge and human capital formation

The implications of a climate policy[9] for the energy sector and energy-saving innovation are similar to those that can be obtained with the other two versions of the model. The carbon price signal reallocates resources towards low carbon technologies (nuclear, CCS and renewable energy) and energy-saving R&D.

Contrary to what can be observed using the WITCH model with directed technical change, climate policy stimulates a dedicated form of energy-knowledge without reducing total R&D investments. The reason behind this result is the twofold effect of total R&D. Total R&D increases both capital and energy productivity. The first effect (that on capital) is pollution-using, but it is dominated by the effect on energy productivity, which is energy-saving. Consequently, climate policy increases total R&D because its energy-saving effect is dominant.

What are the implications for human capital formation? As mentioned above, advancements in labour productivity will have a negative impact on the environment because labour is a complement to energy. Education, which is the engine of human capital accumulation, is pollution-using and therefore when there is a stringent climate constraint, investments are re-directed away from education.

As discussed in Hettich (1998), the effect of an environmental policy on human capital depends on how pollution is modelled and on how education comes into the model. When pollution (in this case emissions) is linked to final output, as is the case in the WITCH model, a tax on emissions reduces the return on both capital and wages, reducing the incentive to invest in education as well.

The negative effect of climate policy on human capital formation is lessened when the contribution of education to the formation of innovation is sufficiently large. In this case, human capital is also pollution-saving, because of the indirect effect on energy productivity. Table 9.5 summarizes the effects of climate policy on human capital and knowledge. Climate policy tends to reallocate productive resources from energy-using sectors (education) to energy-saving sectors (total R&D). As a consequence, the ratio of total R&D expenditure to education is higher in the presence of climate policies and it increases over time.

*Table 9.5* Stabilization trends of R&D and education investments – percentage changes w.r.t. the baseline (no policy) scenario

|                      | *2025*  | *2045*  | *2065*  | *2085*  | *2105*  |
|----------------------|---------|---------|---------|---------|---------|
| Total R&D (%GWP)     | 1.95%   | 3.84%   | 3.75%   | 3.86%   | 4.26%   |
| Education (%GWP)     | −1.31%  | −2.82%  | −4.56%  | −5.18%  | −5.63%  |
| Total R&D/education  | 3.92%   | 8.40%   | 12.05%  | 13.26%  | 13.83%  |

## 5 Concluding remarks

The analysis that has been proposed in this chapter focuses on the impacts of climate policy on the structure of the economy. Whereas the issue of policy costs has been analysed at length, less attention has been paid to structural changes that may be induced by climate policy. The trilogy of modeling approaches to endogenous technical change proposed in this chapter has shown how climate policy can have different impacts on innovation and human capital formation.

Although different formulations of endogenous technical change have only a minor influence on climate policy costs, the macroeconomic effects on knowledge and human capital formation can vary greatly.

As soon as technical change is allowed to take different directions endogenously, other factors overlooked by state-of-the-art climate-economy literature come into play. In particular, complementarity among factors determines the direction of induced technical change. Given the complementarity between energy on the one hand, and labour and capital on the other hand, any form of technical progress that increases the productivity of the capital-labour nest is energy-using and therefore has negative implications on the environment.

Since climate policy tends to reallocate productive resources from energy-using sectors towards energy-saving sectors, both the accumulation of pollution-augmenting knowledge stock and human capital formation slow down. Although a stabilization policy provides stimulus for energy-saving innovation, the overall effect can be a reduction of the knowledge and human capital intensity of the economy.

# Appendix: the production nests and the elasticities of substitution

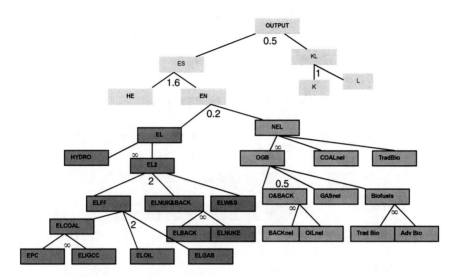

*Figure 9.3a* WITCH: basic set-up.

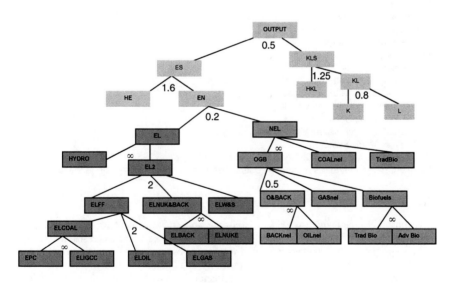

*Figure 9.3b* WITCH: directed technical change.

182   *C. Carraro* et al.

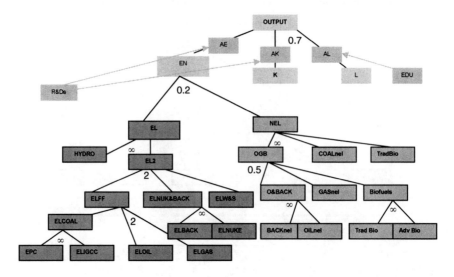

*Figure 9.3c* WITCH: human capital.

Model variables are denoted with the following symbols:

*Y* = production
*K* = final good stock of capital
*ES* = energy services
*KLS* = capital–labor services
*LK* = capital–labor aggregate
*HE* = energy knowledge
*EN* = energy
*EL* = electric energy
*NEL* = non-electric energy
OGB = Oil, Gas and Biofuel nest
ELFF = Fossil fuel electricity nest
W&S = Wind and Solar
ELj = Electricity generated with the technology j
TradBiom = Traditional Biomass
Kj = Capital for generation of electricity with technology j
O&Mj = Operation and Maintenance costs for generation of electricity with technology j

## Notes

1 Technical change is *input-saving*, or *input-augmenting*, if the input cost share decreases at constant factor prices. It is *input-using* if the input cost share increases at constant factor prices. Technical change is *neutral* when it does not save relatively more of one of the inputs of production, e.g. the productivity of all inputs is equally increased.
2 Past literature has distinguished technical change from technological change, which is the application of new techniques of production to a broad spectrum of economic activity (Binswanger and Ruttan, 1978). However, current literature, including this chapter, uses the two terms interchangeably.
3 Binswanger and Ruttan (1978) define input bias as the rate of change in the share of input over production when input and output prices are held constant. By factor-augmenting technical change we refer to an increase in input productivity.

4 In concrete terms, Top Down and Bottom Up models differ mainly with respect to the representation of the energy system and its interactions with the rest of the economy. Whereas Top Down models represent the whole economic system, Bottom Up models are partial model of the energy sector. This distinction has become increasingly blurred and hybrid efforts, such as the WITCH model, are being developed. Loschel (2002) gives a taxonomy of the different model types.

5 The 12 regions are USA (United States), OLDEURO (Western Europe), NEWEURO (Eastern Europe), KOSAU (Korea, South Africa, Australia), CAJAZ (Canada, Japan, New Zealand), TE (Transition Economies), MENA (Middle East and North Africa), SSA (Sub-Saharan Africa), SASIA (South Asia), CHINA (China and Taiwan), EASIA (South East Asia), LACA (Latin America, Mexico and Caribbean).

6 This is the world carbon price that emerges in the international carbon market when a 450 ppm long-run $CO_2$ concentration stabilization target is imposed.

7 Following Acemoglu (2002) technical change is input-biased if it increases the marginal product of one particular input relative to other inputs.

8 The dynamics of factor-augmenting technical change have been inferred by observing the time and spatial variation of conditional input demands, derived from an aggregate non-nested production function.

9 The climate policy is a stabilization target aimed at stabilizing $CO_2$ concentrations at 450 ppm.

# References

Acemoglu, D. (2002). 'Directed technical change', *Review of Economic Studies*, 69, 781–809.

Berndt, E. and Wood, D. (1979). 'Engineering and econometric interpretation of energy-capital complementarity', *American Economic Review*, 69, 342–354.

Binswanger Hans, P. and Ruttan, V.W. (1978). *Induced Innovation: Technology, Institutions and Development*. John Hopkins University Press, Baltimore, MD.

Bosetti, V., Carraro, C., Galeotti, M., Massetti, E., and Tavoni, M. (2006). 'WITCH: A World Induced Technical Change Hybrid Model', *The Energy Journal*, 13–38.

Bosetti, V., Massetti, E., and Tavoni, M. (2007). 'The WITCH model. Structure, baseline, Solutions'. Fondazione ENI Enrico Mattei, Nota di Lavoro 10–2007, Milan.

Bosetti, V., Carraro, C., Massetti, E., and Tavoni, M. (2008). 'International Energy R&D spillovers and the economics of greenhouse gas atmospheric stabilization', *Energy Economics*, 30, 2912–2929.

Bosetti, V., Carraro, C., Massetti, E., Sgobbi, A., and Tavoni, M. (2009). 'Optimal energy investment and R&D strategies to stabilise atmospheric greenhouse gas concentrations', *Resource and Energy Economics*, 31(2), 123–137.

Blankenau W. and Simpson, N. (2004). 'Public education expenditure and growth', *Journal of Development Economics*, 73(2), 583–605.

Bovenberg, A.-L. and Smulders, S. (1995). 'Environmental quality and pollution augmenting technological change in a two sectors endogenous growth model', *Journal of Public Economics*, 57, 369–391.

Brock, W.A. and Taylor, M.S., (2004). 'Economic growth and the environment: a review of theory and empirics', NBER Working Paper, No. W10855.

Carraro, C., De Cian, E., and Tavoni, M. (2009). 'Human capital formation and global warming mitigation: evidence from an integrated assessment model', Fondazione ENI Enrico Mattei, Milan, mimeo.

Carraro, C., Massetti, E., and Nicita, L. (2009). 'How does climate policy affect technical change? An analysis of the direction and pace of technical progress in a climate-economy model.' Fondazione ENI Enrico Mattei, Nota di Lavoro 08–2009, Milan. Forthcoming in the *Energy Journal*.

Clarke, L.E., Weyant, J.P., and Edmonds, J. (1999). 'Issues in modelling induced techno-logical change in energy, environmental, and climate policy', *Environmental Modelling and Assessment*, 4, 67–85.

De Cian, E. (2009). 'Factor-augmenting technical change: an empirical assessment', Fondazione ENI Enrico Mattei, Nota di Lavoro 18–2009, Milan.

Gerlagh, R. (2008). 'A climate change policy induced shift from innovations in carbon-energy production to carbon-energy savings', *Energy Economics*, 30: 425–448.

Goulder, L.H. and Schneider, S.H. (1999). 'Induced technological change and the attractiveness of $CO_2$ abatement policies.' *Resource and Energy Economics*, 21, 211–253.

Gradus, R. and Smulders, S. (1993). 'The trade-off between environmental care and long-term growth-pollution in three prototype growth models' *Journal of Economics*, 58(1), 25–51.

Griffin J. and Gregory, P. (1976). 'An intercountry Translog model of energy substitution responses', *American Economics Review*, 66, 845–857.

Grimaud, A. and Tournemaine, F. (2007). 'Why can environmental policy tax promote growth through the channel of education?' *Ecological Economics*, 62(1), 27–36.

Grubb, M., Köhler, J., and Anderson, D. (2002). 'Induced technical change in energy and environmental modeling: analytic approaches and policy implications.' *Annual Review of Energy and the Environment* 27, 271–308.

Hettich, F. (1998). 'Growth effects of a revenue-neutral environmental tax reform', *Journal of Economics*, 67(3), 287–316.

Hudson E. and Jorgenson, D. (1974). 'U.S. energy policy and economic growth, 1975–2000', *Bell Journal of Economic Management Science* 5, 461–514.

Jaffe, A.B. and Palmer, K. (1997). 'Environmental regulation and innovation: a panel data study,' *The Review of Economics and Statistics*, 79(4), 610–619.

Ikazaki, D. (2006). 'R&D, human capital and environmental externality in an endogenous growth model', *International Journal of Global Environmental Issues*, 6 (1), 29–46.

Kemfert, C. (1998). 'Estimated production elasticities of a nested CES production function approach for Germany'. *Energy Economics*, 20, 249–264.

Lopez, R. (1994). 'The environment as a factor of production: the effects of economic growth and trade liberalization', *Journal of Environmental Economics and Management*, 27, 163–184.

Löschel, A. (2002). 'Technological change in economic models of environmental policy: a survey', *Ecological Economics*, 43, 105–126.

Markandya, Anil and Pedroso-Galinato, Suzette (2007). 'How substitutable is natural capital?,' *Environmental & Resource Economics*, 37 (1), 297–312.

Nerlove, M., (1967). 'Recent empirical studies of the CES and related production function', in Brown, M., ed., *The Theory and Empirical Analysis of Production Function*, New York, Mar. 1971.

Nordhaus, W. D., and Yang, Zili (1996). 'A regional dynamic general-equilibrium model of alternative climate-change strategies', *The American Economic Review*, 86(4), 741–765.

Pautrel, X. (2008). 'Environmental policy, education and growth: a reappraisal when lifetime is finite', Fondazione ENI Enrico Mattei, Nota di Lavoro 57–2008, Milan.

Pielke, R., Jr, Wigley, T. and Green, C. (2008). 'Dangerous assumptions', *Nature*, 452 (3), 531–532.

Popp, D. (2002). 'Induced innovation and energy prices' *American Economic Review*, 92(1), 160–180.

Pyndyck, R.S. (1979). 'Interfuel substitution and industrial demand for energy: an international comparison', *Review of Economic and Statistics*, 61, 259–289.

Sue Wing, I. (2003). 'Induced technical change and the cost of climate policy.' MIT Joint Program on the Science and Policy of Global Change, Report No. 102, September 2003.

Sue Wing, I. (2006). 'Representing induced technological change in models for climate policy analysis', *Energy Economics*, 28(5–6), pp. 539–562.

van der Werf, Edwin (2008). 'Production functions for climate policy modeling: an empirical analysis', *Energy Economics*, Elsevier, 30(6), 2964–2979.

# Part III
# Sustainability

# 10 Confronting consumption

## Challenges for economics and for policy

*Tim Jackson*

## Introduction[1]

Modern society is organised around a particular model of how to pursue human well-being. Broadly stated, this model contends that increasing consumption leads to improved well-being. This conception of progress has a strong intuitive appeal and a powerful hold over the electorate, which goes some way to explaining why the pursuit of the Gross Domestic Product (GDP) has become one of the principal policy objectives in almost every country in the world in the last few decades. Rising GDP traditionally symbolises a thriving economy, more spending power, richer and fuller lives, increased family security, greater choice, and more public spending. A declining GDP, by contrast, is bad news. Consumer spending falls, business go bust, jobs get lost, homes are repossessed and a Government which fails to respond appropriately is liable to find itself out of office.

The question of why precisely people value consumption goods and services is a critical one. In conventional economics, transactions in the market are assumed to represent the rational choices of informed consumers. In this 'rational choice model', the consumer is conceptualised as a 'rational actor', attempting to maximise well-being or 'utility' within the constraints of the market, according to his or her own individual preferences. This broadly utilitarian model has become so widely accepted that most modern economic textbooks barely even discuss its origins or question its authenticity. Mas-Colell *et al.* (1995), for example, assert that 'it is logical to take the assumption of preference maximisation as a primitive concept for the theory of consumer choice'. Begg *et al.* (2003) simply 'assume that the consumer chooses the affordable bundle [of goods] that maximises his or her utility'.

Economics itself tends to be silent on the precise nature and origins of individual or collective preferences. Consumer choice theory, following Samuelson (1938), has restricted itself largely to deriving demand functions for consumer goods on the basis of 'revealed preferences' in the market. In other words, according to this theory, the best we can say about consumer preferences is what we can infer about them from the patterns of expenditure on consumer goods in the market. If the demand for a particular brand of car or household appliance or consumer electronic is high, then we can infer that consumers, in general, prefer that brand over other brands. The reasons for this preference remain opaque within economics, as do the reasons for choosing Sports Utility Vehicles, patio heaters and DVD players over, say, eco-holidays or leisure activities.

Ironically, practitioners in the field have been considerably more inquisitive about the nature and origins of consumer motivations than economic theorists have. New areas of inquiry such as consumer psychology, marketing and 'motivation research' have developed a rather rich body of knowledge – a 'science of desire' (Dichter 1964) – for producers, retailers, marketers and advertisers wanting to know how to design and sell products that consumers will buy. Little of this research concerns itself explicitly with the environmental or social impacts of consumption. But its insights are crucial to a proper understanding of consumer behaviour. Much of the inspiration for this body of research is drawn from outside economics, in disciplines such as humanistic psychology, sociobiology and anthropology. A part of the function of this chapter is to explore some of these insights.

Though convenient as a rationale for the status quo, the conventional economic assumption that consumption growth is the root to social progress has come under increasing scrutiny in the last few decades. Three related problems (Jackson and Michaelis 2003, Jackson 2006a, Jackson 2007a) have raised the stakes in debates about the rightness or wrongness of the underlying model. The first problem is the failure of the ensuing system to remain within environmental limits. The second is the failure of the model to ensure social justice – or distributional equity. The third is the failure of consumption growth consistently to deliver the improvements in wellbeing predicted for it by conventional economic theory.

These failings have not gone unnoticed either by economists or by policy makers. The concept of sustainable development arose in part as a response to the first two failings (DETR 1999, Defra 2005, Atkinson *et al.* 2007). The recent upsurge of interest in wellbeing and happiness (Layard 2005, Marks *et al.* 2006, Dolan *et al.* 2006) bears testament to the importance of the third. These two phenomena – the emergence of sustainable development and the interest in happiness – hold an interesting relationship to each other. If the existing system failed on environmental and social goals but still in fact served to make us happier, it would be unfortunate. We would be faced with an uncomfortable trade-off between improving human wellbeing and reducing environmental impact. That the two things fail together – at least in developed countries – is potentially more tragic. But it is also potentially more hopeful. It raises the distinct possibility that we might do better; that society might devise different ways to pursue wellbeing which are fairer and have less environmental impact; that we might live better, in other words, by consuming less.

The full ramifications of this hypothesis are beyond the scope of the current chapter. Indeed as I have argued elsewhere (Jackson 2005b, 2006b, 2007b), the task of devising a better model – in which it is possible to live better, to share more equitably and yet to remain within environmental limits – demands a sustained and committed engagement at many different levels of society. In this chapter I want simply to explore in a little more depth the foundational aspects of this challenge. In particular, I want to open out the underlying question of rational choice on which the conventional model hangs and expand on some of the alternative perspectives that have been discussed in its place. In the process, I will inevitably have to question the assumption of consumer sovereignty. Along the way, I will discuss the implications of these failures, both for conventional economics and for policy.

## Rational choice

The rational choice model is so widespread and so deeply entrenched in the institutions and structures of modern (Western) society, that it tends to have an immediate familiarity to us. The basic tenet of the model is that we behave in such a way as to maximise the expected benefits to ourselves (as individuals) from our actions.

A premise of the rational choice model is that human behaviour is a continual process of making deliberative choices between distinct courses of action. Faced with such choices, according to rational choice theory, we weigh up the expected benefits and costs of the different actions, and choose the one that offers the highest expected net benefit or lowest expected net cost to us.[2]

In travelling between home and work, for example, I am faced with a choice whether to go by car or to take public transport. I choose to go by car, because the journey is (generally) shorter, the marginal cost is (usually) lower and I like listening to the radio. Or alternatively, perhaps, I choose public transport because it is (generally) more environmentally friendly, (often) less stressful, and I enjoy the company of strangers.

The process of establishing the net costs and benefits of different alternatives is supposed to have two distinct components. One is a set of expectations about the outcomes of each choice. The other is an evaluation of those outcomes. In the example above, for instance, my choice to travel by car depends both on my expectations (that the journey will be cheaper and shorter) and my (positive) evaluation of those outcomes. This feature of the model often leads to rational choice models being referred to in the literature as expectancy-value models (Fishbein 1973).

One of the key features of the rational choice model (especially in its application to consumer behaviour[3]) is an emphasis on the individual as the unit of analysis. It is individuals who make choices in the model, on the basis of rational deliberations that consist of individual evaluations of subjectively expected outcomes.

The value attached to an outcome is often called the 'utility' of that outcome for the given individual, and the rational choice model is therefore one of a more general class of models sometimes referred to as subjective expected utility (SEU) models. The individual-centred approach of these models is referred to as methodological individualism (Elster 1986, Hodgson 2007). Social behaviour, in this view, is the sum of a collection of individual behaviours, each of which results from deliberative choices based on the subjective expected utility of the individual.

One of the reasons why rational choice theory may seem familiar is that it closely resembles and indeed draws heavily on the intellectual underpinnings of classical economics. Cost–benefit analysis, for example, is nothing more than a highly quantitative form of rational choice model. As we shall see in the following sections, economics certainly does not have the monopoly on rational choice. But the rational choice model is so deeply embedded in the economic theory of consumer preference that it is instructive to make that the starting point of our overview.

### Consumer preference theory

The common economic theory of consumer preferences (see, for example, Begg *et al.* 2003) has four basic elements to it: the consumer's available income, the price of goods on the market, the consumer's tastes or preferences and the behavioural assumption of 'utility maximisation'. Given a limited income, a specific range of goods to choose from, and a potentially infinite set of (exogenous) tastes or preferences, the consumer chooses goods from those available in such a way as to maximise his or her subjective expected utility within the constraints of his or her available income.

Several elements of this model are worth commenting on in more detail. The first is the assumed 'rationality' of consumer choice. Rational consumers are those who make reasoned choices that maximise their expected utility over the set of possible purchases. This is the same concept of rationality, clearly, that is embedded in the rational choice model. In order to achieve this utility maximisation, however, consumers need to be in possession of a certain set of information. In particular, and this is the second point, they will need to know the range of possible goods they could choose from, and the prices of each of these goods. Thus, information plays a key role in the actual behaviour of consumers in real-life situations. 'Rational' choices are only possible in the context of 'perfect' market information.

Next, it is important to note that the preferences or tastes that underlie consumer choice lie outside the model itself. They are assumed exogenous to it. The consumer preference model has little or nothing to say about the nature, structure or origin of consumer preferences. Since Samuelson's (1938) work, the most that economics attempts to say about the structure of individual or collective preference is what is 'revealed' about these preferences through the actual decisions that rational consumers make in the market place.

Finally, it is instructive to note that economic theory has an important assumption of 'non-satiety'. In other words, economics assumes that there is no limit to the desires that consumers have for goods and services. The underlying wants and needs are assumed to be potentially infinite. This requirement is structurally important not just to the operation of the consumer preference model – without it the concept of constraint in relation to utility maximisation would not

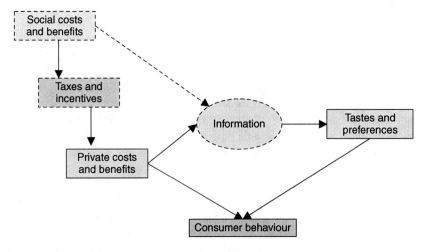

*Figure 10.1* The 'market failure' model of policy.

work – but at one level to the entire project of economics as the science of the allocation of scarce resources.

When it comes to the question of influencing consumer behaviour, the consumer preference model has, at least, the virtue of simplicity. The key influences in any given situation are the range of private costs and benefits and individual taste or preference (Figure 10.1). In addition, of course, the model envisages a key role for information, in allowing consumers to make 'rational' choices. But there still only appear to be two rather limited points of intervention in the model, for policy makers seeking to achieve social goals. One is to ensure that consumers are provided with the requisite information to make rational choices. The other is to adjust private costs and benefits to reflect the existence of social costs and benefits that may lie outside the realm of individual choice.

There is a variation on the consumer preference model that is worth mentioning briefly. This variation was originally proposed in 1966 by Kelvin Lancaster and is hence often referred to as the Lancaster model or sometimes the Attribute model of consumer preference.

Lancaster's suggestion was that consumer preferences for goods are not formed on the basis of the products themselves, but on the attributes that those products possess and the values of those attributes for individual consumers. The economic theory of choice constructed from this suggestion has proved considerably more complex than conventional preference theory. Nonetheless, it has been widely employed and developed to explore consumer preferences for product attributes in sectors as diverse as food (for example, Crawford 2003, Philippidis and Hubbard 2003), luxury cars (Anurit *et al.* 1999), health care (Ryan and Bate 2001), and renewable energy investments (Bergmann *et al.* 2004).

### Rational choice in non-purchasing behaviour

Consumer preference theory – and its extension to 'attributes' – was developed to apply specifically to economic transactions: that is, basically, to a consumer's purchasing behaviours. But the rational choice model has also been applied to people's non-purchasing behaviours. Perhaps the best-known application of rational choice to non-purchasing behaviours is the work of Gary Becker, whose (1976) *Economic Approach to Human Behaviour* and (1981) *Treatise on the Family* won him the Nobel Prize. Becker used the concept of human capital to understand apparently non-economic household behaviours such as divorce, the increase in women's participation in the labour force and the distribution of child-rearing and household labour between men and women.

Consistent with its roots in anthropological theories of social exchange (Homans 1961), rational choice models see exchange as a fundamental determinant of human behaviour. The trade in economic goods and services is only one aspect of social exchange. At a broader level, according to this extended rational choice model, we exchange a variety of different goods (time, gifts, labour, critical appreciation, sexual services and so on) in the expectation that (at least over the long-term) these exchanges will benefit our own self-interest.

In principle, therefore, and to the extent that it is a valid model of behaviour, rational choice theory ought to be useful in describing a wide variety of environmentally relevant behaviours. Establishing the individual costs and benefits of non-purchasing behaviours (recycling, for example) is as important as understanding people's purchasing behaviours (buying recycled goods, for example).

Moreover, the distinction between purchasing and non-purchasing behaviours very often breaks down under careful analysis. More often than not, as the travel behaviour example above illustrates nicely, any such choice will involve both financial and 'non-financial' costs and benefits. Pro-environmental behaviour like many other kinds of behaviour involves both purchasing behaviour and non-purchasing behaviour. The focus on economic exchange inherent in consumer preference theory is to some extent an arbitrary limitation on understanding pro-environmental behaviour. But for the rational choice model, more generally, this is not necessarily a problem. There is a well-established tradition of extending rational choice beyond purchase decisions.

Where we might expect rational choice theory to confront some problems, however, is in relation to moral and social behaviours. Evidence suggests that only a limited proportion of pro-environmental behaviour can be regarded as flowing from a fundamentally self-interested value-orientations. Altruistic, pro-social and biospheric value orientations also appear to be influential in motivating pro-environmental behaviours, and this is particularly likely to be the case where pro-environmental behaviours incur net private costs to those who engage in them.

There are some ways round this problem for rational choice theory, in particular through the concept of extended self-interest. But since the problem of values is part of a wider critique of the rational choice model, we defer discussion of this to the next section.

# Against rational choice

At the heart of rational choice theory lies the image of the self-interested economic person, an image whose roots can be traced back to the writings of Adam Smith, John Stuart Mill and Jeremy Bentham (Russell 2000, Sen 1984). Though powerful as an image, and firmly embedded in many modern institutions, this conception of human action has never been without its critics, and in the last half century the rational choice model has been subject to an increasingly ferocious assault for a variety of reasons.

The rational choice model is built on a number of key assumptions about social action (Scott 2000, Zey 1992, Vatn 2005). These can be categorised under three main headings: (1) that choice is rational; (2) that the individual is the appropriate unit of analysis in social action; and (3) that choices are made in the pursuit of individual self-interest. Most of the criticisms of rational choice theory can be categorised as responses to one or more of these assumptions. The rationality assumption has been attacked mainly on cognitive grounds; the individuality assumption mainly on sociological grounds and the assumption of self-interest mainly on moral and epistemological grounds. In the following subsections I address each of these criticisms in turn.

## *Bounded rationality, habit and emotion*

One of the most famous critiques of the rational choice model lies in the Nobel Prize winning work of Herbert Simon. Simon (1957) argued that in decision-making situations actors face both uncertainties about the future and costs in acquiring information about the present. These two factors, he claimed, limit the extent to which rational decision making (in the sense of a comprehensive calculation of net costs and benefits) is possible. Not only do I simply not have the time to amass all the information necessary to make a thorough comparison between choices; some of that information is simply not available to me, because it concerns events that lie in the (uncertain) future.

Environmental issues in particular raise new kinds of uncertainties for consumers because in many cases the impacts of our actions are distanced from us, either in space or in time. In acting sustainably, consumers are required to take account of agricultural, manufacturing, economic or social processes that take place on the other side of the world – or only become relevant at some point in the future. Moreover, it is often the cumulative effect of many people's actions over time that is problematic rather than my own actions per se.

The problem here is structurally similar to the problem of carrying out a systematic review. In the face of limited resources, a systematic review of the evidence required for 'rational' decision making (policy making) is not always possible, indeed in Simon's view is frequently impossible. The image of choice as a process of rational deliberation over a complete range of alternatives is unrealistic. Decision making in practice is not like that. It occurs under time constraints and operates under cognitive limitations.

Ordinary people in ordinary situations are simply not capable of processing all the cognitive information required for so-called 'rational' choices. Drawing on evidence of the actual behaviour of firms, Simon argued instead for a model of 'bounded rationality' in which actors make decisions not by 'optimising' across all possible choices but by 'satisficing' – that is by setting a minimum level, with which if they achieve they will be 'happy enough'.

One of the ways in which people cope with the cognitive demands of choice, particularly where it occurs on a routine basis, is through a variety of cognitive and emotional heuristics and biases – rules of thumb – against which they tend to make immediate and sometimes not even conscious decisions (Tversky and Kahnemann 1974). The existence of such heuristics and biases again potentially confounds the deliberative model of decision making inherent in rational choice theory.

This kind of low-cognitive-effort decision making is most obvious in the case of what we commonly call routine or habitual behaviours. Routine and habit are increasingly regarded by sociologists and social psychologists as an important aspect of ordinary consumer behaviour (Shove 2003, Shove and Warde 1999). A simple – and relevant – experiment will illustrate the point. Try changing the position of the waste bin in your kitchen. Better still, get someone else to change it for you. And then count how many days it is before you stop going to the wrong place to deposit your waste; and how many times you curse whoever it was suggested the experiment.

The existence of habit, its role in decisions, and its apparent departure from the model of rational cognitive deliberation has exercised critics of rational choice for well over a century. From the early writings of Durkheim (1893) to the more recent sociological work of Bourdieu (1990) and the cognitive psychology of Bargh (1994), Aarts and Verplanken (1999) and others, the role of habit has assumed an important place in the critique of rational choice theory and in the development of social-psychological models of behaviour and behaviour change.

In fact, some attempts can be made to recover the concept of rationality in the face of habit. From one perspective habits can be regarded as cognitive scripts whose role is to reduce the cognitive effort required to make routine decisions whose rationality (i.e. optimality from the perspective of self-interest) has already been determined. For as long as these cognitive scripts serve the interests of rational decisions, they can in fact be regarded as rational habits.[4] In particular, of course, one of their benefits is to reduce the transaction costs associated with rational deliberation.

Quite often however, the existence of counter-intentional habits (Verplanken and Faes 1999) interferes substantially with the ability of the individual to make decisions in his or her own best interests. My inability to locate the kitchen waste bin, seven or eight days after it has been moved, is the result of a deeply ingrained habit that now appears to be interfering with my ability to make rational choices. More generally, in any circumstances in which one is attempting to change one's own behaviour (or indeed the behaviour of others) the transaction costs of rational deliberation appear to be reversed by the existence of habitualised behaviour. A distinct cognitive effort is now required to overcome habitual behaviour, *even where the new behaviour carries substantial benefits to the individual concerned.* In a later section, we shall return to the importance of this issue for policy making.

Quite apart from the role of habit in ordinary behaviour, critics of rational choice theory have also pointed to the emotional or affective dimensions of decision making. I choose to buy this, that or the other shirt, not on the basis of rational calculation of the costs and benefits of a range of options, but because I have an affective response to the colour blue (say). Or to take another example, I decide to keep, rather than give away or have put down, an elderly cat who has suddenly begun to urinate in my study and cause me untold frustration and extra housework, not because I have totted up the costs and benefits of keeping it, but because I have an overriding affection for another creature who has shared a part of my life with me.

Of course, rational choice theory can attempt to recover rationality in these cases by capturing my affective responses to cats and the colour blue within the concept of individual utility, and perhaps even attempt to impute an economic value to these affective responses on the basis of the time and money foregone in cleaning up cat's mess. But from the perspective of those critics of rational choice theory who highlight the role of emotion (Zey 1992, Etzioni 1988), this is an almost futile and potentially tautological attempt to protect a crumbling theory from its own limitations.

In fact, in some constructions, the recognition of emotion as an important influence on human choice threatens to dethrone cognitive deliberation from behaviour altogether. Some attempts have been made to construct a theory of rationality in which reason itself – far from being a deliberative process – is viewed as a set of conditioned responses to patterns of learning laid down as 'emotional markers' in the body (Damasio 1994, 1999). Reason itself, in this model, is a construct of our emotional responses to situations. We make decisions on the basis of our cognitive responses to affective (emotional) states which are themselves the result of physiological triggers in the body, that are built up from both innate responses and learned behaviours reinforced over the history of the individual life.

A slightly different model has been elaborated by Libet (1993) who discovered that people's conscious decisions to initiate bodily movements are preceded by a 'readiness potential' which is involved in sending signals to the muscles to move. In other words, Libet's work supports the hypothesis that unconscious processes initiate choices before cognitive deliberation occurs. Emotion precedes cognition. Libet argued that decision making is the act of choosing to allow or disallow an action to continue, after the action itself has been unconsciously initiated.

Though clearly a long way from rational choice theory, this kind of model does suggest some explanation for the much-lamented (by economists) irrationality of ordinary behaviour. It is also a part of the common wisdom of marketers. The relationship that marketers attempt to establish between brands and consumers is a fundamentally affective one (Roberts 2004, Dichter 1964).

## The argument against individualism

A second strand of the argument against rational choice theory concerns the assumption of individuality. The unit of analysis in rational choice theory is the decision-making process of the individual. Individuals themselves are defined as rational self-interested maximisers of subjective utility. Social behaviour is explained, in rational choice theory, as an emergent property of the individual behaviours and actions of which it is composed. 'The elementary unit of social life is the individual human action,' claims Elster (1986, 13). 'To explain social institutions and social change is to show how these arise as the result of the action and interaction of individuals.'

Of course this critique is not confined to rational choice theory. Many social-psychological models of human behaviour and of behaviour change also presuppose that there is a workable concept of *individual* agency.[5] It makes sense to talk about my individual attitudes and beliefs, the values that I hold personally about the environment, and the way in which those values and beliefs influence my individual deliberations to act in certain ways. It is also defensible to assume that where my personal intentions are strong enough, they will trigger specific individual actions.

I am a committed environmentalist, with a profound belief in the holistic integrity of the earth, and as a result I renounce materialism, invest only in ethical companies and recycle everything. Or, alternatively, I believe that humans hold dominion over the earth and that science and technology hold the key to humanity's continued progress. As a result I resist what I perceive as Luddite attempts to control technology and go out of my way to trade in my performance car for a newer faster model every 18 months. In both cases, the antecedents to my action are generally assumed to be the values, beliefs or preferences that I hold – as an individual.

Again, this kind of 'methodological individualism' is familiar to us because it is deeply embedded in the institutions of the modern economy. The concept of individual choice, the rights of the individual, and the supremacy of individual preference occupy a central role both in the structure of market economies and in the culture of Western society. That there might be any alternative to this conception is, in itself, something that we sometimes have a hard time grasping.

Nonetheless, there is a very long-standing critique of methodological individualism which argues that it is an 'undersocialised' account of human agency and overlooks both our understanding of the relationship between self and other and the nature of decision making and choice in real life (Granovetter 1985, Zey 1992, Hodgson 2007, Vatn 2005). Although it would be impossible to do justice to the complexity of this critique, it is worth highlighting three dimensions of it here.

First, the notion of the individual as an autonomous entity is itself challenged by the social psychology of identity. From the early work of George Herbert Mead, social psychology has proposed a notion of self which is socially constructed. For Mead (1934), the self is the result of 'social conversations'. Indeed, in this view, social interaction is formally antecedent to identity. We learn to construct a sense of self, an identity, but we do so only through our interactions with others (Burr 2002). At the very least, according to social psychology, the relationship between self and other must be regarded as dualistic. Though the concept of an individual 'self' capable of engaging with others and thereby influencing the nature and structure of social conversations is at one level coherent, it depends for its existence and its development on social interaction, on the social conversations that it also plays a part in perpetuating.

This conception of self makes the assumption of individual rationality hard to defend, however. As Zey (1992, 14) contends: 'habits of mind and behaviour develop in a social and cultural context'. Our 'individual' decisions are influenced by our relation to others at a level that is beyond our conscious control. Individual choice in this framing of identity is helplessly mired in the fabric of social norms, expectations and interactions.

A second avenue of criticism against methodological individualism flows from organisational studies of decision making. This avenue points to the fact that in practice a good many decisions are made in a collective, organisational setting. Individual rationality is compromised in this context by the need to account for the wishes and desires of others. But more importantly, organisational psychology suggests that in group situations – where many decisions are made – individuals adopt social roles that are defined by the particular context and situation in which they find themselves. Moreover, the identity of the group itself becomes a key determinant of group behaviour and of the social processes that exist within the group (Tajfel 1982). These intra and inter-group processes undermine the very possibility of individual rationality in such a context.

The final element of the critique against individualism flows from the long-standing concern of sociology with problems of social action and social structure. The question of understanding how social structures arise, how they change and how they influence human behaviour has been central to sociology for at least a century (Giddens 1984). If every social structure could be reduced to the actions of particular individuals, then it might be possible for methodological individualism to account for it. Sociologists argue that this is not the case. In particular, they point to the existence of social structures which do not appear to benefit any particular individual, the longevity of social structures over time (sometimes exceeding many individual lifetimes), the behaviour of individuals in associating themselves with groups that do not appear to support their own self-interest, and the apparent deference of individual behaviour to the wishes of the group in numerous different kinds of situation.

In place of individualist theories of social action, sociologists and social anthropologists have attempted to build structuralist accounts of social action (Polanyi 1944) or else to devise theories of practice (Bourdieu 1990, Reckwitz 2002), where the units of analysis are the components of structure and practice themselves rather than the individual behaviours subsumed within it. I shall return to some of these theories later.

Critics of the sociological approach (Campbell 1996) have accused it of 'over-socialising' human action, just as critics of rational choice theory accuse it of 'under-socialising' individual choice (Vatn 2005). In fact, it turns out that what we are faced with here is a very long-standing debate between two different units of analysis, commonly referred to as agency on the one hand and structure on the other. Or to be more precise, we are caught between proponents of the view that individual agency is the important unit of analysis in understanding social action and proponents of the view that social structure should play that role. As we shall see below, this long-standing debate is mirrored by a very similar and more recent debate between 'internalist' and 'externalist' conceptions of pro-environmental behaviour.

In any such situation, where a modern debate finds itself piggybacking on the structure of a much more long-standing historical debate, we clearly need to take care in adopting hard and fast methodological positions. On the other hand, the extent to which rational choice theory, and many of the familiar institutions that are built on it, has undersocialised human action is strongly supported from a number of different theoretical frameworks and with quite a considerable body of evidence.

## *The moral critique*

The final major critique of rational choice theory takes exception to the idea that humans act only out of self-interest. Once again this debate is as old (at least) as the history of classical economics. Critics of the concept of the self-interested economic person point both to moral dimensions of individual behaviour and to the acceptance by individuals of the moral dimensions of social structures (Scott 2000). Both of these kinds of influences limit the extent to which self-interest actually operates in society, according to critics of rational choice.

The latter issue is clearly related to the problem of accounting for social structure within methodological individualism. Why is it that as individuals we accept social structures at all? One reason might be, as some opponents of individualism suggest, that these structures are formally antecedent to individual behaviour, and that we, as individuals are socialised automatons, helpless in the face of institutional structure. Another possibility is that – as individuals – we recognise that behaviours dominated by self-interest fail to protect the long-term best interests of society at large. But in accepting either of these explanations we are essentially rejecting fundamental aspects of rational choice theory.

The moral dimensions of behaviour are also visible from within the perspective of individual action. Frank (1988) for example points to the place of moral sentiments in human decisions. We routinely forego narrowly conceived self-interest for the sake of broadly altruistic motives. We invest a great deal of time and energy in looking after our children, our relatives, our close friends and occasionally even total strangers. Even more puzzling perhaps, from the perspective of rational choice, is the existence of self-destructive motives such as vengeance and spite, in which we are prepared to wreak havoc on others even at the cost of harm to ourselves.

Some kind of 'rational' explanation for these types of behaviour is offered by evolutionary psychology (Wright 1994, Ridley 1994), which supposes a series of genetically based mechanisms (kin selection, reciprocal altruism and so on) for both altruistic and spiteful behaviours (Hamilton 1970). But the rationality inherent in these explanations is very different from that inherent in the idea of individual self-interest. The genetic explanation for parental love (and other forms of kin selection) lies in the success of such strategies in securing the survival of genes from one generation to the next. But this 'genetically rational' behaviour is prosecuted through individual behaviours which have little or nothing to do with subjective self-interest. Whether these evolutionary mechanisms can offer any comfort to those seeking pro-environmental behaviour is another matter entirely (Jackson 2002).

Some attempts can be made to rescue the 'rationality' of non-self-serving decisions, even within the structure of a subjective expected utility model. In particular, by assigning individual utilities of various kinds to pro-social behaviours, rational choice theory can, to some extent claim to incorporate them within a subjective expected utility model. I behave in an altruistic way, in this view, because there is a value to me (feeling good about myself perhaps, or the expectation that others will reciprocate) that can be incorporated into the cost–benefit equation of rational deliberation. Once again, however, these attempts to extend the boundaries of subjective expected utility theory into a moral terrain have been cast by critics as vein attempts to rescue a crumbling logic through supplementary hypotheses.

At the very least, the existence in practice of clearly defined and measurable pro-social and pro-environmental values that appear to transcend individual self-interest (Schwartz 1977, Stern and Dietz 1994, Schultz 2001) suggests that not all moral behaviour can easily be subsumed under the rational choice model.

## Towards an integrative theory of consumer behaviour

A particular kind of tension is inherent in the debate about consumer behaviour. It concerns the different kinds of variables modelled by different approaches to behaviour. First, one can distinguish a set of approaches that study and model behaviour mainly as a function of processes and characteristics which are conceived as being *internal* to the individual: attitudes, values, habits and personal norms. Another set of approaches studies behaviour as a function of processes and characteristics *external* to the individual: fiscal and regulatory incentives, institutional constraints and social norms.

The 'internalist' approach has mainly been pursued in disciplines such as social and cognitive psychology; the 'externalist' approach has mainly been the domain of disciplines such as applied behavioural analysis and institutional or evolutionary economics. But disciplinary distinctions are not always hard and fast. For example, some early sociology of consumption characterised modern consumers in terms of 'invidious' behaviours conceived of (largely) as responses to internal cognitive processes. Later approaches to the sociology of consumption have placed a great deal more emphasis on external constraints, consumption 'practices' and the 'social logic' of consumer behaviour. Marketing studies typically adopt a more eclectic approach drawing loosely from both perspectives, but tending to emphasise the importance of 'revealed' economic or ethnographic accounts of consumer tastes and preferences.

The distinction between internalist and externalist approaches is important to the debates about sustainable consumption precisely because each approach suggests very different conceptualisations of individual and societal change. Whereas the former approach envisages that changes in consumption patterns will flow from changes in individual beliefs, attitudes and norms, the latter sees change in external conditions as exercising a vital influence on individual behaviours. In the first perspective, enlightened consumers are free to choose pro-environmental behaviours – assuming that they possess appropriate beliefs or attitudes; in the second, consumers are 'locked in' to consumption choices by a variety of external conditions ranging from genetic conditioning to economic necessity, social expectation, accessibility constraints and the 'creeping evolution of social norms'.

It would probably be fair to say that these kinds of tensions are far from being resolved (Jackson and Papathanasopoulou 2007). There have certainly been some ambitious attempts – for example by Bagozzi and his colleagues (Bagozzi *et al.* 2002) and by Stern and his colleagues (Stern *et al.* 1999, Stern 2000, Guagnano *et al.* 1995) – to construct coherent models of consumer behaviour capable of capturing both internalist and externalist dimensions of pro-environmental consumer choice.

The Bagozzi model (Figure 10.2) is perhaps the most elaborate attempt in recent years to incorporate the range of influences on consumer behaviour into a

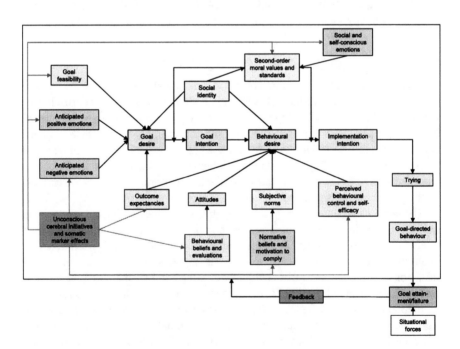

*Figure 10.2* Bagozzi's model of consumer action.

single composite theory of consumer action. What it achieves in terms of heuristic inclusion, however, it lacks in parsimony. Not surprisingly, no attempt has yet been made to apply this theory empirically. Nonetheless, there are a number of studies that test and support many of the individual relations proposed between different variables. Moreover, the model clearly offers a more sophisticated understanding of consumer behaviour than simple expectancy-value theories.

A somewhat more parsimonious attempt to incorporate key features of interpersonal behaviour was developed almost thirty years ago by social psychologist Harry Triandis (1977). He recognised the key role played both by social factors and by emotions in forming intentions. He also highlighted the importance of past behaviour on the present. On the basis of these observations, Triandis proposed a Theory of Interpersonal Behaviour (Figure 10.3) in which intentions – as in many of the other models we have examined – are immediate antecedents of behaviour. But crucially habits also mediate behaviour. Both of these influences are moderated by 'facilitating conditions'.[6]

Equally importantly, intentions are in themselves seen as having three distinct kinds of antecedents. Attitudes – or to be more specific the perceived value of the expected consequences – play a role in mediating intentions, just as they do in Ajzen and Fishbein's (1981) expectancy-value theory. But Triandis is also particularly concerned to include social, affective and habitual factors in the model.

In summary, my behaviour in any particular situation is, according to Triandis, a function partly of what I intend, partly of my habitual responses, and partly of the situational constraints and conditions under which I operate. My

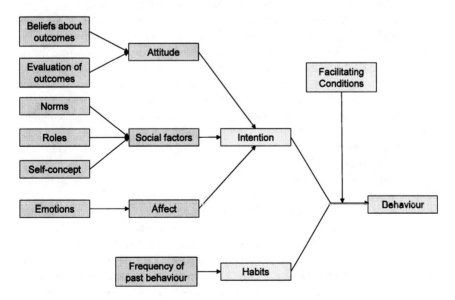

*Figure 10.3* Triandis' theory of interpersonal behaviour.

intentions in their turn are influenced by social, normative and affective factors as well as by rational deliberations. I am neither fully deliberative, in Triandis' model, nor fully automatic. I am neither fully autonomous nor entirely social. My behaviours are influenced by my moral beliefs, but the impact of these is moderated both by my emotional drives and my cognitive limitations.

Triandis' theory of interpersonal behaviour captures some of the criticisms levelled at rational choice theory. It offers a clear heuristic value as a model of social behaviour. It also can be, and has been, used as the framework for empirical analysis of the strengths and weaknesses of the component factors in different kinds of situations. But the internalist–externalist dichotomy in theories of consumer behaviour mirrors a more long-standing, and more deeply entrenched, debate in social science concerning the relationship between agency (or human action) and structure (the social institutions that constitute the framework for human action). The basic dilemma in the agency–structure debate can be expressed in the question: are humans capable of autonomous, directed social action at all; or are they rather locked into historical and social processes over which there is no possibility of individual or collective control?

The dimensions of this problem are complex and involve sociological, biological, historical and philosophical elements. The debate has been explored most thoroughly by sociologists, for whom the attempt to formulate coherent understandings of social action is paramount. This concern with social action, its origins and driving forces, is one of the factors that has led sociology to condemn the one-dimensional rationality inherent in the conventional rational choice model. It has also led some sociologists to attempt to devise more sophisticated forms of 'structuration theory' which attempt to bridge the agency–structure dichotomy and offer more sophisticated, integrative models of social action (Parker 2000).

Perhaps the most well-known form of structuration theory is that of Giddens (1979, 1984) who coined the term 'structuration'. Giddens starting point in trying to build an integrated model of human agency and social structure draws something from the interactionism of Mead and others. Individual subjectivity is mediated through social interaction. Social interaction is what gives individuals access to language, intersubjective interpretation, meaning and knowledge. Only by being embroiled in the social world of others, with whom they can reliably interact, can people achieve 'ontological security' (Giddens 1984, 375). This ontological security provides for a continuing sense of the 'well-foundedness of reality' (Parker 2000, 56).

These propositions allowed Giddens to construct a model of the interconnection between ordinary everyday routine action and the long-term, large-scale evolution of social institutions. Specifically, individual and collective agency provides for the production, regularisation, extension and reproduction of complex patterns of social interaction – or in other words for the 'constitution of society'. But this concept of agency is only possible because actors have access to the 'transformative capacity' of historical social structures, such as language, rules, norms, meanings and power (op. cit., 28–9). These 'rules and resources' are not endowed with agency in and of themselves. But they come to have effect through being known and applied by social actors. Thus, Giddens' model portrays social structure as both the medium and the outcome of people's ordinary social practices.

From the perspective of understanding consumption behaviours, one of the most important elements in structuration theory is a distinction between 'practical' and 'discursive' consciousness. Practical consciousness is the everyday knowledge that people have about how to do things. It depends on a huge wealth of commonly accepted knowledge concerning how to go about things. In fact, Giddens suggests that the bulk of human agency rests in using this kind of practical consciousness in the context of familiar, routine (routinised) situations and behavioural contexts.

In one sense, it is this practical consciousness which allows me to identify the whereabouts of the rubbish bin faultlessly (until it is moved), drive to work without noticing that I have stopped at the lights, and respond effortlessly to many of the trivial tasks that fill my everyday life. Most of this kind of action appears to take place without any recourse to premeditation or conscious, deliberative reasoning.

At the same time, human agency is also characterised by the ability to engage in such reasoning, for example, when asked to expand upon the underlying reasons for (even routine) action. This 'discursive consciousness' consists in everything that actors are able to say about the social conditions of their action. It presupposes both that social actors have an awareness of action and that this awareness has a discursive form – it is prosecuted through social discourse. However, this kind of consciousness does not necessarily describe a process of continual rational deliberation over individual actions. On the contrary, according to Giddens, accounts of intention are generally produced during or after action, rather than before it. Agency is, for the most part, the process of being enmeshed in the repetitive, routine practices of everyday life.

Spaargaren and van Vliet (2000) have used Giddens' structuration theory to suggest a model of consumption as a set of social practices (Figure 10.4) influenced on the one hand by social norms and lifestyle choices and on the other by the institutions and structures of society. They suggest that shifting consumption patterns requires us to 'raise' routine behaviours from the level of practical consciousness to discursive consciousness. Most everyday, routine action is performed in practical consciousness. But there is evidence to suggest that intentional or goal-oriented behaviours require elaboration in discursive consciousness. This insight is particularly important in devising strategies to change habitual behaviour.

In summary, it should be clear that recent understandings of consumer behaviour, and of pro-environmental consumer behaviour in particular, go some way towards answering critiques of the rational choice model. In particular, social-psychological models attempt to account, systematically, for moral, social, symbolic and affective (as well as reasoned) components of consumer behaviour. They show how cognitive processes and unconscious biases impact on goal-directed behaviour. They highlight the importance of habit, both in reducing the

Actors              Human Action            Social Practices            Structures

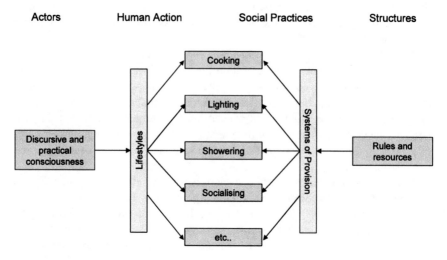

*Figure 10.4* Consumption as social practice (after Spaargaren and van Vliet 2000).

cognitive effort associated with goal-directed behaviour, but also in moderating behavioural intentions.

The issue of habit illustrates very clearly the existence of trade-offs between different components of consumer decision making. Cognitive efficiency – sometimes reinforced by short-run rewards – means that we are often locked into counter-intentional habits, in spite of our best intentions. Affective motivations (emotions) often conflict with moral concerns. Social norms interfere with individual preference. Situational conditions interfere with intention. The broad social and cultural context is a powerful influence on attitudes and motivations.

Choice, in these circumstances, is never a straightforward process of individual rational deliberation. Intentions and desires are continually moderated by social, cognitive, situational and cultural factors.

## Concluding remarks

Policies to encourage pro-environmental behaviour have tended in the past to favour two main avenues of intervention (Figure 10.1). The first avenue is information intensive. It assumes that providing people with appropriate information about (for example) climate change or air pollution will change their attitudes – and hence their behaviours in pro-environmental or pro-social ways. The second perspective attempts to influence the private economic costs and benefits associated with individual behaviours. In this perspective, the aim of policies has been to propose a variety of taxes and incentive schemes to encourage pro-environmental change.

Sadly, the evidence does not support optimism in relation to either of these perspectives – at least by themselves. The history of information and advertising campaigns to promote sustainable behavioural change is littered with failures (Geller *et al.* 1983, McKenzie-Mohr 2000). In one extreme case, a California utility spent more money on advertising the benefits of home insulation than it would have cost to install the insulation itself in the targeted homes (McKenzie-Mohr 2000).

The fiscal approach has also faced limited success in encouraging long-term pro-environmental behaviour changes. Although there is evidence to suggest that price differentials (for example) are sometimes successful in persuading people to shift between different fuels, there is much less convincing evidence of the success of economic strategies in improving energy efficiency overall or in shifting behaviours more generally. Examples of pro-environmental interventions which offer both private benefits to individual consumers are legion. Yet it is well known that people still tend not to take up these options. A variety of different obstacles and barriers are blamed for this (Sorrell *et al.* 2000).

McKenzie-Mohr (2000) argues that the failure of such campaigns to foster sustainable behaviours is partly the result of a failure to understand the sheer difficulty associated with changing behaviours. As a review of the Residential Conservation Service – an early energy conservation initiative in the US – once concluded, most such efforts tend to overlook 'the rich mixture of cultural practices, social interactions, and human feelings that influence the behaviour of individuals, social groups and institutions' (Stern and Aronson 1984).

The evidence reviewed in this chapter tends to support that view. The two conventional avenues of intervention both flow from the rational choice model of human behaviour. The limitations of this perspective have been explored extensively here. The failures of the rational choice model to account adequately for matters of habit, moral behaviours, emotional and affective responses, cognitive limitations, the importance of social norms and expectations and the social embeddedness of individual behaviour have been extensively documented.

The lessons from all this are salutary. Looking at consumer behaviour through a social and psychological lens reveals a complex and outwardly hostile landscape that appears to defy conventional policy intervention. Consumer behaviours and motivations are complex and deeply entrenched in conventions and institutions. Social norms and expectations appear to follow their own evolutionary logics, immune to individual control. Social learning is powerful but not particularly malleable. Persuasion is confounded by the information density of modern society.

The rhetoric of 'consumer sovereignty' is inaccurate and unhelpful here because it regards choice as entirely individualistic and because it fails to unravel the social and psychological influences on people's behaviour. Some behaviours are motivated by rational, self-interested, and individualistic concerns. But conventional responses neither do justice to the complexity of consumer behaviour nor exhaust the possibilities for policy intervention in pursuit of behavioural change.

At one level, the intractability of consumer behaviour is a function of the policy model which has dominated conventional thinking on pro-environmental and pro-social change. But the evidence suggests that this model is inaccurate. Despite the rhetoric of modern 'hands-off' governance, policy intervenes continually in the behaviour of individuals both directly (through taxes, regulations and incentives) and (more importantly) through its extensive influence over the social and institutional context.

One of the key avenues through which Government intervenes in consumer behaviour is in the framing of the economic conditions under which society operates. I started out in this chapter pointing to the model of social progress in which the route to improved wellbeing lies through the pursuit of consumption growth. In setting the pursuit of GDP growth at the heart of policy, Governments have inadvertently created a whole range of situational conditions, institutions and cultural norms which now constrain and shape human behaviour.

At the most basic level, this system is hungry for consumers. The stability of the system itself depends on expanding demands, fast-moving lifestyles, acquisitive habits, competitive behaviours. If everyone actually went out and did what current Government campaigns on carbon emissions appear to ask – drive less, turn off televisions, buy recycled goods, make do and mend, for example – there is every chance that the system itself would collapse. Perhaps its just as well that above-the-line communication campaigns are doomed to failure. Behaviour change cannot happen without institutional change. Institutional change cannot happen without an engaged effort by Government to rethink existing cultural frameworks. One of those frameworks is the one which holds that progress is about increasing consumption.

In short, Governments are not just innocent bystanders in the negotiation of consumer choice. They influence and co-create the culture of consumption in a variety of ways. In some cases, this influence proceeds through specific interventions – such as the imposition of regulatory and fiscal structures. In other cases it proceeds through the *absence* of regulations and incentives. Most often it proceeds through a combination of the ways in which Government intervenes and the ways in which it chooses not to. Sometimes, its roots go deep into our cultural assumptions about the nature of the 'good life'.

As this chapter has tried to demonstrate, a genuine understanding of the social and institutional context of consumer action opens out a much more creative vista for policy innovation than has hitherto been recognised. Expanding on these opportunities is the new challenge for sustainable consumption policy.

## Notes

1  This chapter is based in part on a lecture given by the author to the inaugural meeting of Heednet in May 2004; and in part on a review of behaviour change theories prepared by the author for the Sustainble Development Research Network (Jackson 2005).
2  The literature on rational choice models and criticisms of them is huge. A useful overview of the theory and common critiques can be found in Scott (2000). Key rational choice texts include Becker (1976), Elster (1986), Friedman and Hechter (1990), Homans (1961).
3  The rational choice model has also been applied to the behaviour of entities other than

human individuals, for example, firms. But even in this case, the basic assumption is that the organisation operates as an individual entity in the deliberative framework.
4 Simon (1957) coined the term procedural rationality to refer to the rationality inherent in this context, as opposed to the 'substantive rationality' embodied in the rational choice model.
5 See Jackson (2005a) for an overview of some of these models.
6 Similar notions to 'facilitating conditions' – sometimes called 'contextual variables', 'situational factors' or 'opportunities' – are apparent in a number of other attempts at integrative frameworks for understanding behaviour, including Stern's attitude-behaviour-constraint (ABC) model (Stern 2000, Guagnano *et al.* 1995, Stern *et al.* 1999) as well as the motivation-opportunity-abilities (MOA) model proposed by Ölander and Thøgersen (1995).

# References

Aarts, H., B. Verplanken and A. van Knippenberg 1998. Predicting Behavior from Actions in the Past: repeated decision-making or a matter of habit? *Journal of Applied Social Psychology* 28(15), 1355–1374.

Ajzen, I. and M. Fishbein 1980. *Understanding Attitudes and Predicting Social Behaviour*. Englewood Cliffs, NJ: Prentice-Hall Inc.

Anurit, J., K. Newman and B. Chansarker 1999. Consumer Behaviour of Luxury Automobiles: a comparative study between Thai and UK Customers, Discussion Paper, London: Middlesex University Business School.

Atkinson, G., S. Dietz and E. Neumayer 2007. *Handbook in Sustainable Development*. Cheltenham: Edward Elgar.

Bagozzi, R., Z. Gürnao-Canli and J. Priester 2002. *The Social Psychology of Consumer Behaviour*. Buckingham: Open University Press.

Bargh, J. 1994. The Four Horsemen of Automaticity: awareness, intention, efficiency, and control in social cognition. In R. Wyer and T. Skrull (eds) *Handbook of Social Cognition (2nd edition) Vol 1*: Basic Processes. Hillsdale, NJ: Lawrence Erlbaum.

Begg, David, S. Fischer and R. Dornbusch 2003. *Economics 7th edition*. Maidenhead: McGraw-Hill.

Becker, G. 1981. *A Treatise on the Family*. Cambridge, MA: Harvard University Press.

Becker, G. 1976. *The Economic Approach to Human Behaviour*. Chicago: University of Chicago Press.

Bergmann, Ariel, Nick Hanley and Robert Wright 2004. Valuing Attributes of Renewable Energy Investments, Applied Environmental Economics Conference, 26 March, London: Royal Society.

Bourdieu, Pierre 1990. *The Logic of Practice*. Stanford, CA: Stanford University Press.

Burr, V. 2002. *The Person in Social Psychology*. New York: Taylor and Francis.

Campbell, Colin 1996. *The Myth of Social Action*. Cambridge: Cambridge University Press.

Crawford, Ian 2003. Variations in the price of foods and nutrients in the UK. Working paper No WP03/19. London: Institute for Fiscal Studies.

Damasio, A. 1999. *The Feeling of What Happens: Body and Emotion in the Making of Consciousness*. New York: Harcourt Brace.

Damasio, A. 1994. *Descartes' Error: Emotion, Reason and the Human Brain*. New York: Avon.

Defra 2005. Securing the Future. The UK Sustainable Development Strategy. London: TSO.

DETR 1999. A better quality of life. The UK Sustainable Development Strategy. London: HMSO.

Dichter, E. 1964. *The Handbook of Consumer Motivations: the psychology of consumption*, New York: McGraw Hill.

Dolan, P., T. Peasgood and P. White 2006. A review of evidence on wellbeing. A report to Defra. London: Defra.

Durkheim, E. 1893. [1964] *The Division of Labor in Society*. New York: Free Press.

Elster, John 1986. *Rational Choice*. Oxford: Basil Blackwell.

Etzioni, Amitai 1988. Normative-affective factors: towards a new decision-making model. *Journal of Economic Psychology* 9, 125–150.

Fishbein, Martin 1973. The prediction of behaviour from attitudinal variables. In C. Mortensen, and K. Sereno (eds) *Advances in Communications Research*. New York: Harper and Row, 3–31.

Frank, R. 1988. The theory of moral sentiments, in *Passions within Reason: the Strategic Role of the Emotions*. New York: W W Norton.

Friedman, D. and M. Hechter 1990. The comparative advantages of rational choice theory, in G. Ritzer, (ed.) *Frontiers of Social Theory*. New York: Columbia University Press.

Geller, E., J. Ericksson and B. Buttram 1983. Attempts to promote residential water conservation with educational, behavioral and engineering strategies. *Population and Environment Behavioral and Social Issues* 6, 96–112.

Giddens, A. 1979. *Central Problems in Social Theory*. Cambridge: Polity Press.

Giddens, A. 1984. *The Constitution of Society – outline of the theory of structuration*. Berkeley and Los Angeles: University of California Press.

Granovetter, M. 1985. Economic action and social structure: the problem of embeddedness. *American Journal of Sociology* 91(3), 481–510.

Guagnano, G., P. Stern and T. Dietz 1995. Influences on attitude behavior relationships – a natural experiment with curbside recycling, *Environment and Behavior* 27(5), 699–718.

Hamilton, W. 1970. Selfish and Spiteful Behaviour in an Evolutionary model. *Nature* 228, 1218–1220.

Homans, G. 1961. *Social Behaviour: its elementary forms*. London: Routledge and Kegan Paul.

Jackson, T. 2002. Evolutionary psychology and ecological economics – consilience, consumption and contentment. *Ecological Economics* 41(2), 289–303.

Jackson, T. 2005a. Motivating sustainable consumption – a review of evidence on consumer behaviour and behavioural change. London: Sustainable Development Research Network.

Jackson, T. 2005b. Live better by consuming less? Is there a double dividend in sustainable consumption? *Journal of Industrial Ecology* 9(1–2), 19–36.

Jackson, T. 2006a Beyond the wellbeing paradox: wellbeing, consumption growth and sustainability. Annex in Marks *et al.* (2006).

Jackson, T. 2006b *Earthscan Reader in Sustainable Consumption*. London: Earthscan/ James and James.

Jackson, T. 2007a. Sustainable consumption in Atkinson *et al.* (2007), 254–268.

Jackson, T. 2007b. Where is the wellbeing dividend? Inequality, growth and consumption inequalities. *Local Environment*. Forthcoming.

Jackson, T. and L. Michaelis 2003. Policies for sustainable consumption. London: Sustainable Development Commission.

Jackson, T. and E. Papathanasopoulou 2007. Luxury or lock-in? An exploration of unsustainable consumption in the UK 1968–2000. Accepted for publication in *Ecological Economics*.

Hodgson, G. 2007. Meanings of methodological individualism. *Journal of Economic Methodology*, 14(2), June, 211–226.

Layard, R. (ed.) 2004. Happiness. A report of the Happiness Forum. London: London School of Economics.

Libet, B. 1993. *Neurophysiology of Consciousness*. Boston, MA: Birkhäuser.

Marks, N., S. Thompson, R. Eckersley, T. Jackson and T. Kasser. 2006. *Sustainable development and well-being: relationships, challenges and policy implications. A report by the centre for wellbeing*, nef on Wellbeing Project 3b for Defra. 1–135. London: New Economics Foundation.

Mas-Colell, A., M. Whinston and J. Green 1995. *Microeconomic Theory*. Oxford: Oxford University Press.

McKenzie-Mohr, D. 2000. Promoting sustainable behavior: an introduction to community-based social marketing. *Journal of Social Issues* 56(3), 543–554.

Mead, G. 1934. *Mind Self and Society*. Chicago: University of Chicago Press.

Ölander, Folke and John Thøgersen 1995. Understanding consumer behaviour as prerequisite for environmental protection. *Journal of Consumer Policy* 18, 345–385.

Parker, J. 2000. *Structuration*. Buckingham: Open University Press.

Philippidis, George and Lionel Hubbard 2003. Modelling hierarchical consumer preferences: an application to global food markets. *Applied Economics* 35, 1679–1684.

Polanyi, K. 1944. *The Great Transformation: the political and economic origin of our times*. Boston, MA: Beacon Press.

Reckwitz, A. 2002 Toward a theory of social practices: a development in culturalist theorizing, *European Journal of Social Theory*, 5(2), 243–263.

Roberts, K. 2004. *Lovemarks – the future beyond brands*. New York: Powerhouse Books.

Ryan, M. and A. Bate 2001. Testing the assumptions of rationality, continuity and symmetry when applying discrete choice experiments in health care, *Applied Economics* 8, 59–63.

Samuelson, P. 1938. A note on the pure theory of consumers' behaviour. *Economica*

Scott, John. 2000. Rational Choice Theory, in G. Browning, A. Halcli, N. Hewlett, and F. Webster (eds) *Understanding Contemporary Society: theories of the present*. London: Sage 5, 61–71.

Schultz, P. Wesley 2001. The Structure of Environmental Concern: concern for self, other people and the biosphere. *Journal of Economic Psychology* 21, 327–339.

Schwartz, Shalom 1977. Normative Influences on Altruism, *Advances in Experimental Social Psychology* 10, 222–279.

Shove, E. 2003. *Comfort, Cleanliness and Convenience*. London: Routledge.

Shove, E. and A. Warde 1997. Noticing Inconspicuous Consumption, paper presented to the European Science Foundation TERM programme workshop on Consumption, Everyday Life and Sustainability, Lancaster April 1997.

Simon, H. 1957. *Models of Man*. New York: John Wiley.

Sorrell, S., J. Schleich, S. Scott, E. O'Malley, F. Trace, U. Boede, K. Ostertag and P. Radgen, 2000. Barriers to Energy Efficiency in Public and Private Organisations, Final report, project JOS3CT970022, Brussels: European Commission.

Spaargaren, G. and B. van Vliet 2000. Lifestyle, Consumption and the environment: the ecological modernisation of domestic consumption. *Society and Natural Resources* 9, 50–76.

Stern, P. 2000. Toward a coherent theory of environmentally significant behavior, *Journal of Social Issues* 56(3), 407–424.

Stern, P. and T. Dietz 1994. The value basis of environmental concern. *Journal of Social Issues* 50, 65–84.

Stern, P., T. Dietz, T. Abel, G. Guagnano and L. Kalof 1999. A value-belief norm theory of support for social movements: the case of environmental concern. *Human Ecology Review* 6, 81–97.

Tajfel, H. (ed.) 1982. *Social Identity and Intergroup Relations*. Cambridge: Cambridge University Press.

Triandis, Harry 1977. *Interpersonal Behaviour*. Monterey, CA: Brooks/Cole.

Tversky, A. and D. Kahneman 1974. Judgement under uncertainty: heuristics and biases. *Science* 185, 1124–1131.

Vatn, A. 2005. Rationality, institutions and environmental policy. *Ecological Economics* 55: 203–217.

Verplanken, Bas and Suzanne Faes 1999. Good intentions, bad habits and effects of forming implementation Intentions on healthy eating. *European Journal of Social Psychology* 29, 591–604.

Weitzman, M. 1976. On the welfare significance of thenational product in a dynamic Economy. *Quarterly Journal of Economics* 90:156–62.

Wright, R. 1994. *The Moral Animal – why we are the way we are: the new science of evolutionary psychology*. Abacus: London.

Zey, Mary (ed.) 1992. *Decision-making: alternatives to rational choice models*. London: Sage.

# 11 Social and psychological drivers of energy consumption behaviour and energy transitions

*Lorraine Whitmarsh*

## Introduction

There are several important policy agendas which are converging towards pursuit of a low-carbon society. The most visible and pressing of these is climate change, which is a priority for many governments, including the UK, whose Climate Change Bill commits the nation to cutting its carbon emissions by 80 per cent by 2050 (HM Government, 2008). This political interest is underpinned by scientific evidence of the human influence on climate associated primarily with fossil energy use (IPCC, 2007), and by economic arguments for the importance of action to both mitigate and adapt to climate change (Stern, 2007). At the same time, interest in a low-carbon future is driven by concerns about energy security and competitiveness. At both EU and member state levels, renewables targets and energy efficiency measures are in large part a response to this concern. In the UK, the impending closure of many coal and nuclear plants and increasing energy demand are foreshadowing a 'generation gap' in supply which will need to be addressed by both changes in energy supply and demand. Competitiveness is another element driving low-carbon innovation, and both public and private research and development into new energy sources and carriers (e.g. hydrogen) is in part a response to fear of being left behind in international competition (e.g. Whitmarsh and Wietschel, 2008). Social policy concerns with regard to fuel poverty and obesity similarly feed into the move towards less carbon-intensive and more energy-efficient lifestyles.

The implications of these changes for society are considerable. Clearly, to decarbonise societies to the degree which scientific evidence implies, and which policy targets demand, requires concerted action from all sections of society. Broadly speaking, a transition to a low-carbon society involves at least one (but probably all) of the following changes to energy systems: decarbonising supply, increasing efficiency, and reducing demand. In all three of these areas, there is a role for the public at individual and/or community levels. First, decarbonising supply cannot be achieved without public support – either for new centralised generation and supply infrastructure (e.g. nuclear power) or, more directly, through adoption of micro-generation technologies. Second, on the demand side, there are huge gains to be made through greater efficiency and reduced energy demand by end users. Direct energy use by individuals (for domestic and travel purposes) accounts for around two-fifths of national emissions; and indirect energy use (associated with products and services consumed) contributes yet more (e.g. DEFRA, 2005). Thus, individual choices about – and use of – heating systems, home insulation, appliances, vehicles, lighting, eating, clothing, leisure, travel, and so on, clearly have implications for energy demand and associated emissions. Policies to address energy demand will equally need public support to be workable, not to mention legitimate. But individuals and communities need not be passive in this process, merely resigned to the role of recipients of policy designed by government officials or of technologies developed by industry. Rather, individuals may actively shape – or resist – policies through various processes and channels, and engage in grassroots innovation that may drive wider social change towards sustainability (e.g. Seyfang and Smith, 2007).

In either case – whether the public adopts a passive or an active role in a potential low-carbon transition – there is a need for social science to elucidate the drivers of energy use and of changes in energy use at both individual and broader societal levels. In this chapter, I draw on this social science literature – in particular on psychological, sociological, governance, and transitions research on drivers of energy use, low-carbon innovation and lifestyles, and civic engagement – to consider the roles which the public may play in a potential transition to a low-carbon society. In doing so, I particularly draw attention to the non-rational and often unconscious drivers of energy use, and thus present a perspective on energy behaviour which contrasts with neoclassical economic models of consumption.

## Public engagement with climate change and low-carbon lifestyles

There is a considerable body of literature pertaining to public engagement with climate change (e.g. Lorenzoni *et al.*, 2007; Whitmarsh, 2009b). Surveys indicate that public awareness of climate change has been rising in recent years, and is currently very high. In England, for example, two-thirds of the public say they know 'a lot' or 'a fair amount' about climate change and over half know a lot or fair amount about carbon dioxide (Figure 11.1; Whitmarsh *et al.*, in press). Concern, too, about climate change has been rising (e.g. Upham *et al.*, 2009), although in the context of other day-to-day concerns, climate change is not a priority issue. In general, other personal, social and even environmental issues (e.g. pollution) are more concerning (Poortinga and Pidgeon, 2003). Similarly, while climate change for example, is seen as a risk for society, it is not considered as a personal risk issue. In the UK, 52 per cent believe that climate change will have 'little' or 'no effect' on them personally (BBC, 2004); and most see the most serious impacts as befalling those in other countries (O'Neill and Nicholson-Cole, 2009). Such research findings indicate that climate change is an issue which is perceived by the large majority of individuals as being spatially and temporally remote.

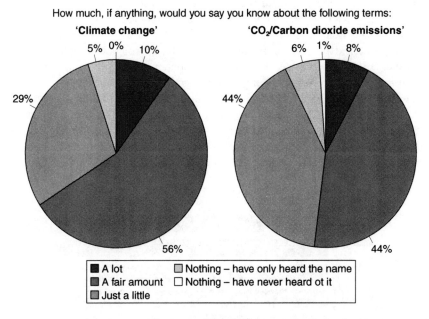

How much, if anything, would you say you know about the following terms:

*Figure 11.1* Public knowledge about climate change and carbon dioxide in the UK (adapted from Whitmarsh *et al.*, in press).

Similarly, public understanding about climate change and carbon remains rather vague and abstract. In general, non-expert publics tend to conceptually integrate environmental issues into one broad category in which 'pollution' is the overriding discourse. Technical distinctions between different issues are blurred; most commonly, ozone depletion and climate change are confused (e.g. Hargreaves *et al.*, 2003), although individuals often make links between climate change and a range of other environmental problems or similar concepts (e.g. waste, carbon monoxide; Whitmarsh, 2009b; Whitmarsh *et al.*, in press). Qualitative research demonstrates, too, that the language individuals use to discuss climate change tends to be fairly generic and abstract. If links are made to particular activities, they are typically industrial processes or deforestation, while little (if any) connection is made to personal choices or actions (Thompson and Rayner, 1998; Whitmarsh, 2009b; Whitmarsh *et al.*, in press). Often, understanding and attitudes about climate change are, to some degree, uncertain; and a significant minority remain sceptical about the reality or human causes of climate change (around 18 per cent in the UK, according to DEFRA, 2007).

Consistent with this lack of public engagement with climate change, few are choosing to adopt low-carbon lifestyles. Although there is widespread stated support for action to tackle climate change (e.g. Poortinga *et al.*, 2006), few are making changes to their own lifestyles to address the issue (Whitmarsh, 2009a). The main responsibility for tackling climate change is located by the public with

216   *L. Whitmarsh*

governments, and individuals appear to identify themselves as passive bystanders. There is greater public support for policies to promote renewable energy and provide low-carbon products and services than for measures to restrict individuals' use of existing carbon-intensive options (e.g. through carbon taxes, road tolls, etc. BBC, 2004; Fortner *et al.*, 2000; O'Connor *et al.*, 2002). The extent to which individuals are currently engaged in – and prepared to engage in – environmentally friendly or low-carbon behaviour appears to be limited to recycling and (to a lesser extent) domestic energy conservation. For example, in a recent English survey, 71 per cent claimed they 'always' recycle, and 67 per cent 'always' turn off lights they are not using. But beyond this, behaviour is largely unchanged. A minority are changing their shopping, eating, or travel habits (e.g.

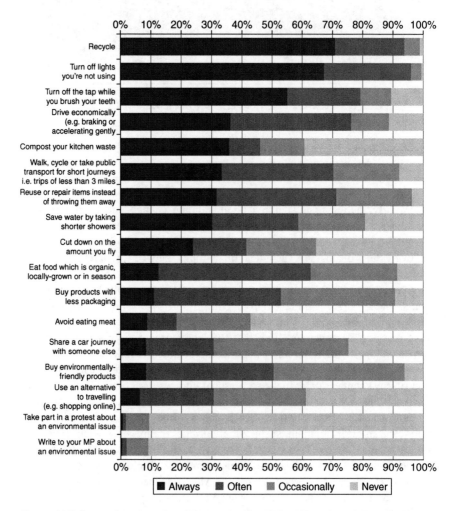

*Figure 11.2* Pro-environmental action amongst the UK public (adapted from Whitmarsh *et al.*, in press).

33 per cent always walk, cycle, or take public transport for short journeys, and 6 per cent always use alternatives to travel, such as online shopping) and political engagement (e.g. writing to MPs or protesting) is lower still (Figure 11.2; Whitmarsh *et al.*, in press). Thus, there appears to be a disparity between awareness about climate change, on the one hand, and individual action to effectively tackle it, on the other.

This 'value–action' gap, as it is often known, is due to individual and institutional barriers to adopting low-carbon lifestyles (e.g. Lorenzoni *et al.*, 2007). These barriers range from individual lack of knowledge and competing values through to cultural norms, systems of provision, and physical infrastructures which serve to lock individuals into more carbon-intensive lifestyles. In the following section, I elaborate on these drivers of energy use and, in particular, argue that the multiple and often unconscious determinants of energy consumption pose particular challenges for those seeking to change it. This contrasts with neoclassical economic models of consumption which construct consumers as rational, consistent, and driven by economic self-interest.

## Social and psychological drivers of energy use

To understand the reasons why individuals are typically not adopting low-carbon lifestyles, we can refer to the social science literature on energy use. Here, I focus primarily on psychological and sociological perspectives since these tend to be overlooked in energy policy (and, indeed, policy in general), which favours economic approaches. However, as I will show, economic models of consumption and consumers are partial and often inaccurate. Psychological and sociological research highlights both individual and structural drivers of consumption. Individual motivations for consumption, including energy use, comprise hedonic, financial, and social desires, as well as material needs. In relation to domestic heating, individuals are typically driven by a desire for comfort (Gatersleben and Vlek, 1998) while choice and use of domestic appliances may be the result of considerations about convenience, aesthetics, re-sale value, and so on (e.g. Layton *et al.*, 1993). Where individuals choose to conserve energy – for example, turn off lights or cycle to work – this is generally motivated by personal (e.g. financial, health) benefits, while environment (if it is considered at all) is more likely to be a secondary motive (Brandon and Lewis, 1999; Whitmarsh, 2009a). Social influences are also important in respect of energy consumption. Consumption practices are often as much about expressing identity and establishing status, as about meeting personal needs or desires. This is particularly evident in car choice and use (Steg *et al.*, 2001), but also in domestic energy contexts (Layton *et al.*, 1993). For example, owning an air conditioning system is associated with affluence and status in some cultures (Wilhite *et al.*, 1997). Similarly, there is a widespread association of car ownership with 'quality of life' (e.g. Black *et al.*, 2001).

Here, the individual and broader structural drivers of energy consumption begin to blur: individuals' stated preferences and 'needs' may be an expression of unexamined social conventions, expectations, and assumptions about what constitutes 'normal' or 'desirable'. Sociological and cultural research has described energy use as embedded within wider cultural trends towards consumerism, insatiable wants transformed into 'needs,' shifting conventions of normality, increasing individualisation, the use of consumption to define the self and, (un)sustainable socio-technical systems of provision or supply (e.g. Jackson and Marks, 1999; Røpke, 1999). Psychologists have not been entirely absent from this view of shifting conventions: Eysenck (1994), for example, has described the 'hedonic treadmill' in which 'people respond to increased prosperity by expecting it to increase, and these rising expectations diminish the happiness that prosperity would otherwise have produced' (p. 96). This description is consistent with evidence that well-being has not increased across society since the 1950s, despite wealth rising significantly since that time (Jackson and Marks, 1999). At the same time, individuals increasingly define and express themselves through material and energy consumption; thus, consumption contributes to meeting innate psychological needs for self-expression and belonging (Dittmar, 1992).

Crucially, though, energy consumption is often *multiply* motivated or determined. That is, individuals often have several reasons for doing something, such as choosing a particular mode of transport or domestic appliance. Social, financial, health, environmental, and other factors may all be considered; as will the various 'roles' that individuals assume (as parent, employee, investor, consumer, citizen, friend, etc.). This complexity of behavioural determinants may lead to actions appearing 'irrational'; for example, someone may cook two meals at once to save electricity, but leave the heating on for the cat (Layton *et al.*, 1993). Indeed, materialist values are often expressed by people with high environmental values (Gatersleben *et al.*, 2008). For example, environmentalists are amongst those who choose to fly, and justify this apparent inconsistency in various ways (e.g. holidays perceived as a break from environmental, as well as social, obligations; Barr *et al.*, 2010). In this context, policy for a low-carbon society cannot rely solely on economic policy; economic signals intended to encourage low-carbon lifestyles will be interpreted alongside other drivers and constraints on behaviour.

It is not only the cultural dimensions of consumption which are invisible. Energy consumption is often embedded in routines which are rarely opened up to scrutiny by the individuals who perform them. This is an area in which psychologists and sociologists converge, though the terminology they use differs. While sociologists speak of 'routines' and 'social practices', psychologists refer to 'habits'. Habits are characterised by frequent and automatic behaviours, which are cued by a stable context (e.g. Verplanken *et al.*, 2008). Energy-use behaviours move quickly from considered deliberations over personal costs and benefits to the habitual sphere, where behaviour can be executed more efficiently and with reduced cognitive burden (Bamberg and Schmidt, 2003). Travel behaviours (e.g. commuting), in particular, tend to be strongly habitual (Verplanken *et al.*, 1998). As such, they are difficult to change, particularly through conventional information-based approaches, such as mass media campaigns, because experimental studies show that habits attenuate attention to new information

(Verplanken *et al.*, 1997). In other words, individuals who habitually drive will tend to ignore information about other modes of transport. Changing habits is most effective when interventions (e.g. information, incentives) are targeted to points in time when individuals are reconsidering their routines, for example when they move house or change jobs and need to plan afresh how to travel to their workplace (e.g. Bamberg, 2006). After such life changes, individuals are also more likely to realign their behaviour to be consistent with their values (Verplanken *et al.*, 2008). Clearly, structural changes – such as road closures, parking restrictions, tolls, and so on – also serve to disrupt habits and routines; and where individuals are 'forced' through such changes to try alternatives, they are more likely to continue using them (thus creating a new habit) (e.g. Fujii *et al.*, 2001).

Summarising this vast literature is a challenge, but there are two key points which deserve particular attention. First, consumption is complex and multiply determined; and second, energy use is often unconscious due to the invisibility of energy per se, the hidden cultural drivers of escalating consumption and energy demand, and the psychological process of habit-formation. The implications for policy are that information-based persuasion appeals will have minimal impact, unless targeted to individuals' (various) concerns, needs and identities and to points in time when they are likely to be reconsidering their routines. Furthermore, policy will need to focus more 'upstream' in order to avoid the establishment of 'bad habits' (i.e., carbon-intensive routines) and to create viable and attractive low-carbon alternatives through changes in systems of provision and infrastructures. Finally, reliance on economic approaches is insufficient to address the multiple drivers of energy use, and individuals' desire not only to maintain, but often to increase, their energy consumption, even in the face of economic disincentives (e.g. taxes) due to behavioural routines, personal aspirations, social expectations, and cultural norms.

## Active role(s) for the public in an energy transition

So far, I have discussed the drivers of energy use and the implications for changing lifestyles. However, this has assumed a relatively passive role in a potential low-carbon energy transition. Recently, research has begun to consider how the public may be more active in societal innovation for low-carbon (or more broadly sustainable) futures (e.g. Nye, Whitmarsh, and Foxon, 2010; Whitmarsh *et al.*, in press). Here, two literatures in particular are relevant for exploring the scope and limitations of public engagement in social change: first, participatory decision making and civic engagement; and second, socio-technical transitions.

### Public participation and civic engagement

UK environmental policy has traditionally sought market solutions to environmental problems and framed the role of the public as 'consumers', typically encouraging voluntary behaviour change by individuals through information campaigns and economic (dis)incentives. Yet, public action to protect the environment can take place in the private sphere (e.g. green consumerism, conservation behaviour) *and* in the public sphere, in the form of socio-political participation (Stern, 2000). The latter is a vital element of democracies that is associated with various benefits, if organised and conducted appropriately (see Dietz and Stern, 2008 for a review). Public participation in environmental decision making can: improve the quality of decision making by drawing on diverse knowledge; allow explicit representation of social values and personal preferences in decisions about what future we 'should' and 'would like to' have; and potentially – through the process itself – foster trust, ownership, and learning amongst participants (Fiorino, 1990; Pahl-Wostl, 2006), and empower groups who feel disenfranchised or might otherwise have few other opportunities to contribute to policy making (Whitmarsh, Swartling, and Jäger, 2009).

In the UK, there is widespread disenfranchisement and lack of political self-efficacy amongst the public (e.g. Grove-White, 1996): less than one-third of people believe that 'when people like me get involved in politics, they can really change the way the country is run' (Hansard, 2008). There has been a decline in electoral participation in recent decades, and while there has also been a rise in non-electoral forms of social participation and protest, this has largely been the preserve of highly educated groups who also vote (Curtice and Seyd, 2003). In many countries, such as the UK, the public often feel their opinions are irrelevant to policy makers (Macnaghten and Jacobs, 1997). When it comes to climate change, the same picture of disenfranchisement and lack of self-efficacy emerges. Although public and community involvement in decision making about climate change is something the public has explicitly stated should happen, when asked whether they would personally like to be consulted in policy decisions about climate change, agreement is much lower (Poortinga and Pidgeon, 2003). This suggests apathy and disengagement from political processes has become customary for many people, who perhaps are sceptical about the utility of contributing to political debates. The majority also lack confidence in the government to tackle climate change, believing it to be unduly influenced by industry in responding to the issue (Poortinga and Pidgeon, 2003). This distrust and perceived governmental inaction in relation to climate change, which is evident across Europe (Querol *et al.*, 2003), undoubtedly influences public beliefs about the need for and efficacy of individual action. Despite some notable examples of grassroots activism for low-carbon change (see below), there remains, in general, little public engagement in climate change policy making (Whitmarsh *et al.*, in press).

The cultural and institutional barriers to civic engagement (e.g. distrust, apathy) limit the (perceived) possibilities for public engagement, and undermine individuals' willingness to participate in efforts to tackle climate change. These barriers may be overcome through citizenship education (Dobson, 2003) but also through encouraging participation by highlighting the diverse benefits (social, environmental, etc.) to individuals and communities. For example, Pattie *et al.*

(2003) conclude: 'people need to be persuaded of the existence of benefits emerging from involvement, and they need to see that their actions are having an effect, at least some of the time' (p. 465). Initial experiences with civic engagement often encourage people to engage through other forms of participation (e.g. Pattie *et al.*, 2003).

## Socio-technical transitions

There is a growing body of literature on 'socio-technical transitions' which offers an interdisciplinary and systems-level perspective on the relationships between energy technology, infrastructure, society, and change in energy systems (e.g. Geels, 2005; Verbong and Geels, 2007). Drawing on science studies, sociology of technology, institutional theory, and innovation studies (e.g. Bijker, 1995; Rogers, 1995), transitions researchers have been concerned with identifying triggers for and impediments to radical social and technological shifts, often seeking implications for facilitating or guiding transitions in socially desirable directions, such as towards a more sustainable future (e.g. Kemp *et al.*, 1998; Rotmans *et al.*, 2001). This approach argues that the co-evolution of technologies, social institutions (including habits and routines), and infrastructures leads to the persistence of particular trajectories of socio-technical change (Dosi, 1984), and to the 'lock-in' of regimes, such as the current carbon-intensive energy and transport regimes. Regimes favour incremental change along these trajectories, and create barriers to more radical change, because of their investment in their particular physical and socio-political systems of provision. Radical innovation emerges in protected spaces outside the mainstream – 'niches' – in which experimental technologies or social innovations are researched and tested (Geels, 2005). Under the right conditions (typically, pressures on the regime and a convergence of niche interests), these radical innovations may diffuse within society and ultimately challenge and replace the regime (Geels and Schot, 2007; Geels, 2005). In contrast to incremental change, this radical change implies not only technological change, but also change in associated institutions, practices, and infrastructures. When a regime has been replaced – for example, in transport, when steam ships replaced sailing ships as the dominant technology (Geels, 2005) – a transition is said to have occurred.

The transitions perspective has been developed and is intended for analysing both technical and social changes symbiotically (Geels and Schot, 2007; Rotmans *et al.*, 2001). However, it has been most commonly applied to technocentric analyses of the diffusion of new niche technologies and resulting changes in the technical fabric of socio-technical systems (Smith *et al.*, 2005). In contrast to these relatively detailed technological histories and models, practical perspectives on the more social aspects of socio-technical transitions remain undeveloped. Although there are some notable exceptions to the general rule (e.g. Van der Brugge *et al.*, 2005), it seems that Rotmans and colleagues' (2001) early calls for more attention to the social and institutional aspects of transitions remain largely unanswered. In a recent trenchant social critique of the transitions approach, Shove and Walker (2007) note that 'for all the talk of socio-technical co-evolution, there is almost no reference to the ways of living or to the patterns of demand implied in what remain largely technological templates for the future' (p. 768). Elsewhere, the 'social' aspects of the transitions perspective have been criticised as excessively functionalistic, ignoring the agency of actors and the importance of social context at the expense of explaining what happens technologically (Smith *et al.*, 2005). Indeed, 'culture' in transition studies is often considered as exogenous to the main (niche-regime) dynamics of social change (e.g. Haxeltine *et al.*, 2008; Whitmarsh and Nykvist, 2008).

Recent work by Nye *et al.* (2010) has sought to help redress this imbalance in the transitions literature, by integrating sociological and psychological literatures on energy use with the socio-technical transitions literature. This work highlights the tendency for energy users to be cast in a supporting or passive role in describing and facilitating low-carbon transition. As outlined earlier, this role includes supporting (or at least accepting) the introduction of new energy generation technologies and supply infrastructure and adoption of energy efficient products. A further role for the public which Nye and colleagues discuss, and which builds on the earlier discussion about the invisibility of energy as an impediment to changing consumption, involves reducing energy demand through methods to 'rematerialise' (i.e. make visible) energy, for example via energy or carbon labels, and smart meters (cf. Burgess and Nye, 2008). Providing informational 'feedback' on energy consumption either directly (via meters) or indirectly (via billing) to energy users enables them to understand and control their energy use, and can result in energy savings of up to 15 per cent (Darby, 2006). While such roles (i.e. supporting energy supply policy, adopting green products, and conserving energy) are certainly important in a potential transition, they cannot be seen as *drivers* of radical change in energy systems. Indeed, such roles tend to assume little change to the overall structure of energy systems or to relationships between social actors within these systems. The current, centralised energy supply system is unchallenged according to this view of the role of domestic energy users (Foxon *et al.*, 2010).

By contrast, Nye *et al.* (2010) point to opportunities associated with transition to a more decentralised, or distributed, energy system for active innovation by energy users and for radical reorganisation of networks and roles. With increased uptake of community or domestic micro-generation (e.g. CHP, solar PVs, wind turbines), energy users become also energy producers and may begin to conceive of themselves as 'energy citizens' (Devine-Wright, 2006). Initial studies of micro-generation also suggest adopters become more aware of their energy use and that micro-generation adoption may be a step towards greening lifestyles (Bergman *et al.*, 2009).

More radical innovation may also arise through grassroots demonstration of the viability and benefits of low-carbon lifestyles, which may stimulate wider shifts in norms and symbolism of consumption, or in the uses of technologies (e.g. Seyfang and Smith, 2007). Groups, such as Carbon Reduction Action Groups (CRAGs) and Transition Towns, are creatively claiming spaces for both

public and private-sphere engagement which appear to highlight viable alternative models of community life, while at the same time contributing to climate
change mitigation (Haxeltine and Seyfang, 2009). Importantly, the motivations
for engagement in these groups are not restricted to environmental concern; individuals get involved for various (e.g. social) reasons (see Howell, 2009; Seyfang
*et al.*, 2007, Whitmarsh *et al.*, 2010). Yet, the extent to which these groups have
influenced policy is debateable. While some argue they act as real-world experiments which demonstrate the viability of policy options like Personal Carbon
Trading (PCT) (Seyfang *et al.*, 2007), their influence is limited while they
remain small-scale grassroots activities which do not threaten dominant interests. At the same time, policy makers are reluctant to regulate because of the
cost involved and because of the fear of public backlash and loss of political
support (Carter and Ockwell, 2007). This political conservatism is a barrier to
radical social change, whereas technological change (even, radical technological
change) tends to be more attractive where it aligns with dominant (economic)
interests (Whitmarsh *et al.*, 2009c).

## Conclusion

Drawing on psychological and sociological literatures, I have argued that there
is currently limited public engagement with climate change and low-carbon lifestyles. Despite widespread awareness of climate change, there is a disparity in
terms of behaviour change due to a range of individual-level and structural barriers to adoption of low-carbon lifestyles. Energy use is determined by multiple
financial, hedonic, social, and structural factors, and is often not conscious or
conspicuous. This view of energy users contrasts with traditional, neoclassical
economics models of consumers as rational, consistent, and economically self-
interested. These findings also pose challenges for changing behaviour, and
undermine reliance on economic and informational measures to encourage voluntary change in lifestyles. A range of measures are needed which speak to the
diverse motivations for energy use, break old (unsustainable) habits and create
new (more sustainable) ones, and provide low-carbon infrastructures and
systems of provision.

There is a role, too, for consumers and citizens to create these new systems
and infrastructures to support low-carbon living. This may be through fora for
participatory policy making and civic engagement to demand and shape change;
and through grassroots radical (niche) innovation in technical systems and experiments in alternative lifestyles. Both of these avenues may, in turn, be supported
through governance structures which encourage engagement and empower citizens. At the same time, new institutional arrangements may be required which
allow for more radical innovation to be considered in policy making (e.g. Whitmarsh *et al.*, in press).

Considering different socio-technical transition pathways is helpful in establishing the different roles – some more active than others – that the public might play
in innovating for a low-carbon future. A transition to a centralised low-carbon

energy system (relying predominantly on a techno-fix approach which alters the energy supply mix) may have little impact on psychological or social aspects of energy use; whereas, a transition to a decentralised low-carbon energy system (i.e. micro-generation) offers potential for an active role for consumers and for restructuring producer–consumer relationships. In the latter case, there are more obstacles involved, but the sustainability benefits may be greater. Crucially, as Foxon *et al.* (2010) argue, we are unlikely to be facing a choice between either a decentralised or a centralised energy supply system; rather elements of both are likely to be needed in a viable, low-carbon energy system. This implies both radical and incremental innovation, and thus various roles for energy users, in a low-carbon transition.

This analysis implies a number of areas in which policy might focus to mobilise the public in a low-carbon energy transition. Drawing on Nye *et al.* (2010), these include:

1   Facilitating deliberate energy conservation via changes in energy visibility, e.g. through smart meters, energy labelling;
2   Changes in habits/routines to more sustainable lifestyles, e.g. through interventions targeted to moments in time when routines are being reconsidered (e.g. relocation) or by altering structures (e.g. road access, parking availability) to disrupt and alter habits;
3   Changes in normative/conventional understandings of proper energy use, e.g. through formal education, deliberative processes, media and NGO campaigns, and grassroots social innovation;
4   Increased demand for, and new uses of, low-carbon and energy-efficient technologies, e.g. through pricing policies, marketing, and user experimentation to identify 'new functionalities' for (and thus, further applications of) green technologies (see Geels, 2005);
5   Influencing the shape of the socio-technical regime, e.g. through provision of opportunities for civic engagement and public participation in policy decisions, creating demand for change in policy and systems of provision through communication (see Ockwell *et al.*, 2009).

These approaches include interventions targeted at individual, community, and wider structural levels, and allow for a range of possible roles for the public in reshaping energy systems towards a low-carbon future.

# References

Bamberg, S. (2006). Is a residential relocation a good opportunity to change people's travel behavior? Results from a theory-driven intervention study. *Environment and Behavior*, 38, 820–840.
Bamberg, S., and Schmidt, P. (2003). Incentives, morality, or habit? Predicting students' car use for university routes with the models of Ajzen, Schwartz, and Triandis. *Environment and Behavior*, 35(2), 264–285.

Barr, S.W., Shaw, G., Coles, T. and Prillwitz, J. (2010). 'A Holiday is a Holiday': Practising sustainability, home and away, *Journal of Transport Geography*. 18, 474–481.

BBC. (2004). *Poll for climate change special*. Retrieved January, 2005, from www.bbc. co.uk.

Bergman, N., Hawkes, A. D., Brett, D. L., *et al.* (2009). Review of Microgeneration in the United Kingdom. Part 1: Policy and Behavioural Aspects. *Proceedings of the Institution of Civil Engineers (Energy)*, 162(1), 23–36.

Bijker, W. (1995). *Of Bicycles, Bakelites and Bulbs: Toward a Theory of Socio-technical Change*. Boston, MA: MIT Press.

Black, C., Collins, A., and Snell, M. (2001). Encouraging walking: The case of journey-to-school trips in compact urban areas. *Urban Studies*, 38(7), 1121–1141.

Brandon, G., and Lewis, A. (1999). Reducing household energy consumption: A qualitative and quantitative field study. *Journal of Environmental Psychology*, 19, 75–85.

Burgess, J., and Nye, M. (2008). Rematerialising energy use through transparent monitoring systems. *Energy Policy*, 36, 4454–4459.

Carter, N., and Ockwell, D. G. (2007). *New Labour, new environment? An analysis of the Labour government's policy on climate change and biodiversity loss. Report prepared for Friends of the Earth.* Centre for Ecology Law and Policy (CELP), University of York: www.york.ac.uk/res/celp/projects/foe/docs/fullreportfinal.pdf.

Curtice, J., and Seyd, B. (2003). Is there a crisis of political participation? In A. Park, J. Curtice, K. Thomson, L. Jarvis and C. Bromley (eds), *British Social Attitudes: the 20th Report*. London: Sage.

Darby, S. (2006). *The effectiveness of feedback on energy consumption. A review for defra of the literature on metering, billing and direct displays.* www.defra.gov.uk/ environment/climatechange/uk/energy/research/pdf/energyconsump-feedback.pdf.

DEFRA. (2002). *Survey of public attitudes to quality of life and to the environment – 2001.* London: Department for Environment, Food and Rural Affairs.

DEFRA. (2005). *Experimental Statistics on Carbon Dioxide emissions at Local Authority and Regional Level.* London: Department for Environment, Food and Rural Affairs.

DEFRA. (2007). *Survey of Public Attitudes and Behaviours toward the Environment: 2007.* London: Department for Environment, Food and Rural Affairs.

Devine-Wright, P. (2006). Citizenship, responsibility and the governance of sustainable energy systems. In J. Murphy (ed.), *Framing the Present, Shaping the Future: Contemporary Governance of Sustainable Technologies*. London: Earthscan.

Dietz, T., and Stern, P. C. (eds). (2008). *Public Participation in Environmental Assessment and Decision Making*. Washington, DC: National Academies Press.

Dittmar, H. (1992). *The Social Psychology of Possessions: To Have is to Be*. New York: St Martin's Press.

Dobson, A. (2003). *Environment and Citizenship*. Oxford: Oxford University Press.

Dosi, G. (1984). *Technical Change and Industrial Transformation*. London: Macmillan.

EST. (1999). *EST Briefing: The Case for the Climate Change Levy*. London: Energy Saving Trust.

Eysenck, M. W. (1994). *Happiness: Facts and Myths*. Hove: Psychology Press.

Fiorino, D. (1990). Citizen participation and environmental risk: a survey of institutional mechanisms. *Science, Technology and Human Values*, 15(2), 226–243.

Fortner, R. W., Lee, J.-Y., Corney, J. R., Romanello, S., Bonnell, J., Luthy, B., *et al.* (2000). Public understanding of climate change: Certainty and willingness to act. *Environmental Education Research*, 6(2), 127–141.

Foxon, T. J., Hammond, G. P., and Pearson, P.J. (2010). Developing transition pathways for a low carbon electricity system in the UK. *Technological Forecasting and Social Change*. 77(8), 1203–1213.

Fujii, S., Garling, T., and Kitamura, R. (2001). Changes in drivers' perceptions and use of public transport during a freeway closure: Effects of temporary structural change on cooperation in a real-life social dilemma. *Environment and Behavior*, 33(6), 796–808.

Gatersleben, B., Meadows, J., Abrahamse, W., and Jackson, T. (2008). *Materialistic and Environmental Values of Young Volunteers in Nature Conservation Projects, RESOLVE Working Paper series 07–08*: University of Surrey.

Gatersleben, B., and Vlek, C. (1998). Household consumption, quality of life and environmental impacts. In K. J. Noorman and A. J. M. Schoot-Uiterkamp (eds), *Green Households? Domestic Consumers, Environment and Sustainability* (pp. 141–183). London: Earthscan.

Geels, F., and Schot, J. (2007). Typology of transition pathways in socio-technical systems. *Research Policy*, 36, 399–417.

Geels, F. (2005). *Technological Transitions and System Innovations: A Co-evolutionary and Socio-Technical Analysis*. Cheltenham: Edward Elgar.

Grove-White, R. (1996). Environmental knowledge and public policy needs: on humanising the research agenda. In S. Lash, B. Szerszynski and B. Wynne (eds), *Risk, Modernity and Environment: towards a new ecology*. London: Sage Publications.

Hansard. (2008). *Audit of Political Engagement – Parliament and Government*. Available from www.hansardsociety.org.uk/blogs/parliament and_government/pages/Audit-of-Political-Engagement.aspx.

Hargreaves, I., Lewis, J., and Speers, T. (2003). *Towards a better map: Science, the public and the media*. London: Economic and Social Research Council.

Haxeltine, A., and Seyfang, G. (2009). *Transitions for the People: Theory and Practice of 'Transition' and 'Resilience' in the UK's Transition Movement*: Tyndall Working Paper 134: www.tyndall.ac.uk.

Haxeltine, A., Whitmarsh, L., Rotmans, J., Schilperoord, M., Bergman, N., and Köhler, J. (2008). Conceptual framework for transition modelling. *International Journal of Innovation and Sustainable Development*, 3(1–2), 93–114.

HM Government. (2008). *Climate Change Bill; Commons Amendments at 3rd Reading*. London: www.publications.parliament.uk/pa/ld200708/ldbills/087/2008087.pdf.

Howell, R. (2009). *The Experience of Carbon Rationing Action Groups: Implications for a Personal Carbon Allowances Policy. Final report for UKERC Demand Reduction Theme*: www.eci.ox.ac.uk/publications/downloads/howell09crags.pdf.

IPCC. (2007). *The Physical Science Basis. Summary for Policymakers. Contribution of Working Group I to the Fourth Assessment Report of the Intergovernmental Panel on Climate Change*. Geneva: IPCC.

Jackson, T., and Marks, N. (1999). Consumption, sustainable welfare and human needs – With reference to UK expenditure patterns between 1954 and 1994. *Ecological Economics*, 28, 421–441.

Kemp, R., Schot, J., and Hoogma, R. (1998). Regime shifts to sustainability through processes of niche formation: The approach of Strategic Niche Management. *Technology Analysis and Strategic Management*, 10(2), 175–195.

Layton, D., Jenkins, E., Macgill, S., and Davey, A. (1993). *Inarticulate science?* Driffield, Yorks: Studies in Education Ltd.

Lorenzoni, I., Nicholson-Cole, S., and Whitmarsh, L. (2007). Barriers perceived to engaging with climate change among the UK public and their policy implications. *Global Environmental Change*, 17(3–4), 445–459.

Macnaghten, P., and Jacobs, M. (1997). Public identification with sustainable development: Investigating cultural barriers to participation. *Global Environmental Change*, 7(1), 5–24.

Nye, M., Whitmarsh, L., and Foxon, T. (2010). Socio-psychological perspectives on the active roles of domestic actors in transition to a lower carbon electricity economy. *Environment & Planning A.* 42(3), 697–714.

O'Connor, R. E., Bord, R. J., Yarnal, B., and Wiefek, N. (2002). Who wants to reduce greenhouse gas emissions? *Social Science Quarterly*, 83(1), 1–17.

O'Neill, S. and Nicholson-Cole, S. (2009). 'Fear won't do it': Promoting positive engagement with climate change through visual and iconic representations. *Science Communication.* 30(3), 355–379.

Ockwell, D., Whitmarsh, L., and O'Neill, S. (2009). Reorienting climate change communication for effective mitigation – forcing people to be green or fostering grass-roots engagement? *Science Communication*, 30(3), 305–327.

Pahl-Wostl, C. (2006). The importance of social learning in the multi-functionality of river basins and floodplains. *Ecology and Society*, 11(1), 10 www.ecologyandsociety.org/vol. 11/iss11/art10/.

Pattie, C. J., Seyd, P., and Whiteley, P. (2003). Citizenship and civic engagement: attitudes and behaviour in Britain. *Political Studies*, 51(3), 443–468.

Poortinga, W., Pidgeon, N., and Lorenzoni, I. (2006). *Public Perceptions of Nuclear Power, Climate Change and Energy Options in Britain: Summary Findings of a Survey Conducted during October and November 2005. Understanding Risk Working Paper 06–02.* Norwich, UK: School of Environmental Sciences, University of East Anglia.

Poortinga, W., and Pidgeon, N. F. (2003). *Public perceptions of risk, science and governance.* Norwich: UEA/MORI.

Querol, C., Swartling, A. G., Kasemir, B., and Tabara, D. (2003). Citizens' reports on climate strategies. In B. Kasemir, J. Jager, C. C. Jaeger and M. T. Gardner (Eds.), *Public Participation in Sustainability Science: A handbook* (pp. 126–152). Cambridge: Cambridge University Press.

Rogers, E. M. (1995). *Diffusion of Innovations* (4th edn). New York: Simon and Schuster.

Røpke, I. (1999). The dynamics of willingness to consume. *Ecological Economics*, 28, 399–420.

Rotmans, J., Kemp, R., and van Asselt, M. (2001). More evolution than revolution: transition management in public policy. *Foresight*, 3(1), 15–31.

Seyfang, G., Lorenzoni, I., and Nye, M. (2007). *Personal Carbon Trading: notional concept or workable proposition? Exploring theoretical, ideological and practical underpinnings. CSERGE Working Paper EDM 07–03.* Norwich: UEA.

Seyfang, G., and Smith, A. (2007). Grassroots Innovations for Sustainable Development: towards a new research and policy agenda. *Environmental Politics*, 16(4), 584–603.

Shove, E., and Walker, G. (2007). CAUTION! Transitions ahead: politics, practice, and sustainable transition management. *Environment and Planning A*, 39(4), 763–770.

Smith, A., Stirling, A., and Berkhout, F. (2005). The governance of sustainable socio-technical transitions. *Research Policy*, 34, 1491–1510.

Steg, L., Vlek, C., and Slotegraaf, G. (2001). Instrumental-reasoned and symbolic-affective motives for using a motor car. *Transportation Research Part F: Traffic Psychology and Behaviour*, 4(3), 151–169.

Stern, N. (2007). *The Economics of Climate Change: The Stern Review.* Cambridge: Cambridge University Press.

Stern, P. (2000). Toward a coherent theory of environmentally significant behavior. *Journal of Social Issues*, 56(3), 407–424.

Thompson, M., and Rayner, S. (1998). Cultural discourses. In S. Rayner and E. L. Malone (Eds.), *Human Choice and Climate Change, Volume 1: The societal framework* (pp. 265–344). Columbus: Ohio: Battelle Press.

Upham, P., Whitmarsh, L., Poortinga, W., Purdham, K., Darnton. A., McLachlan, C. and Devine-Wright, P. (2009). *Public Attitudes to Environmental Change: a selective review of theory and practice. A research synthesis for the Living with Environmental Change Programme, Research Council, UK.* www.lwec.org.uk.

Van der Brugge, R., Rotmans, J., and Loorbach, D. (2005). The transition in Dutch water management. *Regional Environmental Change*, 5(1), 164–176.

Verbong, G., and Geels, F. (2007). The ongoing energy transition: Lessons from a socio-technical, multi-level analysis of the Dutch electricity system (1960–2004). *Energy Policy*, 35, 1025–1037.

Verplanken, B., Aarts, H., and van Knippenberg, A. (1997). Habit, information acquisition, and the process of making travel mode choices. *European Journal of Social Psychology*, 27, 539–560.

Verplanken, B., Aarts, H., van Knippenberg, A., and Moonen, A. (1998). Habit versus planned behaviour: A field experiment. *British Journal of Social Psychology*, 37, 111–128.

Verplanken, B., Walker, I., Davis, A., and Jurasek, M. (2008). Context change and travel mode choice: Combining the habit discontinuity and self-activation hypotheses. *Journal of Environmental Psychology*, 28, 121–127.

Whitmarsh, L. (2009a). Behavioural responses to climate change: Asymmetry of intentions and impacts. *Journal of Environmental Psychology*, 29, 13–23.

Whitmarsh, L. (2009b). What's in a name? Commonalities and differences in public understanding of 'climate change' and 'global warming'. *Public Understanding of Science*, 18, 401–420.

Whitmarsh, L., and Nykvist, B. (2008). Integrated sustainability assessment of mobility transitions: Simulating stakeholders' visions of and pathways to sustainable land-based mobility. *International Journal of Innovation and Sustainable Development*, 3(1–2), 115–127.

Whitmarsh, L., Seyfang, G. and O'Neill, S. (in press). Public Engagement with Carbon and Climate Change: To what extent is the public 'carbon capable'? *Global Environmental Change.*

Whitmarsh, L., Swartling, Å., and Jäger, J. (2009). Participation of experts and non-experts in a sustainability assessment of mobility. *Environmental Policy and Governance*, 19, 232–250.

Whitmarsh, L., O'Neill, S. and Lorenzoni, I. (eds) (2010). *Engaging the public with climate change: behaviour change and communication.* London: Earthscan.

Whitmarsh, L., and Wietschel, M. (2008). Sustainable transport visions: what role for hydrogen and fuel cell vehicle technologies? *Energy and Environment*, 19(2), 207–226.

Wilhite, H., Nakagami, H., and Murakoshi, C. (1997). Changing patterns of air conditioning consumption in Japan. In P. Bertholdi, A. Ricci and B. Wajer (eds), *Energy Efficiency in Household Appliances.* Berlin: Springer.

# 12 Management of North Sea fisheries

*Prashant Vaze*

## 1 Introduction

This chapter summarises research undertaken by the UK Prime Minister's Strategy Unit[1] in 2003 on the incentives upon fishermen in the North Sea and how these give rise to non-sustainable fishing patterns. It looks at the use of the fish resource from the perspective of the economic agents that are exploiting the resource.

Fisheries management has been a perennial interest for natural and ecological economics. It involves issues as diverse as the use of common resources, renewable resource management, technological change and enforcement policy.

The current system of fisheries management in the North Sea is highly complex. The right to exploit the fish stock in the North Sea is shared between many different countries in the EU (UK, France, Netherlands, etc.) and outside (e.g. Norway). Every year the collaborative research body the International Conference for the Exploitation of the Seas (ICES) estimates the population size, recruitment and age distribution of many species of commercially exploited fish in different fishing zones. ICES advises the fisheries managers on the amount of fish that can be safely caught, or whether the fishery should be shut down. ICES draws its conclusions chiefly relying on information collected by scientific research vessels. These take numerous samples each year to build up a picture of the health of each stock. In December the EU fisheries council meets to decide the total allowable catch for different species. As well as setting limits on how many fish can be legally landed each year the Council might also restrict the number of days a month fishermen are allowed to fish (called tie-up), limit the killing capacity of the fleet, restrict the use of small mesh nets or close a fishery. These policies are notoriously difficult to enforce and are often criticised by fishermen as being a bureaucratic fudge and difficult to understand.

In order to manage UK fisheries successfully, managers need to understand a range of inter-linked drivers in the fishery system. The choices made by individual fishermen affect the quantity of fish caught, the amount of profit generated by the industry, the level of investment in new boats and the quality of information used by scientists and fisheries managers on which fisheries management decisions are based. A proper understanding of how fishermen respond to decisions made by fisheries managers is essential to maintaining a sustainable fishing industry. This chapter analyses:

- factors affecting fishermen's decisions
- the fisheries management system
- the resulting key management challenges
- which policies can address these challenges

## 2  Factors affecting fishermen's decisions

This section reviews the key drivers and pressures acting upon fishermen, which in turn affect how fishermen respond to management measures. The review draws upon available literature and face-to-face discussions held with fishermen and experts.

The main incentives facing fishermen can be grouped as:

- Fishermen's attitudes
- Financial and economic pressures
- Management pressures
- Operational attributes

### 2.1  Fishermen attitudes

This section discusses the views and opinions of the fishing industry. No comment is made at this stage about the validity or accuracy of these views.

### Distrust of science

The overwhelming majority of fishermen interviewed by the Strategy Unit, and at all levels of the industry, doubt the validity of the advice official scientists provide to fishery managers. At the most basic level fishermen believe official science underestimates the health of fish stock. More sophisticated criticisms (for instance Kristjansson, 2003) argue that the science is too crude: fishery models typically exclude multi-species effects, ecological impacts (from climate and competition from other species).

The industry and official science are well aware of this tension and have gone some way to ensure there is dialogue. Scientists from the UK Government fisheries science centre (CEFAS) and the industry hold regional meetings prior to the ICES working group meetings and official scientists accompany fishermen to observe discards levels. However, a recent meeting organised by ICES to improve the trust between scientists and the industry concluded: 'the process of incorporation of additional information from the fishery into fish stock assessment should be viewed as a process rather than an act' (ICES/NSCFP, 2003).

The perception of the industry is that official scientists talk at, rather than to, the industry. In response, industry has developed initiatives such as the

Europêche survey (Scottish Fishermen's Federation [2002]) collating the industry view about the state of the stock relative to the previous year. It wishes for a greater role in commissioning the science and gathering data on the state of the stock. The Sentinel fisheries scheme operating in Canada and northeast USA is held up by UK fishermen as a possible model for the future role of the industry.

*Distrust of management*

The industry's views of fisheries management are similarly jaundiced. Broadly, fishermen believe they have too little influence in deciding how fisheries are managed – less than 15 per cent feel involved and two-thirds feel either uninvolved or ignored (Hatcher, 1996). In a recent survey of fishermen operating in the Clyde area (Watson and Bryson, 2003) 72 per cent of fishermen believe involvement of fishermen in management process to be poor or unsatisfactory, 90 per cent believe the degree of local control to be poor or unsatisfactory.

The instruments used to manage fisheries are unpopular. Survey data (Hatcher, 1996) shows most fishermen believe quotas are ineffective at conserving fish stock (84 per cent as they operate now, 60 per cent even if all fishermen complied with their quota). A more recent survey (Hatcher and Gordon, unpublished)[2] echo these viewpoints: only 8 per cent believe quotas are effective in conserving stock, only 37 per cent agree quotas are the best way of conserving stock. In particular, the requirement to discard over-quota fish is unpopular, 99 per cent of fishermen believing it is wrong to discard 'good marketable fish because you are over quota'. Over the past year fishermen have offered to land fish and donate the proceeds to charity rather discard the fish. Fishermen argue that the geographic restrictions of ICES fishing zones, used for assigning quota and some technical restrictions do not reflect fish movements (Nautilus Consultants, 1998). Fishermen express the least concern about technical measures with regards the fishing gear they are permitted to use.

*Compliance*

Most fishermen do not consider themselves criminals for not complying with regulations and quota restrictions. Their communities, and other skippers, tend to be sympathetic when a fisherman is found guilty. (However, this picture does

---

**Court fines fisherman only £4000 sympathetic to his financial distress**

A Scottish procurator-fiscal fined a fisherman only £4000 for landing whitefish worth more than £22,000 at a non-designated port – the maximum penalty was £50,000. The plaintiff successfully argued he and his crew were under tremendous financial pressure as their boat was soon to be decommissioned.

Source: *The Press and Journal*, 2003.

vary across the country: in the West Coast of Scotland there is intolerance to non-compliance). A recent survey (Hatcher and Gordon, unpublished) showed that only 37 per cent of fishermen agreed with the statement 'Quotas should be complied with because they are the law'.

However, the majority of fishermen wish to operate within the rules. Seventy per cent of skippers believed that violating quota restrictions was 'basically wrong, but an economic necessity'. This belief that non-compliance is an economic necessity has been borne out elsewhere.

## 2.2 Financial, economic and operational pressures

### Financial pressures

Fishermen are businessmen. Earnings from fishing have to be sufficient to maintain and invest in the vessel, pay the skipper's and crew's wages and meet all other variable costs. In the UK, individuals and families, as opposed to large and medium-sized companies, own boats. Fishing is a capital-intensive industry and entrepreneurial fishermen can take on significant financial risks. A fisherman, interviewed by the SU, had financed the purchase of his £2.5million whitefish boat from bank loans, by mortgaging his home and borrowing from his family. He is by no means atypical; new whitefish boats cost in excess of £1million. A new entrant into the industry has to purchase not just his boat, but also a fishing license and quota. Often this risk is pooled between the skipper, crew and fishing agents, with each party taking a share in the boat.

### Falling profit margins

Table 12.1 is drawn from a survey by Seafish (Watson and Martin, 2002) and shows the profitability of different segments of the UK fleet. The figures exclude capital charges such as interest and depreciation. If these were accounted for profits would be lower. The figures highlight the huge change in earnings over just three years. Profit margins in 1997/98 were between 15 per cent and 30 per cent but these fell by 50 per cent by 2000/01. The profit margin in the whitefleet segments averaged 5 per cent of revenue.

The box on p. 231 shows that the community and the courts are often sympathetic to fishermen and reluctant to impose penalties.

## 2.3 Management pressures

Our system of management can influence fishermen's behaviour in a number of unwanted ways. This section discusses three of these.

### Short-term planning

At present the management system is geared towards giving annual management advice. This advice is agreed in December to implement the following year. The

*Table 12.1* Comparison of average earnings and profit levels per vessel for 1997/1998 and 2000/2001 across key sectors of the Scottish Fishing Fleet

| Sector | Average earnings 1997/1998 (£) | Average earnings 2000/2001 (£) | Average profit* 1997/1998 (£) | Average profit 2000/2001 (£) |
|---|---|---|---|---|
| West of Scotland Nephrops Trawl | 202,119 | 151,609 | 69,513 | 30,526 |
| North Sea Nephrops | 186,197 | 161,527 | 59,708 | 19,235 |
| North Sea & West of Scotland Twin Rig Whitefish Trawl | 965,878 | 603,294 | 164,905 | 79,990 |
| North Sea & West of Scotland Twin Rig Nephrop Trawl | 506,877 | 270,717 | 96,991 | 14,745 |
| North Sea & West of Scotland Demersal Trawl >24 m | 772,399 | 615,450 | 158,731 | 48,565 |
| North Sea & West of Scotland Demersal Trawl <24 m <300 kw | 326,472 | 210,530 | 49,552 | 20,375 |
| North Sea & West of Scotland Seine Nets | 622,818 | 430,441 | 118,616 | 38,569 |
| North Sea & West of Scotland Demersal Trawl <24 m >300 kw | 526,232 | 361,865 | 80,024 | 18,832 |
| West of Scotland Scallopers | * | 277,705 | * | 63,481 |
| Under 10 m vessels mobile gear | * | 68,353 | * | −438 |
| Under 10 m vessels static gear | * | 47,059 | * | 11,088 |

Source: Watson and Martin, 2002.

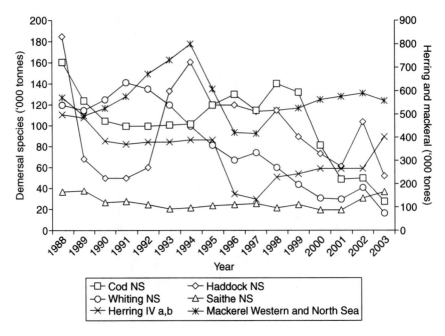

*Figure 12.1* Fishing TACs and quotas agreed by Fisheries Council and non-EU countries fishing in water, 000 tonnes.

total TAC set for a fishery can vary significantly from year to year. The graph in Figure 12.1 shows how the TAC has varied between 1989 and 1999 for a selection of species. TACs for cod, haddock and whiting dropped by 80 per cent, 42 per cent and 64 per cent respectively between 1993 and 2003. As well as this decline in demersal TACs there has been a constant and high degree of volatility. The standard deviation of TAC for the featured species has been around 15 per cent of the average TAC.

This unpredictability of revenue affects fishermen's behaviour. In order to plan, especially for long-term investment decisions like the purchase of new boats, businesses prefer predictability in revenue. Predictability makes it easier to borrow money and hence reduces the cost of borrowing; it makes staff recruitment and retention easier, hence improves the skills and calibre of crew. Without predictability businesses engage in behaviour which gives short-term returns such as reducing crewing levels, or increasing the immediate killing power, for instance by installing twin rigs or increasing non-compliant behaviour. A more rational response by fishermen would be to manage the risks of fluctuating TACs by reducing the volatility of those variables they have control over, and hedging the risks for those variables that are outside their control.

There has been discussion for many years about setting multi-annual quotas to provide fishermen with greater predictability in income. The difficulty in implementing this idea is that a 'precautionary' multi-annual quota that is safe to several successive years of lower than average recruitment would have to be set much lower than the present TACs, further reducing fishing income. This is unpalatable to fishermen.

## *Race to fish*

It is common for many fisheries to be closed for periods of the year. This might be to accommodate the natural migration patterns of fish or maybe to protect juvenile and breeding stocks. As soon as the fishery is opened fisherman have an incentive to fish hard: since stocks will have recovered from the closure and fish will be at their most abundant. The mackerel fishery in North Scotland is open between October and March and the herring fishery June to September. This seasonal access to the fishery creates an incentive for fishermen to fish as early in the season as possible and deplete the fishery in the narrow window of time in which the fishery is open (and indeed to concentrate their efforts as early in the open season as possible, when stocks are at their healthiest).

Even without formal closures there can be a race to fish as a result of cut-off dates. If fishermen are constrained in how much they can catch per year they will ensure they use their quota before the end of the year. Consultees have commented that because the fishing year closes in December fishermen will often fish hard in winter to ensure they use up all their quota – since this is the most hazardous time of the year it can result in fishermen going out in unsafe weather conditions. If this is significant, allowing a small element of carry over from one year to the next, or simply changing the cut-off date, might be an appropriate policy response.

The race to fish can be exacerbated if fishermen are not allocated individual fishing rights, as fishermen vie to do better than their competitors. The anticipation of new management measures can also encourage spiralling volumes of fishing activity. This type of incident was witnessed prior to the introduction of monkfish quotas in 1996 as fishermen strove to establish track-records in anticipation of forthcoming quota controls.

## *Subsidies*

Subsidies can take a variety of forms. They can be designed to support prices, assist investment in new boats or encourage the adoption of more environmentally friendly gear. Subsidies such as price supports and aid for new boat investment provide short-term aid to individual fishermen: increasing revenues or reducing costs. However, in the long-term they are negative as they distort economic signals in the fishery and so encourage over-investment and over-fishing.

The CFP review in 2002 called for an end to government subsidies for new boats or modernisation by 2004. The World Trade Organisation is also looking to introduce worldwide restrictions on damaging fisheries subsidies in the current round of negotiations.

*Decommissioning*

Decommissioning is a form of subsidy intended to reduce the amount of killing capacity. However, if undertaken regularly it can have the perverse effect of reducing the cost of exit and hence incentivise banks and fishermen to make riskier investments. Policy makers have anticipated this problem and to an extent mitigated it by disallowing the decommissioning of new boats, but this has been relaxed in the most recent schemes.

Since 1993, decommissioning schemes have been in operation in 7 of the last 11 years. The vessels decommissioned in the early years tended to be older, less active and less productive than average (Nautilus Consultants, 1997). Therefore, the impact of the scheme on fishing mortality was probably proportionately less than that indicated by the reduction in vessel numbers.

*Super under-10s*

Under-10 metre vessels are more lightly regulated than large boats in order to ease the regulatory burden on smaller, often part-time fishermen. In particular, there is no obligation for under-10 m vessels to record their landings. This has had the perverse effect of encouraging skippers of larger boats to switch to under-10s but to augment their capacity to make them 'super under-10s'.

Over the last decade the size of the under-10 m fleet has decreased significantly from around 7500 boats in 1994 to 5700 in 2002 (Figure 12.2). Despite this reduction in number of vessels, the productive capability of the fleet in terms of its average tonnage and engine power has increased significantly. This

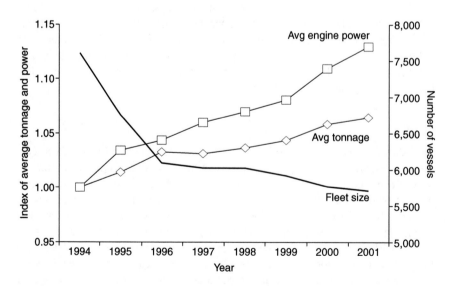

*Figure 12.2* Increased productive capability of under 10 m vessels.

increase in physical capacity and productivity is due to the emergence of a fleet of new, highly powered vessels which are 10 m or less in length.

## 2.4 Operational attributes

### Technical efficiency

The technical efficiency of fishing operations depends on many things (Figure 12.3). The key determinants are the boat, gear and equipment, on-board technology and skill of skipper and crew. It is also important to operate using the right mix of inputs.

Efficiency varies widely between vessels. One study shows that the average otter trawler working in the English Channel is only 47 per cent as efficient as the most efficient (Figure 12.4) (Pascoe *et al.*, 2003). The spread is not so wide in beam trawlers, the best landing around 1.67 times as much as the average.

Personal attributes matter too. Efficient skippers were found to have a strong history of fishing in their family, but were less experienced in terms of time spent at sea, i.e. they were younger or newer to fishing than other less efficient skippers. Efficiency levels and causes were found to vary greatly between fishing gears, areas and skippers.

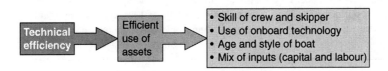

*Figure 12.3* Description of components of technical efficiency.

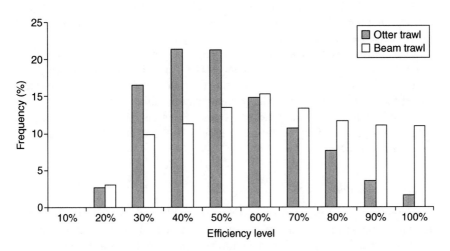

*Figure 12.4* Efficiency range of English Channel vessels (source: Pascoe, 2003).

*Technical creep*

Technological improvements improve fishermen's ability to detect and kill fish. This is not a problem if the fishery manager is using quotas to manage the stocks and enforcement is fully effective. It is an issue if an effort based system is being used to restrict fishing or if compliance if not fully effective.

Table 12.2 shows the specific, often minor low cost technologies are introduced. These increase killing power without significant investment and, quite correctly, without the approval of the fishery manager.

The box below shows the type of technological changes that have occurred within the Scottish pelagic fleet and the impact these have had on killing capacity.

---

**Box 1  Case study of the impact of technological change on the Scottish pelagic fishery**

The Scottish pelagic fishery experienced significant structural change and technological development during the 1980s and 1990s: highly powered, large super-trawlers were introduced and important technological developments were made in fishing-finding equipment, gear design and on-board equipment. However, the estimated impact on productivity was relatively low: 0.38% per year equating to a 5.9% improvement over 15 years. The benefit of the efficiency improvements was being seen in reduced operating costs and onboard storage as opposed to increased catches. The quota management system and market dynamics played an important role in steering the benefits of technological change away from increased landings.

Source: Banks and Reed, 2000

---

In an effort-based system fishermen have an incentive to over-invest in technologies which are not restricted by the licensing authorities. If the fishery manager limits the vessel capacity units (calculated from the size and engine power) then the fisherman might over-invest in detection equipment or gear to enhance killing capacity.

There is theoretical support for this phenomenon (known as 'capital stuffing'), but much less empirical evidence. The Faroe Islands operate an effort system for their whitefish sector restricting the number of days but not the catch. When the policy was first introduced there was an initial increase in investment in the fleet but this fell off after two years.[3] Fisheries managers have reduced effort (days per vessel) by 19 per cent between 1996 and 2003 to compensate for improved technology.

*Capacity utilisation*

Our present management system restricts the number of licenses and the capacity within the fleet segments (pelagic etc). This is a useful and essential management tool. But it might not be enough to restrict effort by itself. Fishermen still have the freedom to decide how much time they spend fishing. The concept of

Innovations affecting CPUE

| Category | Subcategory | Year: 1983 | 1986 | 1989 | 1991 | 1994 | 1997 | 2000 |
|---|---|---|---|---|---|---|---|---|
| Nets | Material | Slow, improvements in strength and durability | | | | | | |
| | Purse design | Greater depth, faster sink rates, large mesh in bunts | | | | | Purse hooks introduced | |
| | Trawl design | | | | | | | |
| | Trawl doors | | Design improvements | | | New lightweight doors | | |
| Propulsion | Kort nozzle | | | Reduced time to and from fishing grounds | | | | |
| | Size/speed | Larger pursers can be used | | | | | | |
| | Bow thrusters | | | | | | | |
| | Hydraulics | Gradual improvements in hauling speed | | | | | | |
| Electronics | Navigation | Increased ability to locate fish | | | | | | |
| | Communication | | | | | | | |
| | Fish finders | Gradual improvements in detection range and species discrimination | | | | | | |
| | Net sensors | Reliable cables | | Cable-less system | | | Extra sensors | |
| Hold size | | Volume more important than quality | | | | Quality more important than quantity | | |

Table 12.2 Improvements arising from technological innovation in the Scottish pelagic fleet (1986–98) (source: Richard Banks Ltd, 2002).

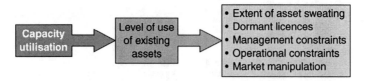

*Figure 12.5* Description of capacity utilisation and its drivers.

capacity utilisation captures the extent to which existing assets are being used to produce output (Figure 12.5). A fleet's 'capacity' can be described in different ways. For example, it is sometimes referred to as the number of vessels, total engine power of a fleet or number of licences in existence.

Estimates of economic capacity utilisation in the Scottish fishing fleet suggest that over 70 per cent of the demersal trawl/seine fleet is operating at between 90 and 100 per cent of the capacity displayed by the 'best' operators (Figure 12.6) (Tingley and Pascoe, 2003). However, even the returns of the 'best' operators are currently constrained by reduced catching opportunities. Small under-10 m vessels appear to be operating with a much wider range of capacity utilisation levels. Around 25 per cent of the fleet is operating at less than half the capacity of the 'best' operators. This result may reflect the fact that some fishermen are currently operating part time. If these fishermen decided to operate full time or were bought out by skippers who then operated the boats full time, a significant shift in fishing productivity of that fleet would occur. If not anticipated, this could undermine the intended effect of management policies.

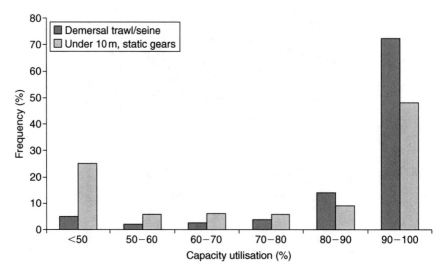

*Figure 12.6* Range of capacity utilisation rates for Scottish demersal trawl/seine and under 10 m static gear vessels (source: Tingley and Pascoe, 2003).

Management measures can also be affected by the existence of dormant licences. Like part-time operators turning full time, if dormant licences were to become re-activated as other fishing opportunities decline, management policies could be undermined.

*Operator profiles and diversity*

Fishing activities can be highly diverse both at the fleet level and the individual boat level. Very different types of operator can target the same species. For example, the mackerel handline fishery in the South West consists of relatively small day-boats fishing in inshore areas and is very different structurally to the mackerel trawl and purse-seine fishery.

At the same time, individual operators within a segment can display a diverse range of attributes and attitudes depending on their age, the vessel's age, transferable skill-set, etc. Geographical and local economic features can also impact upon the success of management policies. For example, in areas where few alternative employment opportunities exist, fishermen may opt to continue using vessels that are old and in need of retirement for longer than they would do if other opportunities were available. The ability of a fisher to access capital, and the level of risk adversity and entrepreneurial spirit they display also shape the way in which individuals respond to management measures or operational constraints.

## 3 Fishery management: system map and instruments

### 3.1 The fishery management system

This section describes how fishermen interact with the fisheries management system. The different organisations within the system are termed 'players' and the interactions between the fisherman and players are termed 'flows'.

At its broadest level the fisheries management system operates to restrict fishing effort to maintain long-term harvest potential of key stocks. Fishermen are at the heart of the fishery system. But there are other players each with roles, objectives and priorities of their own – the objectives of these other players might or might not be aligned to those the fishery manager and the fishermen.

The fishery manager (and the enforcement agencies) determine the total allowable catch (TAC), authorise the issue of new licenses and operate policies to reduce effort and conserve stock. The official scientists assess stocks and provide advice to the fisheries manager. The financial community ('banks') loan fishermen money to invest in new boats and advise the fishermen. The banks are profit seekers and will only invest and advise where they see commercial opportunity.

Within this system four flows between the fisherman and other players are highlighted.

**Information**: Fishermen supply information in their logbooks on the species, location and quantity of fish caught and their fishing effort. In addition, vessels fitted with VMS submit information on their location at sea.

**Profit** is the difference between the revenue earned from fish sales and the cost of fishing. Fishermen also receive funds from the Finance community (loans) and the fisheries manager (Decommissioning grants or subsidies)

**Compliance**: how the fisherman responds to the regulation or restriction set by the fishery manager.

**Entry–exit**: the number of fishermen active within the industry. This is determined by the profitability of the sector, the sentiment within the banking community and any incentives the fishery manager provides enter into or exit from the industry.

Figure 12.7 shows the fishery as a system. The golden arrows depict the four principal properties or flows within the system: information, profits, compliance and entry–exit. In order to manage the system as a whole the fishery manager should address each of these elements.

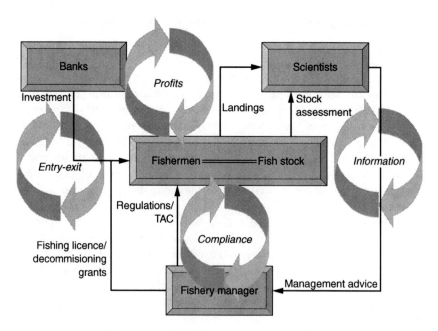

*Figure 12.7* The Fishery Management system showing the main flows between the key systems.

A fully effective management system would influence all of the flows in the above system. Such a system would explicitly take into account the quality of the information being fed in, the size (killing capacity) of the fishing fleet, the likely level of compliance, and the profitability of the industry both presently and following the management change. It would also need to consider whether fishermen have the incentives and are motivated to carry out their part of the deal. Some of these points are worth clarifying.

The information supplied by fishermen to scientists and fishery managers is essentially a by-product of regulations. Information on landings is recorded in logbooks and informs the assessment process. Any misreporting of landings corrupts the information feeding into the assessments.

The management system needs to recognise that individual fishermen have to be profitable to remain in business. It is not essential that every fisherman is profitable every year but on average the bad years must be balanced by the good years. This puts a special obligation on managers since they rather than the market determines how much fish can be landed. This 'cap' on revenue will have knock on effects on other elements of the system especially profitability and compliance.

The level of compliance, or in other words the amount of control a fisheries manager really has, is a crucial element of the fisheries management system. Fishermen do not have an innate incentive to comply with management rules. A good compliance regime would rely on a parsimonious selection of easily enforced rules that are well understood and broadly accepted by the industry.

The size of the fleet is an important parameter within the system. The size of the stock varies significantly from year to year but there is no clear tendency for the amount of biomass to grow over time. The resource is finite and excessive fishing can damage the health of the stock. Left to itself the fleet's killing capacity grows through investment and technological improvements. What incentive does the management system provide to the industry to align killing capacity to the average fish stock?

## 4 Key challenges and options

This section of the chapter analyses the key challenges in aligning the fishermen's incentives to the management priorities and discusses possible approaches to addressing these challenges.

### 4.1 Information

Under the current management system the fisheries manager needs timely and accurate information on the stock, and ideally stock forecasts for the forthcoming year.

ICES carries out stock assessments for most of the key species and fisheries exploited by the UK. These stock assessments and the resulting management advice provided by ICES are highly influential in setting the TAC for the

forthcoming year. From fishery managers' perspective there are several important questions that need to be addressed:

- Is the quality of information fit for purpose?
- Should they be collecting other information?
- What effect does the process of information gathering and stock assessment have on the management system?
- How can we improve the information?

Significant financial and scientific resources are devoted into fish stock assessments but there are still wide margins of error in the current year's stock assessment and even more on the forecast for the forthcoming year. DG Fish has
funded work on the statistical quality of our assessment of SSB. Stocks' standard
error lie between 10 per cent and 30 per cent (EVARES, 2003). This error arises
because of differences in fish abundance from the different sample points on the
bottom trawl survey. Other errors associated with forecasting (assumption on
mortality, recruitment, etc.) further worsen our estimate of current fish
abundance.

This is true even when the system has good quality information on landings.
Figure 12.8 shows successive assessments of the Faroese cod catch. The Faroes
has good quality landings data with little under-reporting of catch. The figure
shows the 1997 catch was revised upwards by about 50 per cent as better

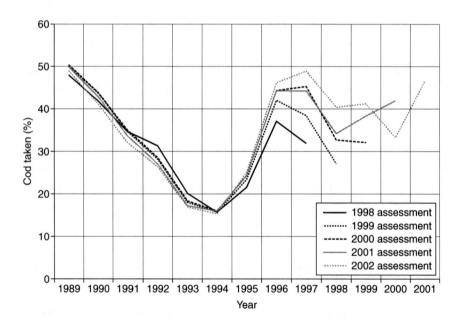

*Figure 12.8* Comparing Assessments 1998–2002 Faroe Plateau Cod (source: Faroese
Ministry of Fisheries).

information came to light. This is not a criticism of the science – fish populations are intrinsically hard to model especially when a high proportion of the fish are very young and are recently recruited. Such changes means makes the TAC advice based upon them unsafe. Rather than trying to modify TAC from year to year in line with supposed changes in stock, other approaches might be appropriate making use of up to date information, e.g. closing fisheries at short notice if too many juveniles are being caught.

As has been mentioned, the fishery manager needs to consider a wider set of issues than just the state of stock when he decides on the appropriate type of management response.

Information about the economic health of fishing operations is also important. Seafish (Watson and Martin 2002), (Watson and Seidel, 2003) and CEMARE (Cattermoul, 2000) have been collating information relating to the economic and financial performance of fleets for several years. Such a data base not only tracks trends, but forms a crucial component of many other types of fisheries economic research and analysis. However, the timing and source of funding is unsteady hindering continuity.

Research into other aspects of the fishing activity, such as the economic and productive efficiency of fishing operations or the fleet's physical capacity, has also been undertaken in recent years. A few studies have been funded at the national level on specific issues, but the majority of funding is provided by the EU. Few national finance routes are available to carry out or encourage in depth academic and policy-related research. Few resources are spent on socio-economics or sociological research. The UK is the only EU country not to have an ongoing contract for research provision and policy advice with a dedicated fisheries economic research organisation.

## 4.2 Compliance

The success of the fisheries management system depends not just on the quality of policy but also on the extent to which fishermen adhere to the measures. In most areas of life people comply with rules without coercion or threat of punishment because the majority regard the rules as useful. Compliance arises as a consequence of trust in the system and social and community pressures.

By its nature there is little hard data about the amount of black landings, but there is a great deal of circumstantial evidence to suggest it is widespread.

In a survey conducted in 2001 (Hatcher and Gordon, unpublished) only 19 per cent of fishermen said that they 'never' landed over-quota fish, 16 per cent of fishermen said they caught over-quota fish 'most of the time' or 'frequently'. We conducted numerous interviews of fishermen and POs and can attest to this.

Lack of compliance is caused by many factors. The risk and cost of being detected and fined is obviously an important issue. The recent NAO report based on the analysis of offences that went to court in 2000–2001 calculated that the present level of fines represents only 1.7 times the value of fish illegally landed and that only 122 fishermen were found guilty over this two year period (NAO,

2003). The SU has speculated that this might represent as few as 0.25 per cent of the illegal landings.

Table 12.3 shows results from interviews of Scottish fishermen conducted in 1997 and 1998. It shows that the example of other fishermen, and financial necessity are the most frequently cited reasons for non-compliance. Evidence presented earlier in this chapter confirms the problems with lack of profitability in the whitefish fleet in 2001. This situation will have deteriorated further since then as a result of the reduction in whitefish quotas. Many fishermen simply could not remain in business if they restricted their catch to quota.

Lack of respect for the rules and biological pressure (they could not avoid catching large quantities of saithe for which they had no quota) are cited as the next two reasons for non-compliance. Fishermen are particularly critical of rules such as lines of latitude or longitude acting as demarcations for stocks, and the need to discard marketable fish, which they cannot avoid catching in a mixed fishery. In autumn 2003 substantial quantities of valuable monkfish were discarded because an underestimate was made of the state of the English Channel stock.

Skippers felt that the court processes provided little deterrent. If the information from the Hatcher and Gordon (unpublished) survey is interpreted as implying 20 per cent of fishing trips result in illegal landings then less than 1 per cent of illegal landings result in prosecution.

The current high level of non-compliance is a problem because it disrupts efforts to recover stocks, because it undermines trust in the system and because it corrupts the incentives within the industry: fishermen who would prefer to be non-criminal have less incentive to remain in the industry. To address the issue of non-compliance it is necessary to address each of the above issues: the lack of profitability, lack of trust in the system and the difficulties in enforcing the current regime.

The key questions are:

- How can we enhance trust in the system so fishermen believe the rules and restrictions placed upon them are in their interests?
- How can we improve profitability in whitefish so most fishermen can make a reasonable profit, most years within their quotas?
- How can the enforcement system be designed so there is a high probability that non-compliant fishermen are efficiently and fairly dealt with?

Legitimacy in the system can only be improved by responding to fishermen's complaints in a constructive and inclusive manner. Leaders of the industry should feel the system is their system and that they play a significant role in determining the management rules. At present they feel remote from the decision process.

The relationship between fishermen and scientists is strained. Fishermen organisations have attempted to bring ideas and information to the table. The Europeche/North Sea Partnership survey in which the SFF participate asked a

Table 12.3 Key motivations in fisheries offences in Scotland

| | North east whitefish trawl | North east nephrops trawl | Shetland whitefish | Pelagic | West of Scotland nephrops | All groups |
|---|---|---|---|---|---|---|
| Age/experience in fishing | 5 | 3 | 4 | 7 | 4 | 4 |
| Financial pressure | 1 | 1 | 5 | 3 | 3 | 2 |
| Biological pressure | 6 | 6 | 3 | 6 | 2 | 4 |
| Inadequacy/irrelevance of legislation | 2 | 5 | 2 | 4 | 4 | 3 |
| Experience of other fishermen's behaviour | 4 | 4 | 7 | 4 | 6 | 6 |
| Inadequacy in enforcement | 4 | 4 | 7 | 4 | 6 | 6 |
| Fear of the court process/community reaction | 7 | 5 | 6 | 6 | 7 | 7 |

Source: Nautilus Consultants (1998).

Notes
1 – most significant, 7 – least significant.

sample of 778 fishermen who fish in the North Sea how the state of the stock changed between the first half of 1999 and the first half of 2000. An assessment by ICES suggests that there was broad agreement in the findings of scientists and fishermen in terms of the change in the state of stocks (ICES 2002). However, there is still very limited integration of fishermen's observations and data into the official system and in some respects *less use is made of fishermen's information* since catch per unit effort is no longer used and official landings data is supplemented with an assessment of unaccounted-for removals.

The situation is arguably worst for species where no formal stock assessments are carried out and 'precautionary TACs' are set based on historic official landings. As we know these often greatly understate real landings or reflect a lack of demand rather than a lack of supply (SFF, 2003) such as landings of nephrops and monkfish in the early 1980s.

Discarding of marketable fish is a particular problem, especially in mixed fisheries where fishermen have little control over what species they catch. Ninety-nine per cent of fishermen regard the discarding of marketable fish as wrong (Hatcher and Gordon, unpublished). This practice also brings the industry into disrepute with the public. The challenge is how to allow fishermen to land accidentally caught fish for which they have no quota, without creating the incentive to target these species.

An enforcement system which gives fishermen a strong incentive to comply requires a number of features, most of which will seem obvious. The rules being enforced should be easy to understand to the fisherman and the enforcement agency. The action that is being restricted should be under the direct control of the fisherman. Non-compliance should be easy to detect. The punishment must be proportional to the crime.

Fishermen regard the present system as being overly bureaucratic. This may or may not be a fair criticism. It is certainly the case that many rules (days at sea, TACs and gear restrictions) apply to particular ICES regions making it difficult to comply with them and difficult to enforce. Species quotas are intended to reduce effort on vulnerable stocks; however, in many fisheries fishermen cannot target species with sufficient discrimination to remain within these quotas – resulting in over-quota fish either being discarded or illegally landed. In such mixed fisheries, the management system is causing non-compliance because the action it seeks to restrain is outside the fisherman's direct control. Lastly landings limits are intrinsically difficult to enforce: fish can be easily disguised by under-reporting the weight of catch, mislabelling the species of part of all the catch, mis-reporting the area or illicitly landing the fish. There are other ways of restricting fishing pressure (effort-days) which are easier to measure and enforce.

Many of these offences occur because non-compliance is now endemic within the system and there is collusion between fishermen, processors and buyers. If compliance is improved this system of collusion will be weakened and many types of illegal activity will become harder to organise. Many of these issues could be addressed by having a more open system of recording information and mechanisms for checking consistency between different information sources.

Even if rules are changed to improve the incentive structure and we successfully deal with systemic non-compliance, a minority of fishermen will continue to break the rules. For them, the level and probability of fines must be sufficient to deter non-compliance. In several other countries non-compliance is handled as by administrative procedure rather than through the courts. Typical punishments include confiscating the fishing license for a defined period of time, or fining. Both of these can be faster to implement and now expensive than the current criminal procedure (the average level of fine paid in England and Wales is £3000 [National Audit Office, 2003]).

Specific measures to address these issues include:

- Allowing fishermen a greater role in the management of the fishery and allowing management decisions to be made closer to home.
- Profitability can be increased by reducing the number of boats active in the fishery, either by permanently removing boats, or by tying up boats for when stocks recover. Clearly a judgement needs to be made about the extent to which stocks will recover in the near future and hence the balance between tie-up and structural removal.
- Stocks which have high bounds of uncertainty or for which no scientific assessment is made should be managed in a more adaptive way. Data can be collected by observers, or from landings data. The management system should also permit a straightforward and routine means of revising the TAC as new data become available.
- Fishermen should be allowed to land fish for which they hold no quota but they should pay a 'deemed value' to the fishery manager so they make no profit or loss from the sale.
- Using administrative procedures rather than criminal fines to punish non-compliance.

### 4.3 Profits

Fishermen are profit seekers. Some operators remain in the industry as they place a high value on the 'way of life' and maintenance of family traditions and connections, however, the overriding aim of being an active fisherman is to generate an economic return. Fishery managers, therefore, do not have to directly encourage actions to improve profits, but it is extremely important that they are aware of the impact that different types of management tools will have on profitability.

Encouraging a sense of ownership of fishing access and use rights encourages a more collective approach to using such rights in a sustainable manner. Individual allocation of rights is the obvious extension of this approach. Allowing individual rights to be fully and freely transferable enables fishermen to adjust their holdings of rights to match their productive capacity. It is well known that an ITQ system encourages fishing rights to concentrate in the hands of a reduced number of operators who are probably the most efficient fishermen and/or the most dynamic businessmen. This concentration may be at the expense of offshore employment numbers[4] or employment in vulnerable communities if these effects are not directly mitigated for. However, ITQs generally result in higher profits for remaining individual fishermen and the fishery as a whole.

An analysis of the extent of excess capacity in the Scottish fishing fleet found that if fishing rights were allowed to be allocated to the most economically productive operators, whilst maintaining their current productive capacities (i.e. boat, engine, gear, etc.) and sticking to traditional species mixes, then 2001 Scottish catches could have been caught by around half of the current number of vessels with around two-fifths less crew (Tingley and Pascoe, 2003). However, the profit gain would have been nearly double that made in 2001 (78 per cent increase).

Input controls that are individually allocated and transferable may stimulate a similar concentration in the hands of the most efficient and productive operators. However, there are added complications, as compared to individual output allocations, which may affect profitability in the long run. The relationship between inputs and expected fishing mortality is difficult to quantify. Fishermen become incentivised to increase their productive capability if input controls are used in isolation. This in turn affects stock levels in the long run and hence profits. Technological developments tend to result in a technical creep that leads to increased fishing mortality, as opposed to cost savings or value-added. Managers need more and different information (on catch per unit effort) to determine appropriate controls and limits on input transferability between vessels and fisheries.

### 4.4 Capital entry/exit

Over-capitalisation is a problem because it reduces the profitability of vessels, inhibits modernisation and puts pressure on stocks. SU analysis suggests a substantial reduction in the whitefish fleet is required to ensure that the fleet is profitable, competitive and sustainable (in terms of its alignment to resources) in the long run.

Fleets become over capitalised for a range of reasons:

- Subsidies directly aimed at increasing the productive capacity of a fleet
- Management policies that do not limit or incentivise fleets to be in alignment with available resources
- Indirect subsidies (i.e. not recovering management costs) incentivise against limiting over-capitalisation
- Technical creep

The fishing industry is structurally prone to 'boom–bust' cycles, driven by biological fluctuations in stock availability and the possibility of generating supernormal profits[5] (also known as resource rents) when stock levels are high. Operating profits in the pelagic industry are substantial – average revenue per boat was £3 million in 2001, while the cost of a new vessel is £10–16 million

meaning capital can rapidly be accumulated through retained earnings and bor-
rowings. If fishing mortality is not restricted, new entrants can be attracted into
the fishery by the potential to make high profits, or existing owners can expand
their own vessels. As new fishermen enter profits become eroded as stocks
decline and the costs of catching extra fish increases. Unless vessels can move
out of the fishery when stocks fall (i.e. into other fisheries or the vessel is decommissioned), the over-investment in productive capacity becomes 'stuck'. It is
therefore, crucial that fisheries are managed to limit fishing mortality and so
protect resources in the long run.

Management policies aim to restrict fishing mortality. This can theoretically
be achieved by either controlling amounts caught, placing limits on the amount
of fishing effort or limiting investment. We argue that the least costly and easiest
to manage option might be to limit the amount of investment so killing capacity
is broadly in line with long-term average stocks.

There are three possible options available to management and/or fishermen to
help minimise the risk of a 'boom–bust' capital cycle:

- *Option 1*: Voluntary withdrawal of capital
- *Option 2*: Industry-organised contributory scheme
- *Option 3*: Tax on resource rent

### Option 1: Voluntary withdrawal of capital

It is normal business practice in any industry to review the size of production
activities and adjust them to align capacity with opportunities. Individual
fishing vessel owners do this at the boat level, e.g. reducing crew numbers
when fishing is poor. However, the individual operator is restricted by the
amount of change that can be made to the size of the operation – a vessel
cannot be cut in half (although many small vessels have been physically
reduced in size to squeeze into the under 10 m length category). Owners who
operate more than one vessel can downsize activities by removing whole
vessels from their fleet. Beam trawl operators, owning more than half a dozen
vessels, used the 1993–1996 decommissioning schemes to rationalise their
activities in this manner (Nautilus Consultants, 1997). Voluntary restraint
occurred at the fleet level in the Australian nephrops fishery: the fleet took a
collective decision to reduce vessel numbers from 300 to 90 on purely commercial grounds. By reducing capacity, stocks were conserved and re-grown
and total fleet profits increased as a result.

Voluntary restraint by the industry works best when there are a small number
of players who are willing to act together, or where many boats are jointly
managed by a single company allowing for actions to be coordinated. This type
of collective action will only work where direct benefits flow back to the group
of operators who are cutting capacity. In the UK context perhaps the pelagic
fishermen are well placed to develop such cooperative actions to restrict capital.
(Clearly the actions need to be consistent with UK and EU Competition Policy

and demonstrate there is no detriment to the consumer in terms of higher prices.) Similarly, some shellfish fishermen may reap the benefits of cooperative action.

*Option 2: Industry-organised contributory scheme*

The second option involves the industry, perhaps through a trade association, paying a share of their profits into a fund when stocks are above average levels so allowing high profits to be made. This would mean there were fewer super-normal profits in circulation which could be used to over-invest in the industry. The fund could be used to self-finance tie-up periods or decommissioning programmes if stocks became depressed or if fleet productivity rose unsustainably.

Mutual insurance is found in other industries. For instance, travel agents assure one another's liabilities through the ABTA[6] scheme, which protects customers against the insolvency of individual travel agencies. A system like the ABTA scheme works well when there are a large number of individual operators and a powerful industry body. Therefore, this type of scheme would be best suited to fisheries that consist of many individual fishermen. Success would be based upon the ability to establish a central organisation to facilitate the mutual insurance scheme and ensure buy-in to the idea by individual fishermen.

*Option 3: Tax on resource rent*

Options 1 and 2 effectively allow fishermen to use all profits to their benefit, even those very high profit levels which can only be generated when stocks are healthy and the fishing is very good. The third option involves fisheries managers actively withdrawing a proportion of super-normal profits (known as resource rents) which can only be generated when stocks are healthy and economic returns are good. By withdrawing money in this way the government effectively reduces the amount of profit left in the industry which could be used to over-invest in capital. It therefore helps to control a build up of capital overhang in the good years, which exacerbates over fishing in the bad years.

Besides helping to minimise capital overhang, there is a point of principle involved in taxing resource rents. Fish stocks are a natural resource and so are effectively 'owned' by everyone, i.e. society. Government is therefore responsible for looking after them and allows fishermen to simply use them, not own them. Other users of marine natural resources (i.e. oil, gas, mineral extraction, etc.) pay charges to government for being allowed to make economic returns by using society's resources. There is an argument that fishermen should be charged in a similar way. Such a charge could be extracted as a tax on high profits and the money 'returned' to the tax-payer, i.e. the real 'owner' of the resource.

Alternatively, the money could be retained by the fisher manager and used to finance management, science and enforcement activities. However, from an economic viewpoint, providing these services free of charge effectively means that the government is subsidising the industry. If the money was used to this end it would be more correct to call it a cost recovery charge, rather than a resource rent tax.

*Cost recovery*

Failure to recover the costs of managing a fishery is a form of indirect subsidy. Therefore cost recovery should be introduced gradually in most fisheries as a matter of course. Many countries with relatively healthy fish stocks recover their management costs. For example, in Australia's offshore fisheries, the industry pays for costs relating directly to the fishing activity. However, costs related to exploratory, collapsed or developmental fisheries are only partially recovered (Tingley and van Santen, 2001). New Zealand operates a full cost recovery programme and Iceland recovers some costs (e.g. quota transfer, fishery monitoring and vessel inspection fees).

## 5 Policy options

Good fishery management should be delivered as a package of instruments. Management tools should not be cherry-picked from a list of alternatives, they should be selected in combination to provide a package aimed at addressing each of the four fundamental flows in the fishery system: profits, compliance, information and capital entry/exit.

The expected impact of management instruments on each of the key flows is not always clear as it depends on the perspective from which an option is being evaluated. For example, the impact on an individual fisher in the short term may be very different to that in the long term. For example, days at sea restrictions in the short term depress a fishermen profits, however if stocks recover in the long term, the impact will be positive. The effect may also be different if the impact is being assessed in a single-species fishery as opposed to a mixed fishery. Table 12.4 provides a brief outline of the expected impact of a range of management options on the key flows within a fishery system. The assumed starting point is healthy stocks levels but excess capacity in the fleet.

## 6 Conclusions

This chapter has examined the problem of managing fisheries from the perspective of the fisherman. The work was part of a larger overall review of fishing industry, which looked in detail at specific issues such as the policies, resources, communities and fleet economics.

To date policy has concentrated on measuring, regulating and enforcing the amount of fish caught. Fishery managers sometimes make the mistake of believing that fishermen take perverse actions against their own long-term interests. We see no indication that this is the case, rather the information available to fishermen or their freedom to manoeuvre is constrained. This chapter argues that a broader range of information needs to be analysed – on profits, fleet structure, quality of information and compliance.

The issue for policy makers is whether fisheries management looks any different when viewed from this broader perspective. This analysis has argued that

*Table 12.3* Effect of management options on profits, compliance, information and entry-exit

| | | Profits | Compliance | Information | Entry-exit |
|---|---|---|---|---|---|
| Output controls | TACs IQs (Non-transferable) ITQs | Individual profits will erode unless allocations are made to individuals. Transferability helps increase profitability. | Individual allocation should encourage sense of 'ownership' but incentive to high-grade or b lack-land is created if quota mix poorly set. | If discarding or illegal landing, info quality will be poor. Especially a problem in mixed fisheries if quotas not aligned to biological mix. | TACs encourage a race-to-fish unless individual allocations are made. ITQs encourage consolidation. |
| Input controls | Vessel licence/VCU restrictions IEQs (Non-transferable) ITEQs Technical measures Area/time closures | Non-transferable effort restrictions depress profits, but transferability helps concentrate quotas in hands of most efficient, profitable operators. | Input controls are easier to enforce than output controls, except where they are too detailed to be practically enforced or easily circumvented. | Should be better quality information on catches if no output restrictions, however input controls still require output information for calibration. | With the exception of transferable effort quotas, incentives are not created for capital to consolidate. |
| Fiscal measures | Cost recovery Resource rent | Cost recovery and resource rent charges increase costs therefore lower individual profits | Resource rent possibly create incentives to mis-report landings if charge is based on this parameter. | Cost recovery should encourage good information and compliance to keep management and enforcement costs down. | Increases cost of fishing, therefore encourages consolidation. |
| | Subsidies | Subsidies tend to decrease costs or increase prices, but specific impact depends on type of subsidy, e.g. decommissioning, rent rebate for use of selective gear device. | | | |

the two most substantial issues facing the industry are the *lack of compliance* and the tendency for the *fleet's killing power to grow beyond the resource base*. Neither concern is easy to address. Both will require a package of approaches that go beyond counting fish and regulating the number of boats and the amount of fish caught.

Some of the ideas sketched out in this chapter are now being actively taken forward. In June 2005 the UK's four fisheries departments Department for Environment, Food and Rural Affairs (DEFRA) and the three other devolved administrations jointly published a report, 'Securing the Benefits', in which they set out future changes to fisheries policy. These include the need to create a new compliance culture within the sector by taking into account the economic drivers that lead to breaches in regulations and undermine sustainability. This includes more active modelling of the profitability of the sector and consideration of selective decommissioning to better align the capital stock with fish numbers.

## Notes

1 See 'Fishermen incentives and policy – A report of the analysis carried out by the Strategy Unit' by Prashant Vaze and Diana Tingley for the full paper on www.strategy. gov.uk.
2 Survey of 70 skippers carried out in 2001.
3 Per comm, Faroese Ministry of Fisheries and Maritime Affairs.
4 But not necessarily onshore or total industry employment.
5 Profits which are larger than 'normal' profits. 'Normal' profits occur when the cost of producing one extra kilo of fish just matches the revenue generated from sale of that extra kilo of fish.
6 Association of British Travel Agents.

## References

Banks, R. and Reed, A. (2000) 'The impact of technological progress on fishing effort: technological progress in the Scottish pelagic fisheries.' Project funded by the European Commission.
Cattermoul, B. and Pascoe, S. (2000) Economic and financial performance of the UK English Channel Fleet: 1994–95 to 1999–00, CEMARE, University of Portsmouth, UK. Survey during 1994/95 funded by MAFF (MF 03 08), 1995–96, 1996–97 funded by EU (FAIR CT 96–1993), 1998–99, 1999–00 funded by EU (TEMEC Project, QLK5-CT 1999–01295).
European Commission (various years) 'Fishing TACS and Quotas' Reference KL 42 02 303 4Q P.
EVARES (2003) 'Report of the International Bottom Trawl Survey Working Group, Lorient, France 25–28 March 2003.' Evaluation of research surveys in relation to management advice (EVARES) – FISH/2001/02 – Lot 1. Project funded by DG Fish.
Fishing News (2003) 'Whitby Court slams DEFRA prosecutions'. 7th Nov 2003, p. 4.
Hatcher A., Jaffry, S., Thébaud, O. and Bennett E. (2000) 'Normative and social influences affecting compliance with fishery regulations.' *Land Economics* 76(3): 448–461. Research undertaken as part of EU funded project: Compliance with Fishery Regulations. 96/090.

Hatcher, A. and Gordon, D. (unpublished) 'Fishery regulation and the economic responses of fishermen: perceptions and compliance; UK Case-Study Report'. Annex to the Final Project Report (not yet approved). CEMARE. Project funded by DG Fish.

Hutton, T., Pascoe, S., Rackham, B. and O'Brien, C. (2003) 'A comparison of technical efficiency estimates for seven English fleets in the North Sea from Stochastic Production Frontier (SPF) and Data Envelopment Analysis (DEA).' In Pascoe, S. and Mardle, S. (eds) (2003) Single-output measures of technical efficiency in EU fisheries. CEMARE report No. 61. CEMARE, University of Portsmouth. TEMEC Project funded by the European Commission.

ICES (2002) 'Report of the ICES Advisory Committee on Fishery Management, 2002' RAPPORT DES RECHERCHES COLLECTIVES NO. 255.

ICES/NSCFP (2003) 'Study Group on the incorporation of additional information from the fishing industry into fish stock assessments' ICES CM 2003/ACFM:14 Ref. D

Kristjansson, Jon (2003) 'On the Management of Cod and Haddock in the Irish Sea' Report for the Anglo-North Irish Fish Producers Organisation Limited.

National Audit Office (2003) 'Fisheries Enforcement in England'. HC 563 Session 2002–03: 3 April 2003.

Nautilus Consultants (1997) 'The Economic Evaluation of the Fishing Vessels (Decommissioning) Schemes.' Funded by the UK Fisheries Departments.

Nautilus Consultants (1998) 'The Costs and Benefits of Compliance with Regulation in Northern European Fisheries'. Study Contract 96/080. Financed by the European Commission Directorate General XIV.

Pascoe, S. and Mardle, S. (1999) 'Supply response in fisheries – North Sea'.Research Paper 143. CEMARE, University of Portsmouth. Project funded by the European Commission.

Pascoe, S., Tingley, D. and Cattermoul, B. (2003) 'Estimating the efficiency of UK English Channel vessels using DEA and Stochastic Production Frontiers.' In Pascoe, S. and Mardle, S. (Eds) (2003). Single-output measures of technical efficiency in EU fisheries. CEMARE report No. 61. CEMARE, University of Portsmouth. TEMEC Project funded by the European Commission.

Scottish Fishermen's Federation (2002). 'North Sea Stocks Survey'.

Scottish Fishermen's Federation (SFF) (2003) 'Submission to UK Fisheries Project Consultation Paper'.

Tingley, D. and van Santen, G. (2001) 'Subsidies in the Fishing Sector in Third Countries: Australia, New Zealand, Iceland, Norway, Canada, USA, Korea and Japan.' Published by MacAlister Elliott and Partners. Funded by European Commission.

Tingley, D. and Pascoe, S. (2003) 'Estimating the level of excess capacity in the Scottish fishing fleet.' CEMARE Report No. 66. CEMARE, University of Portsmouth. Funded by the Scottish Executive Environment and Rural Affairs Department.

Watson, J. and Martin, A. (2002) '2001 Economic Survey of the UK Fishing Fleet'. Published by Seafish, Edinburgh. Funded by SEERAD, DEFRA and Scottish Enterprise.

Watson, J. and Bryson, J. (2003) 'The Clyde Inshore Fishery Study' Seafish, Edinburgh.

Watson, J. and Bryson, J. (2003) 'The Clyde Inshore Fishery Study – Key Findings' Seafish, Edinburgh.

Watson, J. and Seidel, R. (2003) '2003 Economic Survey of the North Sea and West of Scotland Whitefish Fleet.' Seafish, Edinburgh.

# Index

Note: Page numbers in *italic* denote tables.